Darden

*A Pictorial History of
the University of Virginia's
Darden Graduate School of
Business Administration*

Darden

*A Pictorial History of
the University of Virginia's
Darden Graduate School of
Business Administration*

Mark Reisler

DARDEN
BUSINESS PUBLISHING

Darden Business Publishing
© 2005 by the University of Virginia
Darden School Foundation
All rights reserved
Designed by Gibson Design Associates
Printed in China

Library of Congress Cataloging-in-Publication Data

Reisler, Mark.

 Darden, a pictorial history of the University of Virginia's Darden Graduate
School of Business Administration / Mark Reisler.

  p. cm.

 Includes bibliographical references and index.

 ISBN 1-932692-02-9

 1. Colgate Darden Graduate School of Business Administration--
History--Pictorial works. 2. Business schools--Virginia--History--Pictorial
works. I. Title: Pictorial history of the University of Virginia's Darden
Graduate School of Business Administration. II. Title.

HF1134.C654R45 2005

650'.071'1755481--dc22

Contents

A C K N O W L E D G M E N T S

DEVELOPMENT AND PUBLICATION of the Darden School 50th Anniversary History Project, composed of this book and a video history, would not have been possible without the active participation and support of many members of the Darden Community. An invaluable cache of superb source material is the collection of more than three dozen videotaped interviews of key Darden School faculty, staff, and friends conducted between 2000 and 2004. My thanks to all those individuals who willingly shared their candid recollections and observations of life at Darden on tape. The interviewees' names are listed in the sources section of this book. A special note of gratitude goes to Elaine Ruggieri. Not only did Elaine conduct this series of interviews with skill, diplomacy, and good humor, but she also played an important role in the project by organizing and scrutinizing Darden's photography archives for apt materials for this volume and the video history. During her tenure as Darden's vice president for Public and Media Relations, Elaine provided a priceless and foresighted service to the School by establishing and maintaining the institution's photography collection.

My sincere thanks go also to Darden's talented video-production and media group for their dedication and enthusiasm throughout the project: Christina Seale, video producer; Gary Peters, video editor; Victoria Spah, video assistant; and Cary Cheseldine, director of Video Production. This highly professional team was instrumental in the conceptualization and execution of the video history, the production of the interviews, and the digitization of photographs for this book.

It has been a pleasure to collaborate with Jim Gibson of Gibson Design Associates on

this project. Jim's creative-design approach and his appreciation of the Darden School's history and culture have greatly enhanced the visual presentation of the School's first half century. My thanks to Katherine Amato, director of Darden Business Publishing, and her staff for overseeing the production of this book under the proud imprint of Darden Business Publishing. My appreciation goes to Stephen Smith of Darden Business Publishing for his careful and incisive editing of the text. I am grateful to Delores Roberts, who skillfully typed the text in its many incarnations and who has been an absolutely wonderful and unflappably proficient assistant.

I have been honored to serve the Darden School under the leadership of six deans: Bob Haigh, John Rosenblum, Lee Higdon, Ted Snyder, Bob Harris, and Ray Smith (interim dean three times). To a man, all of these leaders contributed to Darden's development and success with integrity, with humanity, and with an abiding determination that Darden, with its unique vision and values, is a special place destined for outstanding accomplishments. The 50th Anniversary History Project was conceived during Ted Snyder's deanship and has been strongly supported subsequently by Ray Smith, Bob Harris, and the Darden School Foundation Board of Trustees, to whom I convey my gratitude.

This book is dedicated to Mary, the love of my life, and to Sara, our daughter, both of whom bring me meaning and joy. I thank them for their unfailing encouragement of Dad and his history.

— M. R.

F O R E W O R D

BY ANY ASSESSMENT, Colgate W. Darden, Jr., was one of Virginia's preeminent leaders and statesmen in the 20th century. As a member of the General Assembly, as a congressman, as governor during World War II, and as a member of the United States delegation to the newly formed United Nations, Mr. Darden's principled convictions, dedication to thoughtful and selfless public service, and visionary approach to excellence gave substance and value to all that he did. He changed all that he touched for the better, and in no area of endeavor has his influence been more profound and enduring than in education.

A bold champion of public education, Mr. Darden strove to improve quality and to afford access at all levels, from primary schools through the system of higher education and (perhaps most obviously) at the University of Virginia itself.

Mr. Darden's commitment to public education led him to pass up what all saw as a sure seat in the United States Senate to accept appointment as the University's third president, in 1947. Mr. Darden saw his mission here as broadening the benefits accrued by the University to Virginia and its people and as enabling the University to deliver for the state leaders and citizens capable of directing the massive postwar economic boom that he rightly predicted. His aim was to fulfill Mr. Jefferson's plan to create an institution, based upon merit, that not only educated the populace for wise self-government, but also generated useful knowledge in the sciences, arts, and commerce that must buttress a free and open society.

Keenly aware of the criticality of economic development to the state and the region, Mr. Darden conceived and led the campaign to create a graduate school of business administration at the University to nurture the farsighted managerial talent essential for economic growth. Astute in his strategy to generate political and financial support and tireless in his advocacy, he succeeded

in establishing the first exclusively graduate business school in the South. Among Mr.
Darden's legacies here at the University, and
there are many, none stands taller than the
graduate school of business administration
that today justly and proudly bears his name.

This volume commemorates the Darden
School's first half century—the period of
its formation and maturation as a major
force among graduate business schools in
this nation and around the globe, and also
as a model of success in triggering exactly
the kinds of economic development that
Mr. Darden imagined would be its natural
product. It outlines the events of five short
decades during which the Darden School
rapidly and impressively evolved from a
concept in the minds of a handful of founders to a robust graduate business institution
that stands among the most respected in the
world. In text and images, this history tells
the story of Mr. Darden's vision and tenacity
in pursuing it, of the temperaments and

accomplishments of those who worked with
him and of those who came after him, of
generations of faculty who have shaped and
sustained the School's unparalleled commitment to excellence in teaching, and,
perhaps most eloquently of all, it tells the
stories of the growing body of loyal alumni
who have gone forth to lead organizations
with integrity for the betterment of society.

One suspects that Mr. Jefferson would
share Mr. Darden's justified pleasure, indeed pride, in the accomplishments of the
women and men whose stories are told
in this record of the Darden School's first
50 years. The entire University of Virginia
family joins me in celebrating this first half
century of noteworthy accomplishments
and in anticipating what is yet to come.

— JOHN T. CASTEEN III
President
University of Virginia

P R O L O G U E

An Institution of Vision and Values

The story of the birth, development, and maturation of the University of Virginia's Darden Graduate Business School is, in essence, a chronicle of institution building. From a bold conceptual kernel in the minds of the Darden School's founding fathers in the early days after World War II to its current recognized place—just a half century later—among the world's outstanding graduate business academic institutions, the University of Virginia's graduate business school has been guided by a clear vision of how best to educate men and women for socially constructive positions of leadership in enterprises across the globe. That vision set the foundation for a distinctive educational organization dedicated to the pragmatic preparation of students for active decision making as they assume positions of leadership in society. The pillars of the Darden School's vision include excellence in teaching, cross-disciplinary curriculum integration, close interaction between faculty and students, an intense, holistic educational experience directly relevant to business, and devotion to ethical behavior.

The implementation of the Darden School's distinctive vision of management education required the development of a remarkably clear-cut and consistent set of values. These values have pervaded the experience of all who have touched or been touched by the School, be they students, faculty, staff, or corporate friends. Despite a rapidly changing global environment over the past half century that has witnessed immense transformations in technology, economic systems, demographics, and international alignments, the core elements of the Darden School's vision and values have endured, to the School's good fortune.

The continuity of the Darden School's distinctive vision and the tenacity of its enduring communal values have served the School well and carried it to the forefront of global management education. They have enabled the University of Virginia to plant and cultivate with care an institution that has educated and will continue to educate outstanding societal leaders whose contributions to organizations throughout the world will be significant indeed.

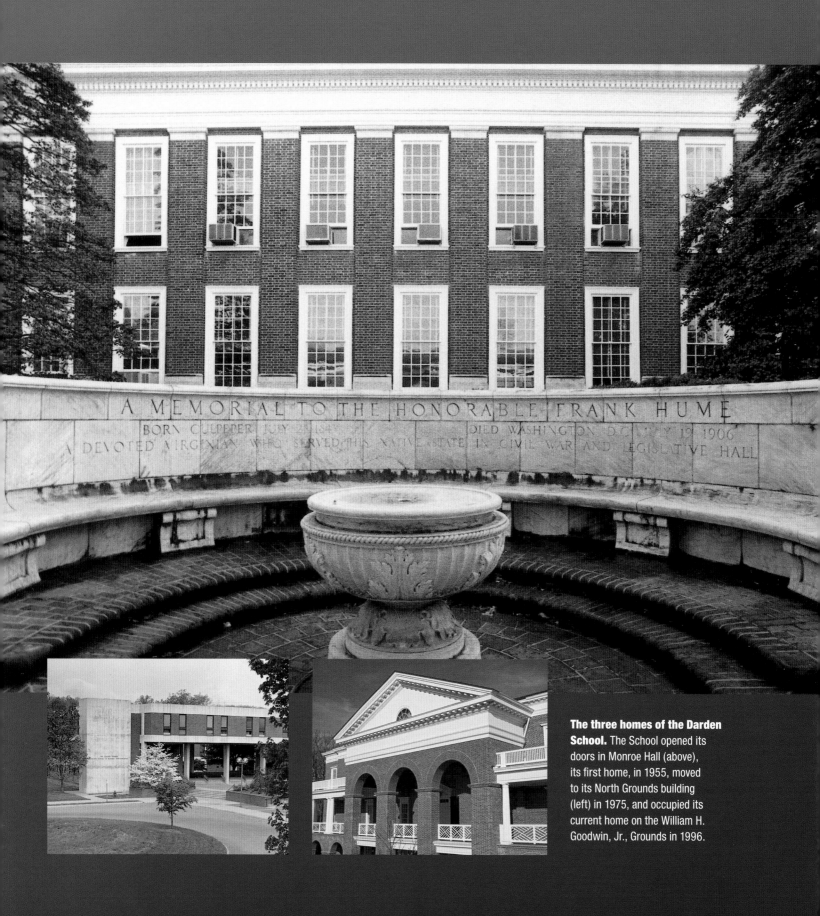

A MEMORIAL TO THE HONORABLE FRANK HUME
BORN CULPEPER JULY 8 1843 · DIED WASHINGTON D.C. MAY 19 1906
A DEVOTED VIRGINIAN WHO SERVED HIS NATIVE STATE IN CIVIL WAR AND LEGISLATIVE HALL

The three homes of the Darden School. The School opened its doors in Monroe Hall (above), its first home, in 1955, moved to its North Grounds building (left) in 1975, and occupied its current home on the William H. Goodwin, Jr., Grounds in 1996.

O N E ❋ *P R E P A R I N G   T H E   S O I L*

The Concept: A Graduate Business School at the University of Virginia

More than any other individual, Professor Tipton Ray Snavely deserves the honor and title of "intellectual father" of the Darden School. A native of Lee County, located deep in the southwestern tip of Virginia, and a 1912 graduate of Emory and Henry College, Snavely received, in 1919, the very first doctoral degree in economics awarded by the University of Virginia. He then joined the faculty of the University of Virginia, where he rose through the ranks and served simultaneously as chairman of the Department of Economics, from 1923 to 1956, and chairman of the McIntire Department of Commerce (later called the McIntire School of Commerce), from 1923 to 1952.

By the mid-1940s, Snavely had become aware of the need for a graduate program in business at the University of Virginia. Believing that the graduate degrees in economics offered by the University were too theoretical to address a growing demand in the business world for an education that could be applied directly to real-life business challenges, Snavely began to ask faculty members and deans their views on the ideal shape that business-related academic programs at the University of Virginia should take. To many University faculty members, Snavely reported, "It seemed unfortunate that there was no institution in Virginia, or indeed in the South, organized as a separate school like that at Harvard or Stanford, and more recently at Chicago, Columbia, and other universities."

In 1946, to help stimulate more-focused thought on the issue, Snavely asked his friend Robert D. Calkins, dean of Columbia University's graduate business school and a scholar whose academic interests included the economic development of the South, to render an opinion on the concept of establishing a graduate business school at Virginia. Calkins responded that there was a clear need for a graduate school that "should materially improve the competence of southern youth for careers in fields which would develop the whole economy of the South." He added the earnest challenge, however, that such a school must be structured and generously supported in such a manner that "it would be equal, or superior, to any school in the North."

Emboldened by his informal talks with faculty members and by Calkins's recommendation,

Tipton R. Snavely, intellectual father of Virginia's Graduate School of Business Administration. Snavely actively promoted the idea that the Commonwealth's economy would benefit from the managerial talent produced by a graduate business school.

McIntire School of Commerce faculty. Led by Tipton Snavely, McIntire faculty supported creation of a graduate business school at Virginia.

that a graduate business school at the University of Virginia would help stem the "brain drain" of managerial talent that plagued the South and inhibited its economy from realizing robust industrial development. The most talented prospective young managers, he contended, abandoned the South to pursue graduate training at prestigious business schools in the North and West and never returned to help transform the South's economy, a requirement if the South were ever to raise its standard of living and free itself from economic subservience to the rest of the country.

Snavely, in the summer of 1946, submitted a formal report to University of Virginia President John L. Newcomb that called for the establishment of a graduate school of business administration. Snavely disseminated his report widely to leaders of the Commonwealth of Virginia's business community, as well as to former Virginia Governor Colgate W. Darden, Jr., and Edward R. Stettinius, Jr., who, after serving first as chairman of U.S. Steel and later as Secretary of State under Presidents Franklin D. Roosevelt and Harry S. Truman, was poised to become the rector of the University of Virginia.

Snavely's report was pragmatic in tone, and emphasized the potential benefits of a graduate business school to the economic development of the South. Observing that the South, in the postwar era, still largely carried the burden and characteristics of a "colonial economy," Snavely argued persuasively

Snavely's arguments in favor of creating the South's first graduate business institution were compelling. The University's senior leadership quickly grasped the significance and urgency of the concept. Appointed rector of the University in August 1946 while serving as the first U.S. ambassador to the newly organized United Nations, Edward Stettinius, in his convocation address in October of that year, proclaimed that Virginia "must have a school of business administration second to none." From such a school, he envisioned, "men would go forth to important business positions throughout the land, and I should hope that, in time, it might become recognized as the educational center of the financial and business community of the South."[1]

With the appointment of Colgate W. Darden to the presidency of the University in mid-1947, Stettinius and Snavely gained an energetic ally and an active leader in the campaign to establish a graduate business school. Darden became an outspoken champion of the proposed school. Henry E. Mc-Wane, president of the Lynchburg Foundry Company, recalled Darden's crucial role in McWane's address to the University of Virginia graduate business school's very first entering MBA class on September 16, 1955: "Let's start at the beginning. The establishment of a business school at the graduate level here at the University was first envisioned by President Darden. Initially he confided his plans, nebulous as they seemed at that time, to just a few of his friends in the business world. We might say that their reactions were not outstanding for their enthusiasm. But among his many other virtues, Mr. Darden packs a full measure of persistence, and this idea persisted in his thinking."[2]

The former governor soon converted a group of important Virginia business-community leaders into ardent supporters of the concept. For example, J. Harvie Wilkinson, Jr., vice president of State-Planters Bank and Trust Company, actively participated in the formulation of recommended principles to guide the new school. Wilkinson believed that a business school in Charlottesville must have a national scope and appeal, must stress the importance of free

enterprise, and must offer "courses which would have a particular applicability to the business of Virginia, the Fifth Federal Reserve District, and the southern states."[3]

The plan for a graduate business school at the University of Virginia also received the endorsement of a number of private-college leaders in Virginia. They asserted that such a school would be a boon to their graduates who wished to pursue graduate training in management but who were compelled to leave the state to seek out MBA programs. President H. Sherman Oberly of Roanoke College represented this view, noting that "the proposed Graduate School of Business at the University of Virginia will undoubtedly fill a great need in the educational and business development of the Commonwealth...."[4]

From the start, the founding fathers—Snavely, Darden, Stettinius, Wilkinson, and McWane—saw a graduate business school at the University of Virginia as an institution that would not only have a keen influence on the economic development of the Commonwealth and the entire South, but also, over time, be counted among the best in the country and, indeed, enjoy a national influence and reputation. Moreover, in the political context of a devastated

Secretary of State Edward R. Stettinius, Jr. Stettinius signed the United Nations Charter on behalf of the United States on June 26, 1945, as President Harry S. Truman looked on. As rector of the University of Virginia, Stettinius strongly endorsed the establishment of a graduate business school.

postwar world witnessing the expansion of the Soviet Union's sphere of influence in Europe and Asia, they envisioned the school as a valued producer of sharp and creative minds that would help lead the dynamic American business enterprises of the future to stem the tide of threatening ideologies.

Finding the Seed Money

While the dream of creating a graduate business school at the University of Virginia was attractive to many, the University would require significant incremental resources to bring this aspiration to fruition. To the University's new president, Colgate Darden, fell the tasks of, first, developing a funding strategy for the proposed school and, second, spearheading a campaign to unearth the necessary resources. In the person of Colgate Darden the concept found an ideal champion. Just as Thomas Jefferson, the political and intellectual father of the University of Virginia, believed that a broadly educated populace was essential to the welfare of the new American nation and to preserving its freedom, so too did Colgate Darden believe that a talented, broadly educated cadre of managers was essential to the economic development of the Commonwealth of Virginia and the South.

Politically savvy and well-connected, both within Virginia and nationally, Darden recognized from the outset that reliance on state support alone to fund a new school would be a long and perhaps futile battle. Instead, he crafted a strategy that called for the simultaneous acquisition of public and private resources. In order to convince the state to allocate public resources to a new business school, Darden concluded that it was imperative to demonstrate palpable support for this initiative from the business community. Thus was born the hybrid model of a graduate business institution reliant on both private and public funding.

Almost from the moment he assumed the presidency, Colgate Darden focused his energies on an embryonic capital campaign at the University designed to raise $7.8 million for the University of Virginia Development Fund. Darden earmarked $1 million of this goal for an endowment for the proposed graduate business school. He traveled throughout the state, appearing before business groups to sell the idea of creating a graduate business school and to raise the necessary money to endow it. By the middle of 1948, in response to Darden's tireless efforts, several key business organizations—including the Virginia State Chamber of Commerce, the Virginia Bankers Association, the Virginia Society of Public Accountants, and the Virginia Manufacturers Association—formally endorsed the establishment of a graduate business school and pledged their support and efforts to fund it.

On the hustings, in appearances before Virginia trade associations and professional groups, Darden emphasized the potential economic-development benefits of a graduate business school to the Commonwealth of Virginia and to the South in general. Noting the loss of what the *University of Virginia Alumni News* termed the South's "mental topsoil" to schools in the North—in 1947, 14 percent of Harvard Business School's students hailed from the South and half never returned—the University's president set as a prime objective improving the South's economy and standard of living through the efforts, leadership, and skills of an educated corps of southern-born managers.[5]

Darden enlisted the help of many of Virginia's most prominent business executives to generate the private resources required for a new school. He established a 24-member funding-campaign steering committee. The committee, chaired initially by Homer L. Ferguson, president of the Newport News Shipbuilding and Dry Dock Company, included J. Harvie Wilkinson as vice chair, Tipton Snavely as a faculty representative, and Darden himself on an ex officio basis.

The committee set a "stretch" fundraising goal of $1.5 million in endowment pledges from the Virginia business community. In making its solicitations, the committee included two important caveats. First, all donations would be returned to the donor unless a total threshold amount of at least $1 million were raised in the campaign. Second (and here Darden's hybrid funding strategy came to the forefront), donations would be returned if the state failed to appropriate re-

sources to support the basic operations and facilities of a new graduate business school.

In late 1948, the steering committee quickly laid its plans, dividing Virginia into 13 geographical regions, each with a target donation level. Its schedule was an ambitious one: to complete the endowment campaign by the end of 1949. This time horizon proved to be overly optimistic. It took three years of intensive work, rather than one year, to attain the minimum goal of securing a $1-million endowment for the new school.

Henry E. McWane, president of the Lynchburg Foundry and past president of the Virginia Manufacturers Association, assumed the chairmanship of the steering committee in late 1949. The committee was renamed the Sponsoring Committee, and McWane appointed an executive board consisting of himself, J. Harvie Wilkinson, Edward H. Lane, and David H. Dillard. Henry McWane also enlisted the help of his brother, Fred W. McWane, in the fundraising effort. The McWanes established an office in the Peoples Bank Building in Lynchburg to serve as command central. "This Committee knew," recalled Henry McWane, "that it had a big job ahead in raising a large sum of money. This *was* a selling job. It must first sell the sound principle behind establishing such a school at the University of Virginia, and then imple-

Henry E. McWane, President of the Lynchburg Foundry, McWane served as the first chair of the Sponsors Board of Trustees and was instrumental in supporting Colgate Darden's campaign to raise private funds for the graduate business school.

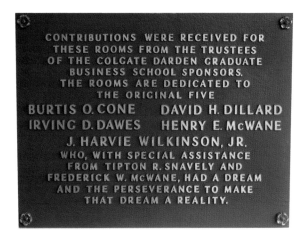

ment this initial promotion with a dollar-and-cents fundraising program. So it was decided to present the project directly to business executives, and to sell the whole package over their desks."[6] With the help of Snavely, the Sponsoring Committee produced a brochure that articulated the case for a graduate business school and disseminated it throughout the Commonwealth's business community. At the same time, McWane and other committee members lobbied the Virginia General Assembly for state funds that would match the private donations being gathered.

The committee's efforts were bolstered by personal appearances by President Darden and Henry McWane at fundraising events throughout the state from 1950 through 1952. As Snavely phrased it, Darden "brought to a high pitch the enthusiasm" of business leaders for a graduate business school. "Mr. Darden," observed Snavely, "deserves full credit as founder of the School.… Without the hard work and the arduous, wearisome trips which he made to all parts of Virginia, the School would not have been established."[7]

Focusing on acquiring several invigorating significant gifts, the committee, in 1952, channeled its energies into courting a limited number of large donors, and set the end of the calendar year as the target date for completing the campaign. Darden, with the help of Henry and Fred McWane and J. Harvie Wilkinson, dedicated enormous energy to bringing the campaign to a successful conclusion. Among the campaign's major donors were member banking institutions of the Virginia Bankers Association, the Reynolds Metals Company, the Norfolk and Western Railway, and Robert R. Young, president of the C&O Railroad. In addition, Colgate Darden contributed $100,000 from the President's Discretionary Fund at the University. At a meeting in Richmond on December 30, 1952, Henry McWane announced proudly that gifts had surpassed $1 million. The campaign ultimately raised approximately $1.25 million to serve as the principal of the new school's initial endowment.

With the requisite private funds now in hand, President Darden allocated space for the new school in Monroe Hall, and successfully lobbied the General Assembly to appropriate operating funds at a level equal to the earnings on the school's newly established endowment.

On the ceremonial opening day of the University of Virginia's Graduate School of Business Administration, in 1955, McWane acknowledged the inspirational leadership of Colgate Darden: "He had a dream and he sold it. He was our outstanding salesman. Whether the call was in New York, or Richmond, or Southwest Virginia, he responded. With the vision of the future for

his beloved Commonwealth always before him, he cheerfully put on his hat and went to work. All who follow us in this worthy enterprise are and ever will be indebted to Colgate Darden for his effective leadership. It would be my humble suggestion that if this University should ever confer an honorary degree, the first should go to him—Doctor of Business Statesmanship."[8]

Private fundraising had been critical to the birth and establishment of the school. It would remain so as Virginia's graduate business school took root and began to flourish. Having attained its minimum goal, the Sponsoring Committee formally dissolved and reincarnated itself as a legally chartered permanent organization—the University of Virginia Graduate Business School Sponsors. This organization, now renamed the Darden School Foundation, continues to play a critical role in the support of the Darden School.[9]

Colgate Whitehead Darden, Jr.: Political Father of the Graduate Business School

In 1974, the University of Virginia's Graduate School of Business Administration was named in honor of Colgate W. Darden, Jr. This accolade could not have been more appropriate. Darden served as the vital catalyst, who personally spurred the establishment of the first exclusively graduate business school in the South. That the Darden School owes its political paternity to Colgate Darden there can be no doubt.

Aptly described by University of Virginia historian Paul Gaston as "a man of uncommon dignity and human sensibility," Colgate Darden was superbly positioned to make the case for and to shepherd the founding of the school that now bears his name. Born on a farm near Franklin in Southampton County, Virginia, in 1897, and educated in the public schools, Darden entered the Uni-

7

versity of Virginia in 1914, where he stayed two years before leaving to join the Allied war effort in France as an American Field Service volunteer ambulance driver with the French army. When the United States entered World War I, in 1917, Darden enlisted in the naval air force and became a pilot with the marines. After his discharge from the military, Darden returned to the University of Virginia to receive his BA degree. Simultaneously, he entered Columbia University Law School, where he earned a law degree and a master's degree in public law. In 1923, he received a Carnegie Fellowship in International Law to study at Oxford University.

Darden came home to Virginia after his study abroad, practiced law in Norfolk, and soon pursued politics, winning election to the Virginia House of Delegates in 1929. In 1932, Tidewater voters elected him to the U.S. House of Representatives as part of the Democratic Party tide led by Franklin D. Roosevelt. He spent two terms in Congress, lost a reelection battle in 1936, and then won back his seat in 1938. He resigned from Congress to run successfully for governor of Virginia in 1941. He served with distinction as the Commonwealth's chief executive during the Second World War.

Veteran political reporter and columnist Guy Friddell of the *Virginian-Pilot*, who covered much of Darden's distinguished political career, observed that "there has never been anybody as popular as he was in the governor's office.... Governor Darden was multifaceted. He followed his convictions and people respected him. He was a scholar and an avid reader." Known as the "Education Governor," Darden's four years at the helm of the Commonwealth were characterized by unflagging support for public education at all levels.

Darden, like Jefferson, believed that an educated citizenry was essential to the success of the American political system. To Darden, the "most powerful thing in the world is an idea. It is not a material thing. In the long run, the thing men follow is a belief, even though it may be bitterly mistaken.... The great moving force in life is the belief in an idea. No system is going to last in the long run unless the people who live under it believe it is worth saving. It is a thing of the spirit."[10]

It is not at all surprising that, upon leaving the governor's mansion, Darden was selected, in 1947, as the third president of the University of Virginia, a post he held until 1959. Darden had rejected the Virginia Democratic Party's attempt to draft him to run for a seat in the U.S. Senate, an election he would almost surely have won, in favor of the University's presidency. His rationale for passing up a Senate seat was simple and consistent with his deepest values: "I felt that altering the course of the University of Virginia, if it were possible for me to do so, would be an infinitely better piece of public work than being a member of the United States Senate."[11]

As president of the University of Virginia, Darden vigorously championed the establishment of a graduate business school. Given his intimate knowledge of the Commonwealth's political process, his close connections with the state's political leaders, and his unique ties to the Virginia business community—bonds solidified through the relationships of his wife, Constance du Pont Darden—Darden crafted a public-private partnership strategy to underwrite the creation of a graduate business school at Virginia.

Recalling his success as president in securing state funds for the University, Darden modestly noted, "I was able to help out because of my knowledge of the Assembly and the governors that were there. They were old friends of mine; but for that I couldn't have gotten the budget help that I got while I was in Charlottesville."[12] Colgate Darden, despite his indisputably pivotal role in creating the University of Virginia's graduate business school, always emphasized the collaborative participation of others—in both the business community and the state government—in his successful endeavor. "Remember," he imparted wisely after a distinguished career in public service, "nobody acts alone in this world. The older I get the more I'm inclined to believe an observation I heard many years ago: There's no end of what can be accomplished if you don't concern yourself as to who gets credit for it."[13]

Working tirelessly to secure both the private and the public funding for the new school, Darden created the school's hybrid character from the outset. This blended fiscal model has served the school named in his honor well for half a century.

Organization of the Graduate Business School

With the private and public resources now identified, President Darden moved rapidly to initiate the organizational activities required to bring the University of Virginia's graduate business school to life. First, in January 1953, he charged a faculty committee, chaired by Tipton Snavely, to recommend the proper organizational structure for the new school after studying the nation's top-rated business-education institutions. In addition, he asked the committee to suggest two or three outstanding persons as potential deans. Darden cautioned, however, that "our program be limited because of the funds available, and that it also be excellent. I have no doubt that further sums will be given us if we demonstrate the value of the School." Simultaneously, Darden sought and received approval, given unanimously, from the University's Faculty Senate to establish a graduate business school. Likewise, the University of Virginia's Board of Visitors, on April 9, 1954, voted to establish the school.

Snavely's committee gathered data and opinions from a number of sources regarding the optimal organization of Virginia's new business school. One fundamental question the committee addressed was how the new school would relate to the University's undergraduate McIntire School of Commerce. In 1952, the University had elevated McIntire from a mere department within the College of Arts and Sciences, dating back to 1920, to a full-fledged, independent school of the University. The obvious question that followed was whether the new graduate school should be consolidated with the McIntire School or stand alone as a separate and distinct entity with its own faculty and led by its own dean. President Darden and the committee favored a graduate school totally separate from the undergraduate commerce school. Recognizing the prominence of the graduate

business schools at such fine universities as Harvard, Chicago, Stanford, and Columbia, both Darden and Snavely concluded that Virginia's incipient effort would grow to distinction only if it could similarly stand on its own as an independent graduate institution.

With this basic issue put to rest, the committee, at times meeting jointly with members of the Sponsors Board of Trustees, invited a number of eminent business educators to Charlottesville to discuss their ideas concerning the proper direction and program for the new school. The committee also sent a questionnaire to those Virginia business leaders who had contributed to the endowment campaign. The purpose of the survey was to gather their views on the new school's strategy and their expectations concerning its activities. Many of the respondents urged the University to model the new school on Harvard's graduate business school. Several, including Harvard Business School graduates, advocated adoption of the case method of instruction. Members of the business community also expressed a desire that the new school offer short, intensive management programs for employees who could not attend the school for extended periods of time. In addition, they stressed the value of training students in the "communication of ideas and cooperation within an organization."

Among the dozen or so experts who spoke to the committee were Professors Charles C. Abbott, George Pierce Baker, and Charles W. Williams of Harvard; Gordon

Colgate W. Darden, Jr., political father of Virginia's Graduate School of Business Administration. This portrait by Ned Bittinger hangs in the South Lounge in Saunders Hall.

Siefkin, dean of Emory University's business school; and C. Stewart Sheppard, assistant dean of New York University's graduate school of business. These distinguished business educators provided their thoughts on the philosophy of graduate business education and the preferred organization of a graduate business institution, while the committee evaluated them as potential candidates for the new school's deanship.

The committee issued its report to President Darden on June 13, 1953. It unanimously recommended that Virginia establish a distinct graduate institution, the first totally separate graduate business school in the South. Moreover, the committee advocated "that the pattern of the Harvard Business School might well be taken as a model for the new school, provided that there is sufficient flexibility for experiment and change." Further, it suggested that the new school "maintain a policy of high scholastic standards for admission and graduation."[14] While acknowledging that the Universities of Alabama, Florida, Louisiana, and Texas had business-education graduate divisions that offered the MBA and PhD degrees, the committee believed that the fact that these graduate activities were tied to large undergraduate programs meant that the graduate programs necessarily were overshadowed and reduced to secondary status by the undergraduate programs. The consequence of a business school's offering multiple degrees was, at best, the diminution of prestige for the grad-

uate program and, at worst, the tendency to "'water down' the quality of graduate work—certainly in appearance if not in fact."[15]

After researching business-school nomenclature used by such universities as Columbia, Cornell, and Stanford, the committee recommended that Virginia name its new venture the "Graduate School of Business Administration" and establish an institution that "should be primarily *par excellence* professional in character." "Both in organization and faculty," the committee advised President Darden, "it should be kept as separate and distinct from the undergraduate school as possible."[16]

In regard to what degrees should be offered, the committee stated without hesitation that the new school should offer only one—the MBA, a full-time two-year experience. While the committee suggested that the new school offer short, intensive courses for practicing managers (who would receive a certificate upon completing a course), it also recommended that there be no intermediate degree, such as a one-year master's degree in science between the bachelor's degree and the MBA. "In due time," the committee predicted, "the School might consider a doctoral degree in business administration," but it should be offered on a cooperative basis with the University's Department of Economics, which already offered a PhD.

The committee also stated its views on the appropriate curriculum for the new school. Graduate students, it counseled, must be exposed to "the 'real' world of business"—perhaps the most salient benefit of the case method of instruction. "We recommend," the committee continued, "the use of the case method of teaching in those subjects in which it seems appropriate…. While it may be that the case system has been carried to an extreme at Harvard, there is no doubt but that the use of the method is highly valuable as a means to disciplining and training the minds of students and of inspiring them to set their course toward executive jobs." The esteemed members of the Harvard Business School faculty had clearly made an indelible impression on the committee, which went so far as to recommend to President Darden that continued consultation with Harvard faculty during the new school's formative years would be of considerable benefit. "Much can be gained," the committee suggested, "by working in close cooperation with Harvard. In saying this, we do not mean that we should seek to imitate or duplicate literally the Harvard plan, but we think that, while the young school is struggling to 'get on its feet,' much can be gained through close relations with Harvard."[17]

In addition to advocating measured use of the case method, the committee recommended that the new school offer a standardized curriculum required of all first-year MBA students, regardless of their educational or employment backgrounds. An educational experience common to the entire student body—divided into "permanently attached" sections for class purposes and into small groups of four or five students for study and problem-preparation purposes—the committee embraced as a powerful technique to promote a cohesive learning environment.

Specialization, the committee advised, should await the second year of the MBA program. While a few second-year courses might be required, students should be free to pursue particular interests in a wide array of business fields, ranging from banking to labor relations. The second year should also include externally focused enrichment activities, such as field trips to factories and lectures by visiting executives. From the start, the committee suggested, Virginia's graduate business school must relate closely to and reflect the actual business environment. "The ties between the School and the business world should be kept as close as possible," concluded the committee.[18] The University of Virginia's graduate business school would follow this cogent advice throughout its history.

The inaugural issue of the *Darden Report* in 1974 pictured Charles Abbott, Colgate Darden, and Tipton Snavely on the cover.

Philosophical Approach to Virginia's Graduate Business School

From its earliest planning stages to the present day, the University of Virginia's graduate school of business has been closely connected to business practitioners and dedicated to instilling a broad management perspective in its students. As Tipton Snavely and Colgate Darden rode the Virginia circuit to promote the idea of establishing a graduate business school, they actively solicited the thoughts of the state's business leaders regarding the nature of the school and its proposed activities. Among the business leaders who accepted this invitation with the utmost diligence was J. Harvie Wilkinson, Jr., vice president of the State-Planters Bank and Trust Company. In February 1953, Wilkinson authored a 15-page memorandum for Snavely's committee titled "A Philosophy of and an Approach to a Graduate School of Business at the University of Virginia," which detailed his views on the objectives and curriculum of the future school and the background of the students it should attract.

Wilkinson's view of management education was quite expansive. The purpose of the new school, he asserted, must be unambiguous: "to train young men for careers of eventual leadership and top policy formation in the world of business."[19] In no sense, he continued, must this new academic enterprise resemble a "trade school." To ensure its efficacy and success, the school, first, must be grounded firmly in a clear philosophical vision and, second, must educate a properly oriented set of promising young people.

Wilkinson theorized that quality managerial education began with an understanding of the nature of man and man's multiple personality facets: spiritual, moral, physical, mental, social, political, and economic. Although business education must focus on the development of "economic man," it must appreciate, nurture, and integrate all the other facets of the human condition. The school's ambitious long-term goal must be to prepare "the business statesman of the last half of the 20th century." Such an individual must comprehend much more than fundamental business principles and techniques. He must understand how to utilize management training effectively by having a thorough familiarity with a broad humanistic tradition, namely, "comprehension of the facts of his own nature, and, hence, the nature of his fellow man."[20]

In regard to a curriculum for the new school, Wilkinson believed that Virginia's future business leaders required instruction in business organization, marketing, finance, personnel relations, industrial engineering, and economics. He observed, however, that a firm grasp of these fields would have optimal utility only if it were grounded in the "basic elements of general education" that would permit the "fusion factor for all of the joints of specialization."[21] It followed then that students entering the new graduate business school should present evidence of previous solid course work in English, mathematics, science, languages, social science (including ethics), history, government, economics, and psychology. "It is exceedingly important," cautioned Wilkinson, "not to turn the business man loose with an M.B.A. degree to fly blind."[22]

In short, Wilkinson argued, the experience of a graduate business student at the University of Virginia must meld specific training in modern management approaches with a broad knowledge of the human condition. This combination would provide the necessary perspective for ef-fective leadership in the world of practical affairs and true business statesmanship.

Selection of Charles Abbott as Dean

President Darden had asked Snavely's committee to consider not only the optimal structure of the new graduate business school, but also its potential leadership. When the committee issued its report, it did not recommend to the president a particular individual for the deanship. It did, however, note its expectation that the school would open for operations "in a modest way" in September 1954. To meet this ambitious date, the committee urged the selection of a new dean with dispatch, acknowledging that "a period of one year is all too short a time for the selection of a faculty, preparation of a curriculum, admission of students, issuing a catalogue, making contacts with businessmen, and other vital matters."[23] The committee recommended a modest operating budget of $100,000 for the school's first year. The budget assumed an enrollment of only 20 entering MBA students. Quick appointment of a dean, the committee advised, would help generate a higher number of student enrollees.

While it did not formally recommend to President Darden a candidate to be the school's founding dean, the committee, in Tipton Snavely's words, "let it be known that it wanted" Professor Charles C. Abbott of the Harvard Business School. Intimately familiar with Harvard's curriculum and a well-recog-

nized, popular, superb teacher at the Boston school, Abbott had traveled to Charlottesville twice to meet with the committee and had exhibited a high level of interest in the planning process for Virginia's business school. Moreover, as the Converse Professor of Banking and Finance at Harvard, he was personally known to Virginia banking executives, who were strong supporters of the new school. Thus, he personified the ideal candidate to lead the University of Virginia's effort to build a graduate business institution influenced by the success that Harvard had achieved.

As early as April 1953, just days after Abbott had met with the committee, Snavely wrote to him to ascertain his interest in the deanship of Virginia's new school. "It seems to me," Snavely observed to Abbott, "that there is a distinct opportunity for the first dean to formulate and model the plan of organization of the School to a notable extent according to his own conception." "I should like personally," continued Snavely, "to express the hope that the opportunity to aid in the founding of the new school might have a strong appeal for you."[24] Abbott responded that he would give some thought to the opportunity.[25]

In May 1953, Snavely invited Abbott to return to Charlottesville for a luncheon with President Darden and several Virginia business representatives at the Farmington Country Club. The gathering went well. As the next step, J. Harvie Wilkinson, Jr., discreetly gathered references on Abbott from organizations with which the Harvard professor had worked closely.

In September 1953, President Darden wrote to Abbott, who at the time was in Berkeley as a visiting faculty member at the University of California's business school on leave from Harvard for the fall semester, inquiring whether he would consider coming to the University of Virginia to help get its graduate business school started.[26] After much soul-searching and after fulfilling his commitment to return from his appointment in California to teach at Harvard during the spring semester of 1954, Abbott made the momentous personal and professional decision to leave Boston and breathe life into the University of Virginia's new graduate business enterprise.

On April 9, 1954, President Darden recommended, and the University's Board of Visitors approved, the appointment of 48-year-old Charles C. Abbott as dean. Abbott moved to Charlottesville with alacrity, and devoted the 1954–55 academic year to putting in place the new school's foundational faculty and curriculum and to preparing its home, Monroe Hall, to receive its pioneering first class of students in September of 1955.

Almost a quarter of a century later, in recounting his years as president of the University of Virginia, Colgate Darden noted, with characteristic understatement,

to journalist Guy Friddell: "We were fortunate in obtaining Professor Charles Abbott from Harvard to head the School."[27]

The Sponsors Organization: "The Equivalent of a Body of Alumni"

Certainly, the financial support of the Virginia business community had been absolutely essential in bringing a graduate business school to fruition at the University of Virginia. The Commonwealth's corporate leaders, however, contributed much more than money to the incipient academic enterprise. They volunteered their counsel and their energy to Dean Abbott and President Darden as the Graduate School of Business Administration took its initial steps to fashion itself into a distinctively value-driven and goal-directed institution.

President Darden encouraged business leaders to establish a separate legal entity, whose mission would be to help organize and sustain the new school, as the primary vehicle through which to channel ideas and advice, as well as money, to the institution. Stepping forward to serve as the original officers of this organization, which became known as the University of Virginia Graduate Business School Sponsors, were Henry E. McWane, president; J. Harvie Wilkinson, Jr., vice president; and Irving D. Dawes (treasurer of the Virginia Carolina Chemical Company), secretary-treasurer. Additional founding trustees of the Sponsors organization were Burtis O. Cone

Dean Abbott converses with Morton G. Thalhimer, an original Sponsor of the graduate business school.

may benefit from the understanding of the responsibilities and problems of the other." More specifically, the organization could assist in "supporting practical and relevant research in management and economic problems of direct significance to business and to the public." From the beginning, supporters of Virginia's graduate business school envisioned an academic institution that would have a direct interest in pursuing real-world issues. It followed logically, therefore, that encouraging use of the case method of instruction, grounded in "actual business situations and problems," to prepare students for "the realities of the business world" was another objective of the Sponsors. Finally, the new organization set as a goal the offering of seminars, programs, and conferences for business practitioners who lacked formal training or who required skill enhancement. From its inception, the Sponsors organization stimulated the School to pursue quickly its executive-education mission.[29]

Providing private funding for the School, of course, had been the primary aim of the Sponsors from the outset. In 1956, the organization adopted the concept of annual giving known as "Sponsorship." Businesses and individuals were invited to make yearly donations of not less than $250 to achieve the status of "Sponsors" of the graduate business school. This annual fundraising approach has continued to the present. In addition, the organization attempted to augment the endowment raised before the School's

and David H. Dillard. The founders of this nonprofit organization, which was separate and distinct from the University of Virginia, believed that it should be the mechanism through which the new school must stay in close touch with the realities of a rapidly changing business landscape. The Sponsors, as J. Harvie Wilkinson put it to his fellow trustees at an organizational meeting in November 1955, would enhance two-way communication between the business community and a school that must always remain "part of the living stream of business life."[28]

The Sponsors set forth a number of objectives in its incorporation documents. A paramount goal was to "bring business and education closer together so that each founding. Early efforts included generating the money necessary to fund the School's first two endowed chairs under the Commonwealth of Virginia's Eminent Scholar Program—the Charles C. Abbott Chair and the Tipton R. Snavely Chair. The organization also raised funds to establish an ongoing Student Loan Fund that has assisted students since the inception of the School.

In short, the Sponsors organization has provided the Darden School's margin of excellence since its birth. "The creation of the Sponsors organization as an independent, tax-exempt body with title to endowment or 'capital' of the School," observed Dean Abbott in 1975, "was a masterstroke. It brought into being at the very beginning a tie with the business community and, in a sense, the equivalent of a body of alumni."[30] Indeed, the Sponsors organization not only has constituted Abbott's original set of "instant alumni," but also has provided unwavering foundational support for the School for a half century.

Samuel A. Lewis, Irving D. Dawes, James L. Camp, and Sydney F. Small (left to right), original Sponsors of the School.

The Tradition of COFFEE

Mary "Pee Wee" Brown, the Darden School's longtime "Coffee Lady," brewed it hot and fresh every morning.

Right: **Coffee in Monroe Hall.** Dean Abbott initiated the coffee period at the outset of the School. Here Dean Sheppard and faculty converse with students in the Monroe Hall library. Said Professor John Colley, "Coffee was another case of Charlie Abbott's genius."

Above right: **Coffee in the PepsiCo Forum, Saunders Hall.** The tradition endures.

In the play *Fiddler on the Roof*, the principal protagonist, Tevye the milkman, extols the virtues of Tradition with a capital *T*. There has been no more cherished tradition at the Darden School than the daily coffee hour that takes place after the first class each morning. Whether in the cramped but revered community-library space (a mere 2,000 square feet) in Monroe Hall on the University's Main Grounds in the 1950s and 1960s; in the cavernous, hard-surfaced lobby of Darden's initial building on the North Grounds in the 1970s, 1980s, and early 1990s; or in the beautifully appointed Jeffersonian PepsiCo Forum in Darden's present Saunders Hall, the ritual coffee break has symbolized the Darden School's dedication to communal learning and close interaction among students, faculty, and staff.

Initiated in the very first year of the

School's existence, the coffee period was established by Dean Charles Abbott to provide students with the opportunity to approach faculty on an informal basis with questions or comments on topics ranging from academics to current events to job searches. In addition, Dean Abbott believed that students would benefit from an institutional practice that mirrored the traditional coffee break in most business settings, a more casual and relaxed time when office colleagues can converse with few constraints. This type of experience, Abbott maintained, was a part of real-world business education. It would help prepare students for important elements of professional success—communication and networking. C. Ray Smith affirmed another benefit of the coffee period: "It was a very efficient way to see people and get things done."[1]

In Monroe Hall, the coffee break took place in the building's library. China cups and saucers were the rule, and freshly brewed

coffee flowed freely. Coffee was prepoured for faculty and students, dressed in coats and ties, who eagerly awaited their morning brew without fail. The tradition moved with the School as it migrated to the North Grounds. Coffee, brewed in large commercial urns, was served in the building's two-story lobby from a counter. For years, Mary Brown, or "Pee Wee" as she was affectionately known, poured tens of thousands of cups of coffee for Darden students, staff, and faculty. As the now more casually dressed students grew in number, china cups were inevitably replaced by the ubiquitous Styrofoam and later by more environmentally friendly paper. But the purpose of the coffee period remained the same, and the volume of conversation and the animation of the crowd of students, facul-

ty, and staff intensified as Darden expanded.

In the design of Saunders Hall—a building conceived as Darden's "Commons"—the goal of preserving and enhancing the ritual of the coffee break was paramount for the architect, Robert A. M. Stern, who created a beautiful central space, the PepsiCo Forum, as the venue for this venerable tradition. Stern's breathtaking octagonal three-story atrium included marble coffee bars and mirrored storage closets, designed specifically to support this daily custom that has been so inextricably bound to the Darden School's values and history. Stern, like Abbott and succeeding generations of students, faculty, and staff, appreciated that coffee serves as a communal glue to help bind the Darden Community together.

"Coffee Lady" Edna McCauley prepares for the 9:30 a.m. onslaught in the lobby of the North Grounds building.

Below: **Coffee in the North Grounds building lobby.** Observed Professor John Snook of the ritual: "When people deal with one another face-to-face while engaging in a socially acceptable pastime, it is difficult for them to perpetuate malice and unkindness, and it is easy to resolve differences and recognize mutual worth."

Monroe Hall. A stone's throw from Mr. Jefferson's Academical Village, Monroe Hall was the home of Virginia's Graduate School of Business Administration for its first 20 years.

VIRGINIA TO OPERATE SCHOOL OF BUSINESS

Special to The New York Times.

CHARLOTTESVILLE, Va., Dec. 1—Colgate W. Darden, president of the University of Virginia, said today that a Graduate School of Business Administration would open to students next Sept. 15.

The school, nearly ten years in the planning, will begin with an endowment of more than $1,000,-000, given by Virginia business, banking and manufacturing interests. Income from this endowment is being matched with appropriations by the state.

Charles C. Abbott resigned as Converse Professor of Banking and Finance at the Harvard Graduate School of Business Administration to become dean of the Virginia school. He is assembling a faculty and planning a two-year curriculum of professional education to prepare men and women for executive careers in business and government. The courses will lead to the degree of Master of Business Administration.

T W O ❧ *P L A N T I N G   T H E   S E E D*

Virginia to Operate School of Business

The article in the *New York Times* on December 2, 1954, was brief and to the point, only a hundred words. Headlined "Virginia to Operate School of Business," the article, with a Charlottesville dateline, reported President Colgate W. Darden's announcement that the University of Virginia would open the doors of a graduate business school in September of the following year after a decade of planning. Moreover, the *Times* stated that Charles C. Abbott had resigned his post as Converse Professor of Banking and Finance at the Harvard Business School to become the new Virginia school's dean. The directness of the *Times*' succinct article reflected the clearly defined and focused purpose of the enterprise: "to prepare men and women for executive careers in business and government."[1]

Dean Charles Abbott.
Abbott relinquished a prestigious post at Harvard for the opportunity to mold Virginia's graduate business enterprise from scratch. Abbott recalled that his first "official caller" at Virginia "was a typewriter salesman trying to sell me a typewriter for the secretary I didn't have."

Dean Charles Abbott

Charles Cortez Abbott was a formidable figure, indeed. In the mid-1950s, the founding dean of Virginia's Graduate School of Business Administration migrated from the hallowed ivy-covered walls of Harvard, on the banks of the Charles River, to the quaintly provincial southern setting of Mr. Jefferson's University with a clear mission in mind. He would establish and cultivate a brand-new academic enterprise that would one day flower into an educational institution rivaling the very best that the Ivy League had to offer.

Through a combination of razor-sharp intellect, powerful personality, and unflagging determination, Abbott planned and implemented an incisive strategy to erect a firm foundation for the South's first graduate business school. From the outset, Abbott's intention was to build a very special learning organization whose influence would pervade the profession of business far beyond Charlottesville and the school's sectional roots. This he would accomplish by recruiting a unique faculty, inculcating a shared sense of mission and values among that faculty and the school's pioneering students and staff, and crafting an ingenious administrative structure that would permit a unit of a state-assisted institution sufficient latitude to compete with the best

Abbott's faithful black Labrador, Hickory, became a fixture seated on a leather chair in the dean's office. The dog was jokingly referred to as the "associate dean."

Opposite: Abbott remained an active and popular teacher of both MBA and executive-education students throughout his tenure. Here, after his retirement, he presents a seminar in 1978 on Sponsors Day.

private business schools in the nation.

Abbott combined the erudition and confidence of a New England Ivy League scholar with the pragmatic bent of a midwestern farmer. He was born in 1906 in Lawrence, Kansas, where his father, Wilbur Cortez Abbott, taught history at the University of Kansas. A distinguished authority on early modern European history and the Cromwellian period in Great Britain, Wilbur Abbott moved his family to New England after joining the faculty first at Yale and then at Harvard. His son, Charles, went to Harvard College, graduating in 1928. Charles Abbott recalled his undergraduate days as a "literary figure." At Harvard, he was president of the *Advocate*, an editor of the *Lampoon*, class poet, and author of the class hymn and the class ode. Simultaneously, economics caught his fancy, and he returned to graduate school at Harvard, receiving a master's degree in economics in 1930 and a doctorate in 1933.

After working in banking in New York and London for brief periods, Abbott was appointed an instructor in economics at Harvard College. He later reminisced with amusement, "I resigned from Harvard College [in 1937]. I think they were going to

fire me, but at least I had the satisfaction of quitting first."[2] The Harvard Business School dean, Wallace B. Donham, wisely saw Abbott's divorce from Harvard College as an opportunity for the business school. He offered Abbott a faculty position at Harvard Business School, where Abbott remained entrenched until 1954, when he departed for Virginia. Abbott rose through the ranks and attained a chaired position, the Edmund Cogswell Converse Professorship of Banking and Finance. A prestigious chair, the Converse Professorship was established by Edmund Converse, president of Bankers Trust, in 1912, four years after the founding of the Harvard Business School, as the first endowed professorship at that institution.[3]

Abbott became a renowned fixture on the Harvard faculty, venturing elsewhere only to serve the nation during World War II as a member of the War Shipping Administration and as a faculty member at the Naval Midshipman Officers Training School at Harvard Business School.

Despite his Harvard pedigree, Abbott never lost his close connection with the land and his early agrarian roots. This pipe-smoking, Beechnut-tobacco-chewing scholar and academic visionary enjoyed nothing more than his Pomfret Center, Connecticut, dairy farm, to which he traveled from Charlottesville each summer for a lengthy and intellectually refreshing stay between academic years.

Serving for 18 years, the founding dean

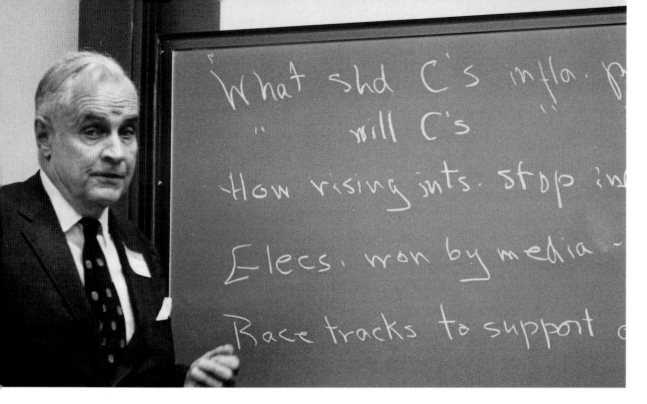

left an indelible imprint on the University of Virginia's graduate business school and its first generation of students. The architect of a compelling curriculum, Abbott was also a powerful magnet who attracted an outstanding set of eclectic professors. He blazed an exceptionally steady and well-defined path for Virginia's graduate business school, a path that has served it well for half a century.

Birth of the Curriculum

While, in theory, Charles Abbott arrived in Charlottesville in 1954 to discover a blank slate upon which he could begin to draw the contours of an imaginative curriculum for Virginia's new graduate business school, a number of strong predilections were already in place that influenced the direction of the school's curriculum. First, the newly appointed dean and President Darden had already agreed that the new

school would have a singular graduate focus and that it would be a unit separate and distinct from Virginia's existing undergraduate McIntire School of Commerce. To Abbott and Darden, Virginia had to develop an exclusively graduate school that would take as its yardsticks the nation's outstanding graduate schools of management: Harvard, Stanford, Columbia, and Wharton.

Second, Abbott brought with him 17 years of experience at Harvard Business School, the intellectual cradle of case-method pedagogy in business education. To Abbott, the case method embodied the essence of the educational process inasmuch as it compelled students to become active participants in their learning venture and prepared them to think on their feet. He proudly transported the case method from Boston to Charlottesville. At Harvard—the uncontested beacon of practical business instruction in the 1950s—the efficacy of the case method

"As in any institution of learning, the character of the curriculum affects the type of faculty it is possible to attract. In turn, the nature of the faculty recruited influences the curriculum."

— Dean Charles Abbott

Abbott selected wooden swivel classroom chairs on wheels to facilitate face-to-face case discussions. These wooden chairs remained the School's classroom standard until fabric swivel chairs replaced them in the School's current building.

had become well established. Likewise, it resonated with the business leaders who nurtured Virginia's efforts to found a graduate business school and who were devotees of a utilitarian approach to education that readied students for managerial decision making. It is thus not at all surprising that Abbott's advocacy of the case method as the core pedagogical approach at Virginia's new school found ready acceptance. Nevertheless, from the outset, it was Abbott's firm view that, at the University of Virginia, "while the Graduate Business School initially will be similar to the Harvard operation, it will differ in important respects."[4]

For Abbott, a hallmark of the case method was the requirement of close intellectual interaction on two levels: faculty to student and student to student. This meant that Abbott would recruit faculty who relished the opportunity to maximize their contact with enthusiastic students. It also meant that the school would assign students to study groups designed to foster intensive teamlike work environments that paralleled the world of business and helped hone organizational and interpersonal communication skills.

A second principle of the case method for Abbott was that it reflect the true complexity of both the general business environment and specific managerial problems. Abbott viewed business holistically. As a result, he was determined to create an integrated curriculum that not only crossed disciplinary

boundaries, but also worked mightily to prevent the erection of barriers between functional fields of study. Consequently, Abbott shied away from creating academic departments at the new school based on such functional fields of interest as accounting, finance, or marketing. Although the curriculum would cover extensively all the core functional fields of modern business, it would do so on an integrated basis, with scholars from the various fields working closely together to craft an interdisciplinary MBA curriculum that would provide the prospective general manager with a broad-based, analytical grounding for realistic and cogent decision making.

A third attractive characteristic of the case method for Abbott was its flexibility. Because change in the business world was constant, it followed that a pertinent business curriculum must necessarily undergo frequent review and revision in light of chang-

ing conditions in the real world of enterprise. Stated Abbott, just one year after the School opened: "Whatever we're teaching three years from now ought to be different from what we're doing today—otherwise we'll be wrong." The easy introduction of new and revised cases into the curriculum allowed the School to respond to the ever-changing business landscape.[5]

The faculty, as Abbott saw it, must be the drivers and producers of a curriculum constantly requiring revision and updating in a world of inexorable change. "Concepts, techniques, and relationships in business are always changing," Abbott reported to President Darden in the dean's first annual report, in 1955. "At the present time, however, technology is advancing, the structure of business is evolving, and the demands upon executives are increasing at perhaps the most rapid rate in history. Appreciation and understanding of these changes require continuous and laborious 'current research' in the realm of practical affairs, and this effort must be expanded both in the library and in the field or clinical investigation." In that same report, Abbott predicted that "much of the future success of the school will necessarily depend upon the quality of the research conducted by the faculty. Continuous scholarly investigation is essential to the well-being and growth of all institutions of higher learning, but it is particularly important in Graduate Schools of Business Administration."[6]

To Charles Abbott, the case method constituted the most logical and effective means to prepare students to assume the responsibilities of leadership. But the case method served as a tool, not as an end in itself. For the founding dean, the case method and the curriculum he built around it were the means to deliver education in its broadest sense—a force to stimulate human progress. Education, wrote Abbott in 1960, "is the essential element in the development of that resource which ener-gizes all others in a community—people."[7]

Abbott's approach to both the broad objective of graduate business education and the pedagogical thrust of the MBA curriculum has endured at the Darden School. Although courses have certainly been modified and augmented to reflect

the vast changes in the business environment since the 1950s, Darden's faculty has remained wedded to an integrated, holistic, student-centered learning process that places the student squarely in the role of decision-making leader. The lasting aim of this process is to prepare students for wise and progressive lifelong leadership.

Monroe Hall classroom. Name tents that clearly identify students have endured throughout the School's history.

The Founding Faculty

Once Charles Abbott was hired, President Darden was eager to push forward rapidly with the establishment of the graduate business school. He wanted the new school to open its doors as early as the fall semester of 1954. The new dean, however, urged a much more methodical course. He needed time, he advised the president, to hire and mold a faculty and to define a distinctive curriculum. Darden agreed to a slower timetable. September 1955 became the target date for the inauguration of classes at the new school.

Abbott's first and foremost task was to recruit an outstanding faculty from scratch by convincing quality instructors to move to Charlottesville and cast their lot with an uncertain, start-up educational venture. Abbott was an accomplished and persuasive salesman. He gathered a small, eclectic group of faculty—a cosmopolitan combination of academics and business practitioners, all of whom had strong personalities and

viewpoints—and lured them to Charlottesville, a community that, in the mid-1950s, was still very much a charming but somewhat bucolic southern town. Abbott imbued the faculty with a powerful and challenging mission: to build a unique institution of higher learning from the ground up.

In his first annual report to President Darden, in December 1955, Dean Abbott noted his success in drawing the faculty "from both the business and academic worlds in roughly equal proportions." He emphasized that the academics he had chosen "without exception, have had some practical contact with business and most of those from the business world have had some acquaintance with teaching." He was satisfied, he told President Darden, that "the range of experience represented by the group is wide."[8]

For Abbott, the most important attribute of a faculty member was skill in the classroom. He asserted his main priority in selecting faculty: "In the first place, he must teach and teach well. Probably this is most important … since the reputation of the school will very largely depend on the product it turns out. High-quality teaching is probably more important in a graduate business school than in a college."[9]

The first member of the new school's faculty was Dean Charles Cortez Abbott himself. This dean would be a hands-on, teaching dean. By necessity, the school's meager budget—a mere $112,000 the first year—left no room for a dean who did not also grace the classroom. More important, not only did Abbott love to teach, but he also envisioned the school as one of excellence in instruction across the board. The dean must, therefore, personally set the tone and standard in the classroom.

John Forbes

John Douglas Forbes was the second member of the new graduate business school's faculty. Forbes arrived in Charlottesville, on September 1, 1954, from Wabash College in Indiana in a yellow Rolls-Royce. He was a Harvard-trained economic historian, who had studied with Edwin F. Gay, the first dean of the Harvard Business School, as well as with Harvard historian Wilbur C. Abbott, Dean Abbott's father. Forbes had taught economic and political history, and also art history, at Wabash. At Virginia's new business school, he taught management communications and business history and served as faculty secretary until he retired, in 1980. Forbes

wrote the new school's initial catalogue and served as its first director of Admissions. While at Darden, Forbes authored biographies of Edward Stettinius, Sr., and J. P. Morgan, Jr. So tied to the Darden School was he that, on the occasion of his retirement, Forbes recalled, "I was carried out kicking and screaming."[10]

Forbes did all he could to foster student creativity and breadth of thinking. Often, his assignments required MBA students to wax poetic. Other times, his assignments forced students to consider issues relating to ethics and the civic responsibilities of business leadership. He bluntly favored the School's emphasis on general management. Opined Professor Forbes in 1956 on the business-education trend toward greater specialization: "If the narrow specialist can't find a narrow hole for himself, he starves. If he gets to the top and runs the works, then everybody starves."[11]

Said Forbes of his quarter century of teaching management communications at the Darden School: "I have tried to give our students an outlook and training which will contribute to two ends: (a) give them competitive advantage over the products of other business schools and (b) strengthen the business community by helping business people to be civilized and responsible."[12] Professor Paul

John D. Forbes. Forbes, the first faculty member hired by Abbott, wrote the School's catalogue, served as secretary of the faculty for a quarter century, and was an uncompromising advocate for effective written communication.

Hammaker observed, "John Forbes, who was versatile and a great teacher, was absolutely dedicated to the idea that when these folks finish, they're going to be darn good pre-senters and analysts."[13] "I just taught them how to write simple English prose without such obscenities as 'input' and 'feedback'; no jargon," Forbes recalled. "What I really taught, I think, was civilizedness."[14]

Dean Sheppard described Forbes, upon his retirement, as "the quintessence of the Renaissance man. His varied interests, his sly pokes with a twinkle in his eye, his creativity and meticulous scholarship, and his generosity of time and money are all left as a heritage to some 2,100 alumni. John has been a leavening agent of the faculty: every school needs one."[15] For more than two decades after his retirement, Forbes annually taught a popular course on art and architectural history in the University of Virginia's School of Continuing and Professional Studies. The course was conducted in a Darden classroom.

Forrest Hyde

Forrest Hyde joined Abbott and Forbes as the third member of the small, preopening faculty group that planned the new school's inaugural curriculum. The trio of Abbott, Forbes, and Hyde held the School's first official faculty meeting on the terrace of Hyde's home in Farmington on September 23, 1954. Hyde, a 1913 graduate of the University of Virginia Law School, had been a

successful New York attorney specializing in trusts. Active in the University's alumni association, Hyde was persuaded by President Darden to retire to Charlottesville and join the business school's embryonic faculty.

Hyde taught courses relating to business and tax law until he retired, in 1958. Tyson Janney (MBA 1957) recalled Hyde as "kind and generous beyond definition. We loved his rambling Wall Street stories and colorful accounts of security transactions."[16] J. Richard Wilson (MBA 1957) attested to Hyde's generosity. In the spring of Wilson's second year, Caterpillar Tractor invited him to Peoria, Illinois, for a job interview. While the company intended to reimburse his travel costs, Wilson, who was subsisting on a tight GI Bill budget, lacked sufficient cash to pay for airfare. When Hyde learned that, as a consequence, Wilson would have to turn down the interview, "Forrest reached into his pocket," Wilson recalled, "and pulled out the biggest wad of bills I had ever seen in my life, peeled off four $100 bills, gave them to me, and said, 'Pay me when you get back.'"[17]

When the School's first MBA class graduated, in May 1957, Hyde invited the entire student body and their families and friends to a celebratory luncheon, which he hosted. Thus began an annual festive graduation event—for which the Sponsors organization later assumed responsibility—a tradition that continues to this day.

Hyde left an enduring mark on the Darden School in one other way. In 1954, in anticipation of the school's opening, he established its first scholarship, the Lieutenant Samuel Forrest Hyde Memorial Fellowship. The scholarship was created to honor Hyde's son, Samuel, a 1950 University of Virginia graduate in commerce and U.S. Air Force pilot, who died in a plane crash near Tokyo, in 1953. This award is presented annually by vote of the faculty to the student who has contributed most to the welfare of the School during his or her first year in the MBA Program and who shows the greatest promise of achieving a useful career. It remains the Darden School's most prestigious award.

Lee Johnston

Lee R. Johnston became the new school's fourth faculty member. He was a Harvard Business School graduate and former assistant to Abbott in Cambridge. Virginia's new dean spirited Johnston away from a faculty position at the University of Kansas to teach finance and investment management in Charlottesville.

He arrived in February 1955, and joined Abbott, Forbes, and Hyde in planning the school's initial curriculum. Johnston played an active and vocal role at Darden, not only in the development of the MBA curriculum and the School's early executive-education ventures, but also as the first director of

Opposite: **Forrest Hyde**. The School's first and most prestigious scholarship was established by Hyde in memory of his son. It is awarded annually to a second-year MBA student selected by the faculty.

Lee R. Johnston. Johnston retired in 1988 as the longest-serving member of the School's founding faculty.

the School's Doctoral Program, from 1966 to 1972.[18] He also formulated the School's initial MBA electives in the entrepreneurial field: Managing Smaller Enterprises, Starting New Ventures, and Venture Management.[19]

Affectionately nicknamed "The Bear," Johnston, a decorated combat veteran of both World War II and the Korean War, was known for his toughness, both inside and outside the classroom, and could cut an intimidating figure at times. "And yet,"

Tyson Janney observed, "once you finally passed his courses and the wounds began to heal, you caught yourself actually liking the guy."[20] Johnston taught at the Darden School from 1955 until his retirement, in 1988.

Almand R. Coleman.
Coleman made accounting come alive, inscribing the equation A=L+OE indelibly in the minds of generations of Darden MBAs.

Almand Coleman

I n June 1976, Almand R. Coleman, the Charles C. Abbott Professor of Business Administration and the School's first chaired professor, retired after 21 years of service at the Darden School. Coleman, a stalwart member of the School's original faculty, developed and taught Darden's course on managerial accounting and control and led the accounting area for two decades.

A native of Smithfield, Virginia, Coleman graduated from Washington and Lee University and received his MBA from Harvard. After working for the federal government, then

as a CPA with a Richmond firm, and finally as an officer with State-Planters Bank and Trust Company, he turned to a career in teaching. He served as a professor of accounting at Washington and Lee University for more than 15 years. During the 1954–55 academic year, while holding a visiting professorship at Harvard Business School, Coleman learned of the University of Virginia's plan to create a graduate business school and of Charles Abbott's search for faculty candidates. Coleman was eager to join this pioneering endeavor. An experienced instructor well-versed in Harvard's case-method pedagogy and a former banking colleague of J. Harvie Wilkinson, Jr., a founding Sponsor of the School, Coleman proved an attractive candidate to Abbott as the new dean struggled to put into place a starting team of formidable faculty members that consisted of both experienced academicians and business practitioners.

Abbott's instincts were sound. From the start, Almand Coleman brought an imposing personality to the classroom. He used a combination of insightful analysis and humor—plus dashes of histrionics—to make accounting, a subject that students in most schools often consider less than inspiring, come alive for countless Darden students. Coleman believed that a successful faculty member must possess "a thorough understanding of the discipline which one is teaching and, just as important, an understanding of the art of teaching."[21] Coleman lived his teaching philosophy; his artistry in the classroom became legendary. With the virtuosity of a maestro leading an accomplished symphony orchestra, Coleman conducted each and every case-method class to elicit the maximum engagement of his students. Yet his objective was remarkably simple and straightforward. "All I want my students to do," he stated after the School had completed its first year, "is to think intelligently with figures. If they need anything at all in the business world of tomorrow, that's it."[22] Said Tyson Janney of Coleman, "He was one of the best professors for humor. And he could make accounting come alive. I don't know any other professor who could do that."[23]

Coleman brought his enthusiasm and teaching proficiency to business practitioners as well as to MBA students. Setting a pattern for future Darden faculty, he emphasized the importance of executive-education teaching as an essential component of a faculty member's set of activities. In 1958, he became a core member of the faculty team that developed the School's inaugural executive program. He continued to stress the importance of working directly with the business community throughout his career. Wrote Dean Stewart Sheppard, in a letter nominating Coleman for a teaching award in 1975: "Blessed with an engaging personality, abounding physical vitality, and irrefutable mastery of subject-matter, Almand has left an indelible mark on all who have been exposed to him in classrooms, executive development halls, and public auditoria. To our alumni and present student body, he represents the prototype of inspirational teacher who should be representative of our University. Certainly no person could be singled out who has had more of an impact on students at this school."[24]

Upon mandatory retirement from the University of Virginia, Coleman continued to teach as a visiting professor at such institutions as Washington and Lee University and Tennessee Technological University, under its dean, William J. Arthur, a member of Darden's first graduating class and the second student to receive a Darden doctoral degree. Remaining amazingly active and vigorous well into his nineties, Coleman—to the surprise of none of his former students and colleagues—won the senior men's U.S. National Track and Field Championship in javelin throwing in 1988 and 1991, exhibiting the same athletic prowess that he had demonstrated as a young college student at Washington and Lee.

George Maverick

In 1955, George Madison Maverick joined the founding faculty. An MIT graduate in chemical engineering and a World War I veteran, he held a PhD in physical chemistry from the University of Geneva in Switzerland. Maverick had taught at MIT and later served as director of Research for Standard Oil of New Jersey (Esso). At Esso, he advanced to the position of director of Employee Relations for the Standard Oil Development Company, the parent company's

research arm, before retiring to his farm in the Charlottesville area. Upon the recommendation of the MIT School of Industrial Management Professor Douglas McGregor, an organizational behaviorist famous for Theory X and Theory Y, Dean Abbott hired Maverick, first as a visiting professor and then as a permanent member of the faculty, to teach interpersonal relations and employee relations, which he did until his retirement, in 1964. Maverick was noted for his emphasis on the practical management of complex organizational issues. He served on the School's first Student Evaluation and Scholarship Committee, a faculty body that assessed students' academic performance.[25]

Maurice Davier

Born in France, raised in New Jersey, and educated at MIT and Harvard, Maurice Davier taught production and industrial management at the Darden School from its opening, in 1955, until his death, in 1964. He had served as vice president and general manager of the Van Cleef Corporation, a subsidiary of the Johns Manville Corporation, before leaving the private sector for academia. A nonacademic, Davier, at Dean Abbott's suggestion, attended the Harvard Business School's "Summer Program on the Writing and Teach-

Above: **George M. Maverick**. A retired executive, Maverick was the School's first teacher of organizational behavior.

Right: Maurice Davier enjoys coffee with students in the School's initial Basic Advanced Management (BAM) executive-education program in 1958.

ing of Cases" for eight weeks in 1955, just before Virginia's new business school opened its doors. He became a quick convert to the case method, and plied his students with case studies of businesses in the throes of making complicated manufacturing and production decisions. From his students, he expected clear, analytical responses that took into account multiple variables and options. He also initiated the annual first-year MBA field trips to industrial plants and businesses in Virginia in order to expose students to the challenges of real-life operations, a practice that continues to this day. Tyson Janney recalled Davier as "a thoroughly decent person who seemed to really know his field of manufacturing and tried his darnedest to teach it to us."[26]

Abraham Zelomek

Abraham W. Zelomek was an experienced business practitioner who was recruited by Dean Abbott to teach the School's initial first-year marketing course as well as electives in marketing and pricing policy and price protection. He was a graduate of the Wharton School and attended the New York University School of Law. He served as an adviser to the Office of Production Management and the War Production Board during World War II. As a member of the founding faculty, Zelomek was actually a visiting, rather than permanent, professor for 15 years, commuting from New York City, where he headed his own business-publishing and statistical-

research firm, the International Statistical Bureau, Inc. Zelomek's organization also consulted with a number of the nation's leading companies, particularly in the retail, textile, chemical, and broadcasting industries. During his tenure at the School, he traveled by train to Charlottesville monthly—and sometimes twice a month—to offer specially structured, intensive block courses in marketing and to deliver guest lectures, until his retirement, in 1971. While in Charlottesville, Zelomek, called "Zel" by his friends, lodged at the University's Colonnade Club and played the role of the new business school's informal ambassador to the faculty of the rest of the University, a faculty often skeptical about the new school's academic pedigree.

Zelomek was a prolific writer, often quoted in the press. He was particularly noted for his annual presentation on Sponsors Day, when he would forecast the prospects for the U.S. economy in the year ahead. Zelomek was an expert scholar in both marketing and economics, and his annual predictions and evaluations concerning the American economy were anxiously awaited throughout the Commonwealth of Virginia and far beyond its borders.[27]

Everard Meade

Everard W. Meade, a University of Virginia alumnus, retired to Charlottesville to pen novels and to continue to write for television after a successful career in advertising at Young and Rubicam, where he was vice president of Radio and Television; at Ogilvy and Mather, where he was also a vice president; and in the radio-broadcasting industry. Immediately recognizing his potential value to Virginia's new graduate business school, Dean Abbott hired Meade as a part-time lecturer to teach marketing and advertising and to assist in a variety of administrative tasks, including oversight of the School's college-visitation program. When Abbott offered him a job, he promised, tongue-in-cheek, to convert Meade into a "reasonable facsimile" of a professor of advertising. Meade's cre-

ativity and wit—in the 1930s, he had written radio scripts and produced shows for Jack Benny, Fred Allen, Burns and Allen, Al Jolson, and Fred Astaire—positively effervesced in the classroom, where he taught advertising and oral communications.

Bringing Meade into the School's family was a major coup for Abbott. Meade's service to the Darden School—always intelligent, diplomatic, and joyful—lasted more than four decades. Upon his retirement from teaching, in 1980, Meade assumed the posts of assistant to the dean and alumni secretary, allowing him to cultivate the School's active alumni network and build strong alumni chapters in cities across the nation. For many years, he wrote the "Alumni Notes" in the School's magazine. Of Meade, Tyson Janney recalled, "He worked wonders in many quiet ways."[28] Upon his death, in 2000, at

38

the age of 90, the Everard W. Meade Fund for Creativity was endowed by his former students and friends to provide an annual award at Darden for creative leadership.[29]

William Rotch

While technically not a member of the School's founding faculty—he was hired by Dean Abbott in 1959, initially as a teaching fellow and assistant to the dean—Bill Rotch embodied, throughout a Darden teaching career that ultimately spanned four decades, the strong and sustained relationship between the School's founding principles, as they were fleshed out in the 1950s and '60s, and their enduring vibrancy over the course of a half century.

A Harvard Business School MBA and doctoral graduate, Rotch assumed a full-fledged faculty position in 1961 at Abbott's invitation. Rotch taught accounting and strategic cost management, and also became the primary advocate and developer of the School's required course on written communication. He served with distinction in a number of capacities. Rotch was the School's first director of Research and the first chair of the Research Committee. He also held the post of associate dean for Academic Affairs, fostered the use of computers in the early days of the School, promoted the School's globalization efforts as director of the Tayloe Murphy Center, and was a tireless champion of high-quality casewriting and case-method pedagogy.

Rotch was also an active, lifelong proponent of fostering international cooperation and understanding. He served for many years on the board of trustees of World Learning, Inc., the organization that runs the Experiment in International Living. That organization's School for International Training named its training center in Brattleboro, Vermont, the William Rotch Learning Center in his honor. Rotch was the Johnson and Higgins Professor Emeritus of Business Administration when he died, in 2002.

Always a refined and consummate gentleman, Rotch made an enormous and lasting contribution to the Darden School's culture and community. Brandt Allen, his

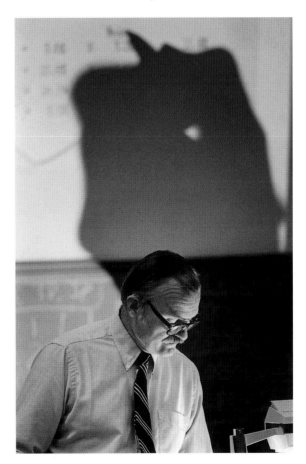

Opposite: **Everard W. Meade.** A favorite of the School's early students and alumni, Meade taught advertising and marketing with wit and real-world savvy. He served as alumni secretary upon his retirement from the faculty.

William Rotch. Rotch was a passionate advocate of case-method pedagogy.

longtime colleague in accounting, said of Rotch: "Bill believed in people. He's the least negative person I've worked with. And he was out at the end of the scale when it came to honesty and kindness. I will always remember Bill for his craft. He loved to write and teach great cases. He was a master casewriter and master teacher."[30]

Paul Hammaker

Throughout its history, the Darden School has successfully identified practicing business executives capable of enriching the MBA Program considerably if they could be enticed to join the faculty on a full-time basis. Paul M. Hammaker was a prominent example of such an executive during the School's formative period. He signed on to the faculty in 1962, after serving first as a senior executive with the Marshall Field Company and then as president of Montgomery Ward and Company.

Hammaker was introduced to Dean Abbott by founding faculty member A. W. Zelomek, who was an economic adviser to Montgomery Ward. While Hammaker brought to Virginia no direct case-method teaching experience, he recalled that adapting to the case-method approach was, for him, "a very natural thing because in business you don't do anything but case method."[31]

Abbott quickly perceived that Hammaker's extensive executive experience would be a great boon in the classroom. University President Edgar Shannon interviewed Hammaker and agreed with Abbott's opinion. In 1977, Hammaker and Louis T. Rader, his Darden School colleague and friend, collaborated on a book titled *Plain Talk to Young Executives*, a compendium of their practical, managerial wisdom accumulated during their many years of senior leadership in private industry. The book sold 30,000 copies, 10,000 of which were the Japanese edition. Hammaker taught business policy and marketing at the School from 1961 to 1973, when he retired from teaching. After his retirement, he continued to serve as a fellow in the School's Olsson Center for Applied Ethics, and maintained an active business-consulting practice.[32] In 1980, Hammaker's service to the School was honored by the establishment of the Paul M. Hammaker Professorship in Business Administration. Central to the funding of the Hammaker Chair were William Goodwin (MBA 1967) and William Welsh (MBA 1970). Wrote Dean Sheppard to Hammaker upon

William J. Arthur   *Wheeler K. Bell*   *Marsden B. Candler, Jr.*   *Donald F. Carson*   *A. Eugene Crotty*   *John H.P. Davis*   *Peter B. Elliman*   *James H. Fields*   *Pieter A. Fisher*   *Harvie W. Fitzgerald*

Lewis B. Flinn, Jr.   *James W. Geissal*   *W. H. Holden Gibbs*   *Tyson L. Janney*   *William T. Kilby*   *E. Lee LeCompte*   *Harry N. Lewis*   *Sidney S. Negus, Jr.*   *Arthur L. Pleasants III*   *Pliny A. Porter III*

Alfred W. Powell, Jr.   *E. Stuart Quarngesser*   *N. Lewis Rawlings, Jr.*   *H. Hansel Ritter*   *James L. Rumsey*   *Collins Snyder*   *Henry W. Sutherland*   *J. Richard Wilson*

The Class of 1957, first graduates of the School.

Opposite: **Paul M. Hammaker.** Hammaker exemplified Abbott's strategy of hiring seasoned business practitioners to balance academic faculty. He smoothly transitioned from president of Montgomery Ward to inspiring case teacher.

the establishment of the chair: "The Chair personifies the aspirations of the school to combine insights into the practical world of affairs with academic standards of excellence. In you we found the perfect match."[33]

On January 25, 2003, Hammaker celebrated his 100th birthday in Staunton, Virginia. Dean Robert Harris and C. Ray Smith visited him on that occasion to convey the Darden School's congratulations. Five years earlier, in his autobiography, Hammaker recalled that his Darden School teaching, both MBA and executive education, "was great, often fun, usually satisfying, and truly wonderful. It was a happy dream that had a happy ending.... I treasure the experience."[34] Paul Hammaker passed away at the age of 101, on April 1, 2004.

The Class of 1957

On Friday, September 16, 1955, a contingent of 38 pioneering students embarked on an academic adventure that they would never forget. All male and all white, these students chose to cast their lot with an untested educational enterprise that promised great benefits, but simultaneously carried great risks.

The School's original Admissions Committee of one consisted of Dean Abbott himself, assisted by Professor John Forbes. The admissions process was straightforward: submission of a simple application followed by an anxiety-producing interview with the dean. Dean Abbott, however, could ill afford to be highly selective if he were to recruit an entering MBA class of respectable size.

High-tech classroom. Paul Farris instructs a laptop-equipped class in a fully wired and video conference–enabled amphitheater classroom in Darden's current facilities.

Inset: **Monroe Hall classroom**. While paper and pencil have been replaced by personal computers and video conferencing as standard classroom technology, the intensive, interpersonal essence of Darden's pedagogy has remained steadfast.

Study groups: a prime feature of Darden's learning culture. Class of 1966 students (left to right) Willard D. Hoskins, Robert H. Carlile, Robert G. Knowles, Harold C. Gosnell, Harvey W. O'Coner, and Douglas S. Luke study in the Monroe Hall library.

A total of 66 candidates applied for admission to the new school. Seventy-three percent were accepted, many of whose undergraduate grade-point averages and standard test scores left something to be desired. James H. Field (MBA 1957) remembered: "It was easy to get accepted [to the School], but very difficult to keep up with the demands of a very tough schedule. We were the guinea pigs on which they built a curriculum."[35]

Of the 38 students who ultimately matriculated in September 1955, 60 percent were Virginians and 26 percent were alumni of the University of Virginia. Another 4 percent hailed from elsewhere in the South. The entering class ranged in age from 21 to 29 and averaged 24½. Significantly, 76 percent were military veterans, and 36 percent were married. The GI Bill was a powerful stimulus for many of Darden's early students to pursue their MBA degrees. To recent veterans in 1955, the School's in-state tuition of $414 and out-of-state tuition of $714 were difficult to digest. Uncle Sam's tuition subsidy was important in helping to fuel the School's early years. But budgets for many students, particularly those who were married and had young children, were very tight. They and their wives eagerly awaited the monthly arrival of their GI Bill checks. "We were literally living on the GI Bill, a lot of us," recalled Tyson Janney.[36]

Of even greater financial importance than the GI Bill to the new MBA students was the Student Loan Fund, established through the hard work of the Graduate Business School Sponsors. The purpose of the Student Loan Fund, the resources of which exceeded $100,000 in the School's first year, was to ensure that the School could help finance the needs of any admitted student "so that no qualified man or woman," in the words of Dean Abbott, "need abandon the idea of graduate education in business because of lack of financial resources."[37]

As the 38 entering students listened to the opening-day remarks of Henry Mc-Wane, president of the Graduate Business School Sponsors, they were jolted by a loud, booming blast. Professor Everard Meade, displaying a devilish flair for the dramatic, had fired a small cannon from the window of his office on Monroe Hall's second floor to celebrate the birth of the School. Little did the students realize that the blast's energy symbolized the rigor and dynamism of the academic program in which they would immerse themselves over the next two years.[38]

The MBA Program was rigorous, indeed: three classes a day, an hour and a half each; Saturday classes until noon, except on those Saturdays when four-hour exams were administered; and 12 papers for the required Written Analysis course. In 1980, from a perspective of 25 years, Tyson Janney recalled the students' experience: "'Incredible,' 'impossible,' 'I didn't believe it,' 'unreal,' and several dozen unprintable adjectives soon became commonplace reactions to the complexity and volume of our daily work-

At the School's thirtieth anniversary, Ev Meade demonstrates the cannon he fired in 1955 to mark its opening day.

load. It was really staggering—especially for those of us who had either spent the previous two to four years in the service or working and were academically rusty."[39]

Life for the School's pioneering students was more than challenging. They reported to classes—all held in the School's sole classroom—six days a week, typically dressed in a blazer, shirt and tie, khaki trousers, and loafers. Janney described the drill: "Every waking moment was spent either in 'the classroom' (which, except for the neat swivel chairs, was about as warm and aesthetically pleasing as the waiting room in a bus sta-

tion), or in the library, with all 216 volumes and 12 dog-eared *Wall Street Journal*s, or our dormitory or apartment rooms. None of us expected such a grind. It was brutal. And the realization soon set in that *this was it*: the constant overload and the uninterrupted pressure, the insecurity of often not knowing how well you were doing."[40]

The students quickly forged close bonds among themselves in the face of the rigorous course requirements. While the workload, in the words of Richard Wilson (MBA 1957), "was truly an overwhelming experience," the students managed to create and enjoy an informal, collegial atmosphere. Gene Crotty (MBA 1957) recalled that the pioneering students "developed an early spirit of the corps, like the Marine Corps. Each buddy is responsible for looking after his friends."[41] The students organized, elected class officers, and drafted a student-association constitution. Students enjoyed frequent interaction with the dean. Said Wilson of Abbott: "I held him in awe the whole time. I mean, he was the epitome of what a top academician should be, what a dean should look like, and the way he should act." Dean Abbott and his wife, Louise, were always open to student contact. They would often invite students to their home, Pavilion VI on the Lawn, for Sunday dinner. Louise Abbott, a Phi Beta Kappa graduate of Radcliffe College, who had been a U.S. Tennis Association national doubles champion in her youth, made a special effort to make students and their spouses feel at home, and was instrumental in founding the Wives Club, a group dedicated to supporting the wives of the always-busy graduate business students. Recalled Wilson: "The morale of the class was always high. We were always on edge. We were, I think, doubly encouraging ourselves to succeed. It was the most intense two years that I've ever spent in my life."[42]

For some, the academic experience proved *too* overwhelming, despite support and encouragement from faculty and staff. Of the 38 students who entered the new school in September 1955, only 28 received their MBA diplomas two years later. "We were small in number," observed Janney in retrospect about the School's trailblazing first class, "but none walked taller" at the School's first graduation ceremony, on June 11, 1957. "There will never be a class any tougher or prouder of the School. For we were the first!"[43]

The 1960 MBA "Business Bowl"

I t did not take long for students at Virginia's new Graduate School of Business Administration to begin to flex their intellectual muscles in national student competitions. As early as 1960, a five-man team from Virginia made an impressive showing in the "Business Bowl," a business-management-game competition in New York City, hosted by IBM at its Park Avenue educational center. Virginia's team—Robert L.

Anderson, Reuben S. Jones, Jr., James R. Peters, John W. Sinwell, and Thomas D. Steel—competed against MBA teams from Columbia, Cornell, Tuck, Wharton, Maryland, Rutgers, Syracuse, and Tulane. The teams

were tasked with managing a mock company that produced "Gizamos" for sale in multiple markets. They had to make quick decisions on a number of variables, including price, production volume, marketing expense, research-and-development strategy, and plant expansion. Decisions were fed into two IBM 650 computers, which evaluated their consequences in the context of preset economic conditions. The computers simulated a changing competitive business economy and rewarded the teams that amassed the most income.

Coached by Professors William Rotch and Almand Coleman, together with Dean Abbott, Virginia's team took top honors—

Virginia's victorious "Business Bowl" team is featured in the press. Standing (left to right): Professor Almand Coleman, Dean Charles Abbott, Robert Anderson, Professor William Rotch. Seated (left to right): Thomas Steel, Reuben Jones, John Sinwell, James Peters.

Hume Fountain adjacent to Monroe Hall.

tying with Cornell for first place—by making sound decisions in a high-pressure situation. The training that the School's students received in their intensive case-method courses clearly demonstrated its benefits in this competitive business simulation.[44]

Virginia's graduate business school had arrived on the national scene.

Monroe Hall

The University of Virginia Graduate Business School's first home was in Monroe Hall, a choice central location on Mr. Jefferson's Main Grounds, just a stone's throw from the Lawn. President Darden had assured the business community that if private funds were raised to help found the new school, he would provide it with space. He was true to his word. The University's Board of Visitors, upon the advice of the president, al-located part of the east wing of Monroe Hall to the nascent graduate business school.

Initially, the School's square footage was quite limited. It consisted of a single classroom, a small library, one study-group room for students, a secretarial office, and faculty offices. The Monroe Hall library doubled as study-and-research space and as a social-gathering spot for the morning-coffee ritual and for informal contact between students and faculty. The Sponsors organization appropriated funds for renovations, and, in 1956, an additional large classroom and two smaller ones were modified and became part of the new school's space. To say that Monroe Hall was intimate is an understatement. "The assumption in Monroe Hall," observed Professor John Snook, "was that everybody knew everybody."[45]

Within a few years of the School's occupancy of Monroe Hall, it became evident that

48

the existing building would quickly become inadequate to handle future growth. While a 1964 renovation of Monroe Hall's west wing, a project jointly funded by the Sponsors and the state, helped improve the facilities, Dean Abbott, in that year, requested $2,000 from the Sponsors to fund an architectural study aimed at enlarging Monroe Hall. Pursuant to this preliminary analysis, Abbott advocated the construction of a 65,000-square-foot addition to Monroe Hall that could accommodate future growth of the student body up to 500. In 1966, the Virginia General Assembly appropriated $35,000 to fund a planning study for a Monroe Hall addition.

The dean's plan to expand the School's initial home was soon derailed, however, by the University of Virginia's more expansive long-range construction plans. The University wanted to develop the Duke tract, a large parcel of wooded land about a mile northwest of the Main Grounds. It viewed this property as a perfect spot for a precinct of graduate and professional schools, a location that could comfortably accommodate new buildings for the Graduate Business School and the Law School, both of which required additional space and were currently occupying prime real estate on the University's increasingly crowded Main Grounds. The University stipulated that if the Graduate Business School were to acquire the substantially expanded space that it wished, it would have to move from its abode near the heart of the Academical Village to the hin-

Professors James C. Dunstan, John L. Snook, and William Rotch. Opposite (top to bottom): Professors Brandt R. Allen, John L. Colley, Jr., John L. Snook, and Neil H. "Pete" Borden.

terland of the undeveloped North Grounds.

The Sponsor Trustees were quick to recognize the value of extensive virgin terrain for the future development of the School. In 1967, together with University President Edgar Shannon and Law School officials, they began to lobby Virginia Governor Mills Godwin and the General Assembly for funding to build major new facilities for the two professional schools. The politicking ultimately proved successful. The University's plan to construct new homes for its graduate business and law schools was included in Governor Godwin's bond issue in the 1968–70 biennium.

The Sponsor Trustees believed that it was the state's obligation to fund the School's facilities while the Sponsors organization would bear the responsibility for seeking private funds to augment the School's operat-

ing budget. The University and the General Assembly accepted this view. During its 1972 session, the General Assembly approved final funding for a new building for the School. On February 1, 1973, ground was broken on the North Grounds for the University of Virginia Graduate Business School's second home.[46]

The First Faculty Generation

Of all the legacies that Charles Abbott bestowed upon Virginia's Graduate Business School, none was more critically important than the faculty members he hired. These professors sank their roots deeply into the soil of Mr. Jefferson's University and developed a powerful sense of ownership of the young institution, which they were instrumental in shaping and sustaining. In the 1960s, as the newborn school grew beyond the modest size of its first few MBA classes, Abbott began to recruit a permanent cadre of faculty to augment the tiny group of "Founding Faculty," who had instructed the School's pioneering students.

This core group of teachers and scholars, who can justly be called the Graduate Business School's "First Faculty Generation," not only has solidified the School's original vision and values, but also has carried them forward steadfastly throughout the life of the School and into the twenty-first century. As in the case of the Founding Faculty he forged, Abbott, in sculpting the First Faculty Generation, created a mix of experienced practitioners and sharp academicians. Seasoned business executives—including John L. Snook (1961) from Standard Oil, Paul M. Hammaker (1962) from Montgomery Ward, Robert R. Fair (1964) from Westinghouse, and Louis T. Rader (1969) from General Electric—enriched the classroom with hands-on business experience as they successfully integrated themselves into the Graduate Business School's faculty. At the same time these business practitioners were joining the School, Abbott was recruiting an extraordinary group of talented young academics, who have formed the backbone of the School's success over the past four decades and who have left their indelible imprint on Darden's MBA graduates as well as its executive-education participants.

Many of these young professors had cut their academic teeth at the Harvard Busi-

ness School. Among these faculty were Frederick S. Morton (1957) in business policy, William Rotch (1959, 1961) in accounting, Neil H. "Pete" Borden (1963) in marketing, Robert F. Vandell (1965) in finance, Alexander B. Horniman (1967) in organizational behavior, William W. Sihler (1967) in finance, Christopher Gale (1969) in marketing, Derek A. "Dan" Newton (1970) in marketing, and Brandt R. Allen (1970) in accounting. These eager and energetic teachers arrived from Boston infused not only with ardor for case-method pedagogy, but also with the zealous determination that they could fashion at Virginia a graduate business institution that delivered a practical managerial education rivaling or surpassing that of any other graduate business program in the country.

Pete Borden reflected the passion of these refugees from Boston: "It was a very different experience than Harvard because it was small. The university was small; there were 7,500 students when I got here

[in 1963].... The business school was so much smaller and it was so much more of a family, and we all, as a faculty, fit in one room, and we could holler and make a lot of noise at one another. It was very different than the Harvard experience where, at Harvard, the marketing group was larger than the Darden faculty. So it was coming down to where the individual made a difference. A lot of that opportunity was size, but the other part was Charlie. Charlie Abbott encouraged the individual initiative of building."[47]

To his recruits from Harvard, Abbott added a number of other enthusiastic young faculty from a variety of different institutions as he wove together the School's First Faculty Generation. Among these professors were John L. Colley, Jr. (1967) in operations, from the University of Southern California; Robert D. Landel (1969) in operations, from the

Georgia Institute of Technology; Eleanor G. May (1970) in marketing, from George Washington University; Leslie E. Grayson (1971) in economics, from the University of Michigan; Alan R. Beckenstein (1972) in economics, from the University of Michigan; and R. Jack Weber (1972) in organizational behavior, from the University of California at Berkeley. In addition, Abbott appointed to the faculty a number of alumni from the University of Virginia. C. Ray Smith, a 1958 MBA graduate, joined the accounting faculty of his alma mater in 1961, the same year that C. Frederick Sargent, a 1959 MBA graduate, joined the finance faculty. Charles O. Meiburg, a PhD graduate in economics, was appointed to the faculty in 1964. James C. Dunstan, a doctoral graduate of the School, who previously had a successful business career, became a faculty member in 1972, teaching marketing, finance, and business policy.

Remarkably, under Abbott's sagacious guidance, the Harvard contingent, the recruits from the University of Virginia and other universities, and the business-practitioner group melded together over the years into a cohesive First Faculty Generation, with a single-minded dedication to ensuring that Virginia's incipient graduate business school would enjoy a sound footing that would enable it to blossom and prosper. That footing encompassed a commitment to deliver an uncompromisingly relevant and rigorous general-management education that prepared students to

meet the challenges of business leadership with skill, confidence, and integrity.

It was the members of the First Faculty Generation who constructed the highly integrated curriculum that has characterized the Darden School since its early days. Professor Pete Borden was instrumental in fashioning the School's academic architecture. "I came in," recalled Borden, "as a guy who had really bought into the case method and interactive pedagogy. So, after being here for a year, I made it my business to see if I could push toward an integrated program. It took quite a few years to get thorough integration in the program.... I said, 'We have to have one assignment sheet, one program that goes out each week.' Before that, everyone sent out their own stuff, which was kind of conventional academic. I said, 'No,

let's try it with an integrated program.' I thought if everybody could see what everybody else was doing, we could move toward more integration. And we eventually got it.... Pretty soon, we had enough believers so we became much more case method and the program became more balanced."[48]

Borden's contemporary, Professor William Sihler, described the result of this integrative process for the Darden School: "The curriculum is a program, not a collection of courses, and it is developed as an entity, in which the courses rely on one another to develop the subject matter.... The total impact of the program is also planned to develop the 'action abilities.' These skills are not learned by the student who takes one course at a time."[49]

The First Faculty Generation expended

Robert R. Fair welcomes The Executive Program (TEP) Class of 1985. Fair directed Darden's executive-education unit for more than two decades as it became a major enterprise.

tremendous time and energy to develop and refine a holistic curriculum designed for delivery by master teachers whose goal was instructional excellence. By 1970, after a decade and a half of evolution, the School's MBA Program was ready for external scrutiny. In that year, Professors Borden and Snook prepared an application for accreditation of Virginia's MBA Program by the Association of American Collegiate Schools of Business (AACSB). In February 1971, after a two-day visit by an evaluation team, the AACSB pronounced Virginia's MBA Program formally accredited.[50] It has remained so ever since.

Executive Education

From the earliest discussions of the need for a graduate business school at the University of Virginia, there was no doubt that executive education would play a prominent role in the institution's objectives, activities, and development. In fact, in his September 1955 address celebrating the opening of the graduate business school, Henry McWane, chairman of the Sponsor Trustees, stated that, while the initial primary focus of the School would be to serve resident, full-time graduate students, the School also had an obligation to meet the needs of its many corporate supporters throughout the Commonwealth, "who rather eagerly await the inauguration of a program of intensive short courses in special subjects for established business practitioners."[51]

Just two months later, the fledgling

Sponsors organization, in conjunction with Dean Abbott, incorporated executive education explicitly into the new school's fundamental mission. The Sponsors perceived the School to be an ideal vehicle "to bring business education and business closer together so that each may benefit from the understanding of the responsibilities and problems of the other."[52] From a practical standpoint, observed J. Harvie Wilkinson, vice president of the Sponsors, an operating objective of the School must be "to bring together representatives from different businesses and from government, and to exert a broadening influence upon men with diverse specializations." The School would accomplish this objective by arranging "conferences, seminars, and advanced management programs for men in business who may not have had formal training in the colleges, but who have had business experience."[53] The business leaders who helped give life to the new school hoped to benefit not only from a crop of young managers who would emerge with MBA degrees after two years of intensive study at the University of Virginia, but also from brief, focused, practical business-education programs that would enhance their current employees' skills and bring more-immediate results.

Thus, executive education became a foundational pillar of the University of Virginia Graduate Business School. Robert R. Fair, the longtime leader and catalyst of Darden's executive-education activities, recalled that Dean Abbott believed that the MBA Program

and executive education "were equal objectives. In fact, if he [Abbott] had his way, he said he would have started executive education before he started the MBA Program."[54]

In actuality, the new school's initial foray into executive education came right on the heels of the arrival of the School's first class of MBA students. The School's inaugural executive-education program took place in November 1955. It was a one-week program requested by the Young Presidents' Organization, a national group comprising midsized corporations whose presidents were under the age of 40. The topic of the seminar, delivered to 40 participants, was "How to Acquire Working Capital"; its faculty leader, not surprisingly, was Dean Charles Abbott himself, an expert on the subject. This first program ushered in a 12-year relationship between the Young Presidents' Organization and the School. In 1956, a second executive-

education program—a three-day seminar on sales management—was conducted for the American Textbook Publishers. The dean and his supporters in the business community were of one mind regarding the importance of the School's continuing-education efforts. Dean Abbott stressed to his small faculty, as well as to President Darden, the need for the School to develop quickly in this area. To help spark activity, two groups sprang into action. In early 1956, the Sponsors organization formed the Committee on Management Short Course Programs, chaired by Sture G. Olsson, president of the Chesapeake Corporation, to advise the School on program needs and to help promote the School's programs to the business community. At the same time, the dean encouraged the faculty to generate creative ideas for fostering permanent short-course activity at the School. In 1957, the faculty established the Short Course

Committee, chaired by Forrest E. Keller, an economist who had been the assistant director of Economic Research for the U.S. Chamber of Commerce before his appointment as the first executive secretary of the Sponsors organization. The committee's charge was to plan for a balanced array of short courses, seminars, and conferences.

Significant executive-education activities burgeoned in the early years of the School, as programs for such industry groups as the Virginia Press Association, the Virginia Bankers Institute, and the Virginia Manufacturers Association were presented. While these early programs clearly had a strong Virginia orientation, it was not long before the faculty set its sights on a broader potential executive-education clientele.

In 1959, the faculty codified the School's executive-education objectives. First and foremost, the goal of executive education was to provide professional development to middle- and top-level managers. Second, the School intended to seek participants from companies nationwide, while acknowledging a "special responsibility to Virginia and the Southeast." Third, executive education was designed to encourage close relationships between business practitioners and the faculty, relationships aimed at enriching the faculty's teaching and curriculum-development efforts. At the same time that it set objectives for its "Short Course Programs," the School established criteria for accepting program proposals. A number of these criteria have

endured. Among the most important are the following: a program must be relevant to the needs of a "substantial section of the business community"; a program must accept participants from multiple companies; a program would ordinarily be taught exclusively by the Graduate Business School's own faculty.[55]

Frederick S. Morton. Morton chaired the committee that planned the Basic Advanced Management Program (BAM).

The Sponsor Trustees' Committee on Management Short Course Programs recommended, in 1956, that the School develop a short course emphasizing "basic, rounded, professional training in the fundaments of business operations." A faculty planning committee took up the challenge. Chaired by Professor Frederick S. Morton, the committee created the Basic Advanced Management Program (BAM) as the School's most notable executive-education activity. An integrated program rather than a series of disparate courses, BAM was designed for business people on the threshold of senior-management responsibility in their companies. A faculty team—comprising Morton as faculty leader and Almand Coleman, Maurice Davier, Edward O. Malott, Arthur B. Moss, and Dean Abbott—delivered the first BAM to 35 participants, representing 29 companies and seven states plus Washington, DC, over the course of four and a half weeks in the summer of 1958. At the closing ceremony, Ralph K. T. Larson, managing editor of the *Virginian-Pilot*, who had been elected BAM class president, cited the effectiveness of the case method in expanding the horizons of the attendees. On behalf of the class, he presented to the School a lectern made from the wood of a walnut tree that dated back to James Monroe's ownership of the land on which Monroe Hall, the Graduate Business School's home, stood.[56] A summer general-management program, geared to rising corporate stars, has been conducted by the School ever since.[57]

As the School's executive-education activities began to blossom and the need for administrative support became apparent, Dean Abbott, in 1961, established a specific unit within the Sponsors organization, the Division of Management Programs, to plan and oversee all nondegreed educational activities. The dean appointed Fred Morton, who already chaired the faculty Short Course Committee, as the division's initial director. When Morton went on leave in 1964 to teach abroad, he passed the director's baton to Robert Fair.[58]

Fair's appointment was auspicious. He came to the School from a division of Westinghouse, where he had been responsible for management development, the process of identifying and nominating promising corporate employees for university and in-house educational programs to enhance their skills. Fair's connections to Virginia's

Alan R. Beckenstein.

Graduate Business School antedated his appointment. He had received his bachelor's degree in engineering from the University of Virginia and his MBA from Harvard, where he had known Charles Abbott, then a faculty member there. In 1953, as a Harvard MBA graduate, Fair had met with the faculty committee planning Virginia's new graduate business school as part of the committee's effort to interview University of Virginia alumni who had enrolled in out-of-state schools to pursue graduate business degrees. Five years later, after Abbott had moved to Charlottesville and was seeking faculty with business experience, Fair was recommended to the dean by Joseph L. Vaughan, provost of the University of Virginia, who had been Fair's humanities professor in the Engineering School. Abbott tried to entice Fair to join the faculty of the young business school for several years. Finally, in 1964, he succeeded, when Fair accepted the combined posts of associate professor and director of Management Programs.

Fair assumed the directorship with relish, and set to work on a career that spanned more than three decades, during which he elevated Darden's noncredit instructional programs to international stature. Under Fair's leadership, the School's management programs charted a number of promising directions. First, Fair quickly propelled his division from a money-loser to a profit-generator by increasing both price and volume and initiating a series of executive seminars—short programs of two to four days covering specific topics—to supplement BAM's offerings.[59] To further expand its executive-education potential, the School

began to transport its programs beyond Charlottesville. Initially conducting programs elsewhere in the United States—in such cities as Norfolk, Williamsburg, Chicago, Atlanta, and New York—the School then leapfrogged to foreign venues. During the 1970s, faculty taught programs abroad in a number of different locations, including Mexico City, London, and Cardiff, Wales. In 1979, Darden extended its reach to Australia with the launch of its Australian Management Program. Taught at the University of New South Wales, near Sydney, this seminar was a two-week policy-oriented program that integrated marketing, finance, accounting, and organizational behavior.[60] The School's Australian program continued for 16 years. The overseas programs benefited the Darden School not only by providing it with exposure

Neil H. "Pete" Borden.

abroad, but also by presenting the faculty with opportunities to learn firsthand about the international business environment.

Darden's executive-education ventures gained greater prominence during the 1970s and 1980s. The School's flagship program, Basic Advanced Management, saw an increase in enrollment, participant heterogeneity, and length—to six weeks, in 1967. Originally drawing students primarily from Virginia and the South, BAM soon attracted participants from across the United States and, ultimately, from around the world. In 1973, the name of the program was changed to "The Executive Program" (TEP) to reflect these new dimensions. In the same year, TEP witnessed its first female attendee, Joanna Fiori of First National City Bank. For many years, TEP served as the premier

offering of the School's rapidly developing executive-education initiative. The success of TEP was further reflected in the creation of an additional two-week general-management program, Managing Critical Resources (MCR), designed as a briefer, lower-cost option to appeal to companies in Virginia and the South. First offered in 1968, MCR, renamed the Management Development Program in 2004, is conducted several times a year, just one of many programs in Darden's stable of executive-education offerings.

Both TEP and MCR, as well as Darden's growing number of other executive-education programs, were characterized by a carefully thought-out, highly integrated curriculum taught by Darden faculty, who not only excelled in the classroom, but also went out of their way to involve themselves

Derek A. "Dan" Newton.

intensively in participants' educational and social experiences at the Darden School.[61] George Bricker, a leading management consultant to executive-development programs, judged Darden's MCR to be "the best two-week general management program in the country." The remarkable amount of personal attention and time that Darden faculty devoted to the School's executive-education activities paid dividends for the School by building both its reputation and financial resources. In 1976, just 20 years after the School opened its doors, *BusinessWeek* described Darden's Division of Executive Programs as "one of the best in the country."[62]

Darden's executive-education activities accelerated greatly in the last quarter of the twentieth century by offering both open-enrollment programs and single-company (or government-agency) sponsored programs. The School's flexibility permitted it to capitalize on creative ideas for new and experimental programs. A notable example was a series of seminars, created and administered by a partnership of Darden Executive Programs and the School's Center for the Study of Applied Ethics, that were conducted at Richmond's Union Theological Seminary in 1979. Intended for both theologians and business executives, the well-received seminars, led by Professor Louis Rader, were designed "to foster informed dialogue between those engaged in business and those engaged in professional ministry regarding value considerations in business as they affect both the

Leslie E. Grayson.

corporation and the church."[63] A more recent example of Darden's executive-education capabilities was a series of intensive programs in e-business that the School conducted for such clients as Citibank and PricewaterhouseCoopers in the late 1990s during the nation's Internet boom. In addition, Darden, as an integral part of the University of Virginia, has developed executive-education programs in conjunction with the University's Institute of Government, Curry School of Education, and Health Sciences Center. In 2004, for example, the Darden-Curry Partnership for Leaders in Education, a program that trained public-school administrators in strategies to help turn around schools with performance challenges, received financial support from Virginia Governor Mark Warner and the Microsoft Corporation as well as significant national attention.

By the late 1990s, Darden's executive-education programs were enrolling more than 4,000 participants in approximately 50 offerings annually. Under Robert Fair's leadership—as well as that of his successors as associate dean for Executive Education, C. Ray Smith and Brandt Allen—Darden Executive Programs has remained true to its principles throughout its remarkable growth. The programs continue to be taught primarily by full-time Darden School faculty who invest themselves totally in the program experience. The courses provide practicing managers with intensive learning experiences in a university setting. Continuing-education activities generate rich, contemporary case materials that later often find their way into the MBA Program. The faculty and the School benefit from close interaction with practicing managers, who then take their learning back to their companies for relevant applications to real-world business problems. Now 50 years old, Darden Executive Programs continues to fulfill the vision of the School's founders.

The Doctoral Program

While Virginia's Graduate Business School was founded with a clearly focused dual mission—delivery of an MBA program and executive-development courses for practicing managers—as a graduate school at an increasingly prominent national university, it was not long before the question whether to offer a doctoral degree emerged. In fact, less than 18 months after the School's first MBA class enrolled, Dean Abbott raised the possibility of developing an advanced graduate degree in business to President Darden, who advised the dean to consider the idea methodically and to concentrate the School's attention and resources initially on the MBA Program. In 1956 and again in 1957, Abbott formed

committees of his small faculty to study the doctoral-program concept. Both committees advised against establishing a doctoral program, believing it to be a challenge that was too much for the fledgling school to confront at this early date in its existence.

In 1961, still warm to the idea of a doctoral program, Abbott appointed yet another committee to advise him on the notion. This time, Abbott selected Dean Frederick D. G. Ribble of the Law School to chair the group, which included Dean Frank A. Geldard of the Graduate School of Arts and Sciences and the University's rector, Frank Talbott, Jr., as well as business-school faculty members Almand Coleman, Almarin Phillips, and William Rotch. The Ribble committee recommended establishing a doctoral program. The Graduate Business School faculty, however, fearing insufficient resources to support both an MBA and a Doctor of Business Administration (DBA) program, failed to support the committee's recommendation. This rejection came despite the fact that the University, from a strategic perspective, favored the creation of a doctoral program in business administration because there was, as yet, no such program in the Commonwealth, and the University of Virginia might lose its chance to offer the degree to another state institution if it failed to act quickly.

The issue continued to simmer, however. Professor Lee Johnston, the staunchest faculty advocate for a doctoral program, continued to champion the concept and, in

Professors Charles O. Meiburg and William W. Sihler.

the fall of 1963, convinced his colleagues to design a program. Johnston chaired the committee that crafted a DBA program. The faculty approved the DBA degree in April 1965, and Dean Abbott appointed Johnston the School's first director of the Doctoral Program. The program's objectives were codified by the faculty in 1971: "To offer a high-quality Doctoral Program for a selected number of very promising candidates with the aim of preparing these men and women to be superior teachers, course and curriculum designers, and researchers with deep interest in the realities of business, and with a sympathetic understanding of the problems of executive leadership."[64]

The School's Doctoral Program has remained small throughout its almost 40-year life-span. While the program, over time,

has opened a number of doctoral fields of study—Finance (1966), Quantitative Methods (1969), Marketing (1969), Accounting and Control (1974)—not all these fields of study have been open simultaneously, and the total number of doctoral students enrolled in the program at any one time has seldom exceeded a dozen. In recent years, the field of Management, with its subfields of Entrepreneurship and Business Ethics, has been the most active in producing doctoral graduates.

Throughout its existence, the Doctoral Program at Virginia has required candidates to demonstrate a broad knowledge of the core areas of business and to graft upon that knowledge a penetrating mastery of a particular field through close collaboration with one or more faculty mentors. Johnston was succeeded as director of the

Doctoral Program by Professors William Sihler, Robert Landel, and Edgar Pessemier, all of whom advocated increasing the analytical rigor of the program and the exposure of doctoral students to state-of-the-art methodological approaches in university departments outside the School. In 1986, under Pessemier's directorship, the degree's designation was changed from DBA to PhD to reflect its deeper methodological emphasis. Subsequent Doctoral Program directors Paul Farris and Philip Pfeifer, as well as the current director, Patricia Werhane, have all emphasized the importance of producing doctoral graduates who are not only outstanding researchers, but also fine teachers who can effectively serve as missionaries for the case method of instruction at institutions where they conduct their careers.

The Institute of Chartered Financial Analysts

Not many years after the birth of Virginia's Graduate Business School, the Financial Analysts Association, an organization of financial professionals based in New York, developed a set of objectives designed to enhance significantly the credibility and standards of their profession. An important goal of this professional society was the establishment of an ancillary organization that could lend academic respectability to the formal certification of practitioners who wished to promote themselves as credible professional financial analysts. A second goal was to initiate quality educational programs aimed at upgrading the knowledge base and skills of financial analysts. Finally, the association recognized the need to commission an estimable group of financial professionals to craft and promulgate a formal code of ethics and to self-regulate the profession.

In 1961, the Financial Analysts Association created the Institute of Chartered Financial Analysts (ICFA), and elected C. Stewart Sheppard, then dean of the Graduate School of Business and Public Administration at Cornell, as its first director. Simultaneously, Sheppard left Ithaca to accept an appointment in Charlottesville as a professor at the University of Virginia Graduate Business School. Dean Abbott recognized the potential synergies between his young business school and the financial analysts' initiative, and was eager to have Sheppard and the new ICFA housed at Virginia, a plan supported by President Edgar F. Shannon. After considering a number of other competing business schools, the Executive Council of the Financial Analysts Association selected the University of Virginia as the home of the ICFA, owing mainly to the respect that the team of Sheppard and Abbott had earned in the financial community.

Sheppard soon brought aboard C. Ray Smith, who, like Sheppard, joined the School's faculty in 1961, as assistant director and head of certification testing at the ICFA. Sheppard and Smith wasted no time

in rolling out a certification-examination program. Candidates for certification were required to pass rigorous examinations at three levels in order to demonstrate their mastery of a body of knowledge that would henceforth enhance the public image of the financial analysts' profession. The CFA designation, or charter, quickly became the acknowledged elite professional credential for career financial analysts. Many states recognized it in lieu of licensure. By 1975, more than 4,000 individuals—including 22 Darden School graduates—had received certification as "chartered" financial analysts thanks to the work of Sheppard and Smith.

The ICFA's examination program grew in popularity and prestige, and the organization's activities expanded swiftly. The ICFA sponsored publication of the *CFA Digest*, conducted continuing-education courses—at times, in conjunction

with the Darden School—for its already-credentialed members, disseminated standards of professional conduct, investigated consumer complaints, and levied disciplinary sanctions when necessary.

In 1972, when he became dean of the Darden School, Sheppard relinquished his ICFA leadership post, handing the reins to W. Scott Bauman, who became executive director and also a member of Darden's faculty. Bauman resigned as executive director of ICFA in 1978. The post was then filled by O. Whitfield Broome, an associate professor at the University of Virginia's McIntire School.

As the ICFA prospered and grew, in both chartered membership and staff, it became independent from the Darden School. By 1980, it administered examinations to almost 2,000 candidates in 90 locations in the United States, Canada, and overseas. It has, however, remained headquartered in

C. Stewart Sheppard, founding director of the Institute of Chartered Financial Analysts (ICFA). Nurtured at Virginia's Graduate School of Business Administration, the ICFA has become the premier organization providing certification of financial analysts worldwide.

Charlottesville, and continues to acknowledge its roots at the University of Virginia. In 1976, the ICFA created an award in honor of Sheppard. The C. Stewart Sheppard Award is granted annually to the ICFA member who has most significantly rendered outstanding service to the Institute.[65]

When Stewart Sheppard died, in 2002, at the age of 86, Thomas A. Bowman, president and CEO of the CFA Institute, the successor organization to the ICFA, said of his organization's founding director: "All that the CFA designation has become is due, in no small part, to the vision and continuing efforts of Stewart Sheppard." At the present time, more than 45,000 investment professionals worldwide hold the CFA charter. An additional 100,000 individuals in nations across the globe are candidates for the prestigious credential.[66]

The Tayloe Murphy Center

The Tayloe Murphy Center has been an important outreach arm of the University of Virginia Graduate Business School for nearly four of the School's five decades of existence. Like the School itself, the Tayloe Murphy Center was created through a joint public/private effort to secure resources for aiding the economic development of the Commonwealth.

In 1944, the Commonwealth of Virginia established the Bureau of Population and Economic Research as a unit of state government and located it at the University of Vir-

University Professor Charlotte H. Scott. Scott conducted banking studies for the Tayloe Murphy Institute.

ginia. Supported by state funds and directed by Lorin A. Thompson, the Bureau undertook a series of studies on topics concerning the demographic, economic, and industrial development of Virginia and its localities. The freestanding Bureau and the young Graduate Business School were brought closer together in 1964, when Charles O. Meiburg, a PhD graduate (in economics) of the University of Virginia, was appointed both associate director of the Bureau and a faculty member at the School. In 1966, when Thompson assumed the post of chancellor—and, later, first president—of George Mason College, in Northern Virginia, Meiburg was promoted to director of the Bureau. During the 1960s, the Bureau of Population and Economic Research actively pursued its research mission and, in 1967, Governor Mills E. Godwin, Jr., designated it the official state agency for population estimates.

While the Bureau was collecting and disseminating data about the demographic and economic trends in the state, a campaign in memory of W. Tayloe Murphy was raising contributions to support an entity designed to undertake studies to promote commercial development in the Commonwealth. W. Tayloe Murphy was an important figure in Virginia politics and business. A native of Westmoreland County, in Virginia's Northern Neck, Murphy served in Virginia's House of Delegates in the 1940s and '50s for 14 years and as treasurer of the Commonwealth from 1942 to 1947. In the business world, Murphy held the posts of president of Northern Neck State Bank and president and chairman of the Tidewater Telephone Company. When he passed away, in 1962, a close friend anonymously pledged a million dollars to establish the W. Tayloe Murphy Institute at the University of Virginia in recognition of Murphy's public service and his "unfaltering support of the Graduate School of Business Administration." A provision of the pledge required matching gifts of $600,000 from other donors.[67]

The University's Board of Visitors formally established the Tayloe Murphy Institute in 1965, and Dean Abbott was named its director. The campaign to raise the matching funds succeeded in attracting generous support from a number of Virginia banks and business people. In 1967, University President Edgar Shannon announced the completion of the requisite funding, and the Institute became fully operational.

Abbott appointed Maurice Nelles, a business-school professor who had managed research programs at such major companies as Borg-Warner, Westinghouse, and Lockheed and had been deputy director of the War Production Board during World War II, as the Tayloe Murphy Institute's first executive director. While the Institute undertook a number of studies in its formative years, a difference of opinion arose between the University and the Institute's Advisory Council, a panel of prominent Virginia business leaders, regarding the Institute's strategy and jurisdiction. Nelles resigned in 1970, and Abbott resumed active leadership of the Institute as he attempted to define more specifically the Institute's role at the University.

One initiative of the Institute was clear, however, and it concerned retailing. Convinced that the Commonwealth could benefit from research on retail business, Abbott recruited Eleanor G. May, director of Research at the Washington, DC, department-store chain Woodward & Lothrop, to be the Graduate Business School's first female faculty member and a senior researcher at the Institute. May initiated a major series of retail and sales-tax

Charles O. Meiburg, director of the Tayloe Murphy Institute. Under Meiburg's leadership, the Institute became widely recognized for its studies of banking, retailing, economics, and demographics in Virginia.

Eleanor G. May, Darden's first female faculty member, conducted valued economic studies for the Tayloe Murphy Institute.

studies that became some of the Institute's most widely recognized and anticipated products over the next two decades.

In an effort to put aside internal philosophical differences and put an end to turf battles, President Shannon appointed a committee in 1971 to consider how the University should most effectively organize its public-affairs research and service programs. The committee, chaired by Department of Government Professor Frederick C. Mosher, recommended the consolidation of the Bureau of Population and Economic Research and the Tayloe Murphy Institute.

When Stewart Sheppard became dean, President Shannon asked him to implement the consolidation of the two units. Sheppard appointed Charles Meiburg as the director of the combined entities, which assumed

the name Tayloe Murphy Institute. Meiburg organized the new institute into three units: the Population Studies Center, the Economic Studies Center, and the Business Studies Center. Led by William J. Serow (and, later, by Julia Martin), John L. Knapp, and Eleanor G. May, respectively, as research directors, and aided by University Professor Charlotte H. Scott, the three centers produced a series of well-regarded studies for the benefit of both business and government in the Commonwealth. Among the most notable studies published were *Virginia Annual Gross State Product, Distribution of Virginia Adjusted Gross Income by Income Class, Estimates of Population of Virginia Counties and Cities, Retail Sales in Virginia, Deposit Statistics for Banks and Thrifts in Virginia Communities, Consumer Price Indicators for Virginia Metropolitan Areas*, and *Virginia Statistical Abstract*. These practical, ongoing studies helped the Tayloe Murphy Institute become a household name in the press and in government and business circles throughout Virginia over the next decade and a half.[68] Charles Meiburg served as director of the Institute from 1972 until 1983, when he stepped down to accept the post of associate dean for Academic Affairs at the Darden School. He was succeeded as director by Darden Professor James C. Dunstan.

In 1987, in an effort to better coordinate the University of Virginia's overall efforts to serve the Commonwealth's governmental entities and the public, the Tayloe Murphy Institute was reorganized. The University merged the Economic Studies Center and the Population Studies Center, both of which were state-funded, with the College of Arts and Sciences' Institute of Government, forming a new unit called the Center for Public Service, which reported directly to the provost.

The Darden School retained the Business Studies Center, which was funded by endowment income and which continued to operate, under the slightly revised name of Tayloe Murphy Center. In accordance with its mission to help promote the commercial development of Virginia and consistent with both the Commonwealth's and Darden's growing interest in the global economy, Dean John Rosenblum asked the Tayloe Murphy Center to take on a new and important international focus. In September

1987, Professor Leslie E. Grayson, a strong proponent of the Darden School's global activities, assumed the directorship of what, for a time, was renamed the Tayloe Murphy International Business Studies Center.

Under Grayson and his successors, Professors Mark Eaker and William Rotch, the Center became an active participant in the Virginia Department of World Trade's International Market Planning Program. This program was a cooperative venture between the Virginia Department of World Trade—and, later, the Virginia Department of Economic Development—and the state's graduate business schools. Its objective was to help Virginia companies identify and develop overseas markets for their products. As part of this program, and under the guidance of Professor Robert W. Haigh, several dozen Darden students participated in research studies, for Virginia firms, that examined a variety of key business topics, ranging from market-entry strategies to joint-venture possibilities. A number of Darden student teams won the Governor's Award for Excellence in International Market Planning in annual competitions to identify outstanding student-written business plans. In addition, the Center sponsored research studies on the investment strategies and plant-location decisions of foreign companies in the United States and

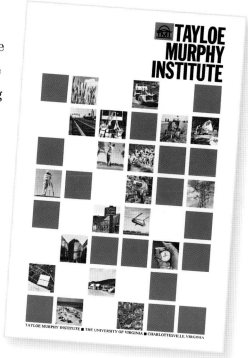

on export and joint-venture opportunities abroad for Virginia companies. At the same time, the Center expanded its role within Darden to help the School intensify its efforts to bring a global perspective to its instructional, casewriting, and research programs.

In 1994, Dean Leo Higdon appointed Brandt Allen as director of the Tayloe Murphy International Business Studies Center. Allen and his successors, Professors Robert Conroy and Jay Bourgeois, encouraged the Center's support of Darden's MBA student-exchange programs with international business schools as well as its international research activities. With the Center's strong support, the Darden School forged formal student-exchange relationships with 15 institutions abroad: the International University of Japan; the Hong Kong University of Science and Technology; China Europe International Business School (CEIBS); the Solvay School of the Université Libre de Bruxelles; Hitotsubashi University (ISC), in Japan; Rotterdam School of Management of Erasmus University, in the Netherlands; the Instituto Panamericano de Alta Dirección de Empresa (IPADE), in Mexico; the Stockholm School of Economics; Beijing University; Melbourne Business School, in Australia; the International School of Management of the University of Navarra (IESE), in Barcelona, Spain; the School of Management of the Universidad Austral (IAE), in Argentina; London Business School; Indian School of Business; and Cheung Hong Graduate School of Business.

In its role as a stimulus to the Darden School's globalization efforts, the Tayloe Murphy Center has also supported the School's participation in the MBA Enterprise Corps. A consortium of more than 20 leading graduate business schools, the MBA Enterprise Corps sends newly minted MBA graduates to Central and Eastern Europe, where they work with local firms in former Soviet-bloc countries. Under the aegis of this program, Darden graduates have served in Bulgaria and Russia.

In addition to overseeing the Darden School's formal student-exchange programs and other student-learning and -service opportunities around the globe, beginning in the 2000–01 academic year, the Tayloe Murphy Center assumed the administration of Darden's innovative Global Business Experience course. This course originated as an intensive one-week elective abroad during spring break that permitted Darden students to take a class on a global topic directly related to the location where the course was conducted. Later, a three-week international course model was also introduced. Darden students have taken the Global Business Experience course in a number of different locations, including Barcelona, Brussels, Shanghai, Mexico City, Prague, Stockholm, Riga, and Bahrain. Since the program's inception, more than 500 Darden students, in both their first and second year of the MBA Program, have benefited from the Global Business Experience opportunity.

Finally, as an additional initiative to help globalize the School, the Tayloe Murphy Center began, in 2001–02, to sponsor international visiting faculty members, who offer Tayloe Murphy Global Seminars at Darden as electives in the MBA Program. These three-week courses, taught by an international expert, focus on a topic pertinent to a particular area overseas. The Tayloe Murphy Global Seminars have covered such topics as "Latin American Financial Markets," "Venture Capital and Strategic Entry in the Asia Pacific," "Surviving and Thriving in Central and Eastern Europe," and "The View from Europe: The Role of Innovation in the Changing Business-Environment Relationship."

Since its birth, the Tayloe Murphy Center has played an integral role in the Darden School's service to Virginia business and government. In more recent years, its additional international focus has recognized not only the impact of the global economy on the economic health of Virginia and the United States, but also the importance of the Darden School's increasingly worldwide scope and stature.

The Olsson Center for Applied Ethics

Thomas Jefferson founded the University of Virginia to serve as an institution of higher education dedicated to fostering leadership and integrity in the minds and hearts of the leaders of a bold, new democratic society. When the University gave birth to its Graduate School of Business Administration some 136 years after Jefferson secured a charter for his beloved public academy, the mission of its newest offspring fit perfectly with Mr. Jefferson's intention. The Graduate Business School's founding fathers, like the University founder himself, believed in an educational process

that embodied the promotion of leadership and integrity as an academic institution's highest calling. It is not surprising that, from the start, given its dedication to producing outstanding leaders in the world of practical affairs, Virginia's Graduate Business School deemed it a prime institutional objective to teach students to appreciate the broad moral and humanistic imperatives of integrity-based leadership. As J. Harvie Wilkinson, Jr., put it in 1953, in his philosophical blueprint for the University's proposed graduate business school, "It is desirable and necessary for the development of top leadership in business that there be at least a minimum awareness of the religious or spiritual aspect of man and as something above that minimum there should be a nurturing of the spiritual seed."[69]

Just 11 years after its inception, the School initiated planning for a program in ethics that would come to represent a signal manifestation of its devotion to this essential leadership quality. In 1966, a gift from Mrs. Signe M. Olsson of West Point, Virginia, in memory of her husband, Elis, founder of the Chesapeake Corporation, endowed a chair for stimulating "public interest in and understanding of the ethical implications that necessarily adhere to the exercise of authority in both public and private life."[70] The chair would, moreover, seek to improve leadership's "standards of behavior and emphasize the essentiality of integrity in reconciliation of the dignity of the individual and the moralities implicit in free markets."[71]

The establishment of the Elis and Signe Olsson Professorship became the springboard for Dean Abbott's efforts to develop the Center for the Study of Applied Ethics at the Graduate Business School. President Edgar Shannon embraced the concept, and the University of Virginia formally recognized the Center in 1969. Dean Abbott appointed Professor Alexander B. Horniman as the Center's executive director. Horniman established an advisory board and set the Center's initial agenda, which included the publication of benchmark bibliographies in business ethics and the development of seminars and cases emphasizing ethical issues.

In 1973, Dean Sheppard named Frederick E. Nolting, Jr., as Olsson professor and executive director of the Center. He also appointed Professor Paul Hammaker, upon his retirement from the faculty, as a senior fellow with the Center. Nolting, a former banker, who held a PhD in philosophy and had served as the U.S. ambassador to Vietnam, introduced the elective Ethics in Business, Law, and Government as the School's first ethics course. Nolting encouraged the Center to sponsor conferences on such topics as the duties and responsibilities of corporate trustees, the teaching of ethics in business schools, and pension reform. As Nolting conceived it, the Darden School's Center for the Study of Applied Ethics must be firmly "grounded upon personal value standards. Its emphasis upon the importance of personal integrity springs naturally from the environment of the University of Virginia."[72]

The pace of the Center's research quickened in 1977, when Dean Sheppard

appointed Professor Louis T. Rader as executive director. Rader had joined the Graduate Business School faculty in 1969, after a distinguished career in industry, where he had held such positions as president of the Univac Division of the Sperry Rand Corporation, vice president of General Electric, and group vice president of International Telephone and Telegraph. Simultaneously, Rader was appointed to the University of Virginia's School of Engineering faculty, where he served as chair of the Department of Electrical Engineering until 1976. Given his substantial experience in corporate life, Rader focused the Center's attention on the highly relevant topic of corporate standards of conduct. In conjunction with Hammaker, Horniman, and research associate Henry Tulloch, Rader initiated a research study of the top 700 companies in *Fortune* magazine's listing

Patricia H. Werhane.
An internationally known business ethicist, Werhane was appointed the Darden School's first female chairholder.

of the largest 1,000 industrial and 300 nonindustrial companies. The Center's study found that 90 percent of America's largest companies had put in place a formal standards-of-conduct policy that was enforced. The study also discovered that the upper echelon of management—usually, the chairman and president—most often formulated the corporate standards-of-conduct policy, as well as served as its enforcers.[73]

In addition to supporting the Center's practitioner-oriented research, Dean Sheppard emphasized the importance of introducing ethical issues into the MBA curriculum in a more focused way, and encouraged, in 1980, the incorporation of "specific modules of instruction in business ethics in our required first-year MBA Program."[74] Henry Tulloch, who played a key role in the Olsson Center's activities from its earliest years until his retirement, in 2004, discussed the importance of ethics in management education: "Every decision has an ethical dimension, and the issue is to be able to recognize it and then take consistent action."[75] After his retirement from the University of Virginia, Sheppard himself taught courses in managerial ethics at Stetson University, and became a senior fellow at Darden's Center for the Study of Applied Ethics.

Dean John Rosenblum shared the commitment of Deans Abbott and Sheppard to the importance of ethics in business and to the key role the Center could play in the School and in society by highlighting that importance. Upon Rader's retirement, in 1983—when Rader, too, became a senior fellow at the Center—Rosenblum asked Alexander Horniman to return as the Center's director. Horniman not only agreed to take on leadership of the Center once again, but also introduced, in 1984, an MBA elective, Business Ethics and Managerial Decision-Making, as well as a module of four ethics courses in the first-year MBA Program.[76]

Darden became a trailblazer among graduate business schools in implementing a required course in business ethics. Teaching ethics, however, Horniman observed, is not without its difficulties: "The subject of ethics is such a controversial issue.... If someone says you have an ethical issue, it's like I've done something wrong.... The challenge is to present to graduate students a way of thinking and the issues and consequences in a way that they can make some choices about themselves. To teach ethics as 'here's how you ought to do something,' I don't think works very well.... It's easy to perceive someone teaching ethics as telling someone else how to behave. That's not the intention. The intention is to provide the students with ways

Sture G. Olsson. President of the Chesapeake Corporation and a member of the Sponsors Board of Trustees, Olsson believed that Virginia's young business school should make ethics a priority in the training of managers.

R. Edward Freeman. As director of the Olsson Center, Freeman spearheaded conferences, research, and teaching programs that have brought international recognition of the Darden School as a thought leader in business ethics.

first step in his ambitious plan to attract two or three of the world's leading thinkers in business ethics to the Darden School.

Having taught previously at the University of Minnesota and the University of Pennsylvania's Wharton School, Freeman, who had a PhD in philosophy from Washington University, was a trained ethicist who recognized the enormous potential of Darden's Center for the Study of Applied Ethics with respect to both teaching and research. A highly regarded scholar in ethics and strategy, Freeman was widely recognized for his book *Strategic Management: A Stakeholder Approach*, which developed a strategic framework that advised corporations to become far more attentive to all their stakeholders. Freeman defined stakeholders as the key internal and external groups with which business leaders must be in tune over time if their enterprises are to flourish.

Dean Rosenblum had lured Freeman to Darden from Minnesota as a visiting professor in the hope of ultimately keeping him in Charlottesville permanently. Rosenblum knew that Freeman's passion for engaging students intellectually and his innovative talents as a teacher—he had won prestigious teaching awards at both the University of Minnesota and the University of Pennsylvania and later did likewise at the University of Virginia—represented a perfect fit with Darden's pedagogy. Moreover, Freeman's distinguished practitioner-oriented research could move Darden's Center for Applied

of framing very difficult situations and inviting those students to think about them in new ways. Hopefully, they'll use those thought processes later when they leave us."[77]

In 1986, the Center's efforts to introduce a wider range of course work in business ethics into the MBA curriculum and to undertake pathbreaking research and idea-generation received impetus from two events. First, Sture G. Olsson, chairman of the Chesapeake Corporation and a 1942 graduate of the University of Virginia's School of Engineering, building on his mother's formative gift to the Center, pledged an additional $650,000 as a matching challenge grant in an effort to beef up the Center's endowment. The match was rapidly attained. Second, R. Edward Freeman joined the Darden School as a visiting associate professor. Appointing Freeman was Dean John Rosenblum's

Ethics to another level. Rosenblum's tactics worked. In 1987, Freeman became a permanent Darden faculty member, and was appointed Olsson Professor of Business Administration and director of the Center for Applied Ethics, which was simultaneously renamed the Olsson Center for Applied Ethics in honor of the Olsson family. Upon assuming the directorship, Freeman predicted, "We are dedicated to being the leading source of thinking about business ethics. That was the original intent of the Olsson family."[78]

Freeman moved the Center's agenda forward without delay. In the spring of 1988, the Center sponsored the initial Ruffin Lecture and Monograph Series in business ethics. The series was funded by a $500,000 gift from the Peter B. and Adeline W. Ruffin Foundation, and was named in honor of Peter Brown Ruffin, chairman of the Galbreath-Ruffin Corporation, who had served as a Darden Sponsors Trustee from 1964 to 1973. The Ruffin Series aspired to bring to the Darden School the leading thinkers in the world "to discuss," as Freeman put it, "the state of the art in business ethics."[79]

In April 1988, the initial Ruffin Lectures attracted business ethicists from around the world to Charlottesville to consider the series' theme, "Business Ethics: The State of the Art." The keynote speakers were such notables in the field as Kenneth E. Goodpaster of Harvard, Thomas Donaldson of Loyola University, Norman E. Bowie of the University of Delaware,

and Ezra Bowen of *Time* magazine.

On the heels of the success of the inaugural Ruffin Lectures, the Olsson Center, under Freeman's leadership, forged a partnership with Oxford University Press to develop a Ruffin Series that would encompass publication of the proceedings of the Ruffin Lectures as well as additional books on ethics of interest to business academicians, ethicists, and practicing managers.[80]

In subsequent years, the Ruffin Lectures explored such themes as "Business and the Humanities" (1989) and "Ethics, Entrepreneurship, and the Foundations of Capitalism" (1999) in conjunction with the Batten Center for Entrepreneurial Leadership. By 1998, 14 volumes had been published in the Oxford University Press Ruffin Series.

The dynamism of the Olsson Center paid dividends to Darden's students. In 1989, the Darden School hosted the national Graduate Business Conference, an annual gathering of student leaders from the nation's leading MBA programs. The conference's topic was business ethics, with the keynote address delivered by the popular management consultant and author Tom Peters. Peters told the 125 student representatives from the world's top MBA schools, "What Darden is doing and what you're doing is just stunningly important. Thank God, you're here. Thank God, you're worrying about these things."[81] Further, since the spring of 2000, the Olsson Center has helped sponsor Darden's Values-Based

ON THE 25TH ANNIVERSARY OF THE DARDEN SCHOOL
"...I CANNOT RESIST A SUGGESTION WHICH EMBODIES ALL OF MY HOPES FOR THE SCHOOL. IT IS THAT NOTHING WILL EVER INDUCE US TO LAY ASIDE INSTRUCTION IN THE ETHICAL FOUNDATIONS OF AMERICAN BUSINESS. WITHOUT A FIRM ATTACHMENT TO UNIMPEACHABLE INTEGRITY, IN OUR BUSINESS AS WELL AS IN OUR PERSONAL AFFAIRS, WE BUILD ON SHIFTING SANDS AND THERE CAN BE NO FUTURE FOR ANY OF US."
COLGATE W. DARDEN, JR.
SEPTEMBER, 1980

Ethics at the core. The School commissioned a bust, sculpted by Chase S. Decker, to honor its founder and his devotion to ethics. Originally sited in Bankers Courtyard in the North Grounds building, the bust now rests in the Darden Garden on the Goodwin Grounds.

Leadership Conference, an annual student-organized and student-initiated event that focuses student attention on the importance of values both in their future careers as leaders and in their personal lives.

Even more significant, in January 1989, the first-year curriculum of Darden's MBA Program expanded the earlier module of ethics courses into an in-depth, required, graded course in business ethics, designed, as Freeman put it, "to make ethical considerations an integral part of each student's decision-making process." This landmark curriculum transformation reflected the Darden faculty's appreciation of the premise that "the dynamic and global environment for which Darden's business students are being prepared requires skills in ethical reasoning right along with financial analysis."[82] "We

really took a huge step," recalled Freeman, "by saying that ethics is as important as the other subjects."[83] Darden's pathbreaking required course in ethics—the first graded MBA course in ethics at a major graduate business school—tackled such difficult issues as corporate social responsibility, managing diversity, equitable negotiating, and ethical advertising from a number of conceptual frameworks, including stakeholder analysis, harms and benefits, and rights and duties. In introducing the course, Freeman said, "We will not grade what a student's ethics are, we will grade on how well they reason, because the course is really about moral reasoning."[84] Since 1989, Darden students have confronted their own personal values in the context of managerial and social responsibility while broadening their understanding of the complexity of the role of accountable, integrity-focused leaders.

The vigor of the Olsson Center's teaching and research programs took on even more energy in 1993, when Patricia H. Werhane joined the Darden School faculty as the School's first holder of the Ruffin Professorship in Business Administration, a chair in business ethics funded by the Peter Ruffin Foundation. An internationally known scholar, Werhane was the Darden School's first female chaired professor, and had held the post of director of the Center for Values across the University at Loyola University of Chicago. She teamed up with Freeman to propel the Olsson Center into further prominence for its teaching and scholarship in business ethics. Werhane founded and has served as the longtime editor of the *Journal of Business Ethics*, the leading journal in its field, and has also served as editor of the Kluwer Series on International Issues in Business Ethics. Werhane and Freeman, together with their newest professorial colleague in the Olsson Center, Andrew C. Wicks, have authored more than 200 cases in business ethics, and their teaching materials are recognized globally as being at the forefront in the instruction of business ethics.

Both Freeman and Werhane were determined to carry the influence of the Olsson Center beyond the University's North Grounds. They developed a rich business-ethics concentration in Darden's Doctoral Program, which has produced some of the nation's most promising young business ethicists since the late 1990s. In addition, they have worked tirelessly to build relationships between Darden and the other schools at the University of Virginia, including Law, Medicine, Engineering, and Arts and Sciences, not only by teaching undergraduate and graduate students on the Main Grounds, but also through Olsson Center cosponsorship of conferences and seminars with other university programs that have a strong interest in ethics. The Olsson Center, for example, is a charter partner in the University's Institute for Practical Ethics. Bridge-building, open inquiry, and intellectual vibrancy have become the hallmarks of Darden's Olsson Center.

THE CASE METHOD

By the time graduate business education arrived at the University of Virginia, the case method of instruction had enjoyed a long and distinctive history. Developed originally in the 1870s at Harvard Law School by Dean Christopher Columbus Langwell, this pedagogical approach substituted active student discussion and analysis for formal professorial lectures. Believing in the efficacy of this method for educating students in business, the founding dean of the Harvard Business School, Edwin F. Gay, was a strong proponent from the founding of his institution, in 1908. While some of the Harvard Business School's early faculty were less than enamored with this approach, Harvard progressively produced a substantial body of case studies in a variety of business disciplines, and the case method began to pervade its curriculum.[1]

When Charles Abbott and the other refugees from Boston whom Abbott enticed to the University of Virginia arrived in Charlottesville, the case method of instruction was second nature to them. While their Harvard experience had convinced them that case pedagogy should be transported to Virginia—a point of view shared by the Snavely Committee, which had recommended use of the case method and Harvard's approach as a model—they were not advocates of simply replicating what was done in classrooms on the banks of the Charles River.[2] Instead, Abbott and the School's enthusiastic Founding Faculty and its First Faculty Generation would imbue the case method with a strong tinge of their own personal brand of highly interactive classroom instruction and rigorous student-centered problem solving.

The members of the University of Virginia's young business-school faculty internalized the case method as fundamental to the educational process, and took case teaching to the level of an art form. They carefully studied both the strengths and shortcomings of this pedagogical approach, appreciated its nuances, and worked continually to enhance their ability to orchestrate it for maximum effect.

When queried about the centrality of the case method to quality business education, Darden faculty have emphasized a number of features of the process itself, as well as their thoughtful self-consciousness in regard to their role as instructors and discussion leaders. Most fundamentally, the case method has been attractive to Darden faculty because it reflects the actual world of business. Paul Hammaker, a senior career executive who became an accomplished

instructor at Darden, encapsulated the view of Darden's faculty across the generations, be they academicians or practitioners: "I spent many years preparing [for the case method] because in business you are faced with situations regarding decisions day after day, and the case method is nothing except new material portraying a specific situation with facts, sometimes with a lot of figures, and the student is expected to analyze and come up with conclusions and ideally to say there are several possible answers or alternatives, and that of the alternatives, I think the one I prefer is this."[3]

In mirroring the real world of business, the case method sets forth situations that—like reality—are often characterized by countless unknowns and deep-seated uncertainties. For the Darden faculty, tackling cases with implicit ambiguity provides students with a strong dose of what they will face in the trenches as managers. The case method teaches students that information is fragmentary and incomplete and that there

Real-life experience. Richard M. Davis (MBA 1981) speaks on horsemanship to his Analysis and Communications class in 1980. Davis led his horse, Aracne, up the steps to a second-floor classroom in the North Grounds building.

are no pat answers to intrinsically complex situations. Charles Abbott explained this important facet of managerial education to President Colgate Darden in his very first report as dean: "Thus, viewed realistically, education for business and administration becomes an eclectic process. Concepts, techniques, and points of view must be gleaned from many disciplines and reassembled for the purpose of preparing men to analyze perceptively specific situations in which both known and unknown factors are present, to think in concrete terms, and to act decisively with wisdom."[4]

Whether members of the Founding Faculty or of succeeding faculty generations, Darden instructors have been unanimous in their devotion to the case method because it fosters positive, interactive learning. This pedagogical approach compels students to become active participants in analysis and debate. There

is no hiding or passivity in a case-discussion classroom. The student becomes an actor in and an integral component of the learning process. As Robert Bruner, Distinguished Professor of Business Administration, observed, "Fundamentally, we place the burden on the students for their learning, asking them to shoulder the responsibility for drilling down into cases and trying to find truth and trying to find the application of ideas."[5]

At the core of the case method are the students themselves. Christopher Gale, longtime marketing professor at Darden, explained the concept: "The whole point of the case method is to let the students be the stars.... My role as leader of the class discussion is to somehow keep five or six or seven or eight balls in the air all at the same time without giving a clue as to what I want.... Every contribution could be useful no matter how short.... But the students are the stars. That's the beauty of the case method. They are the ones having to pull, to tug, to try to get the thing to make sense."[6] The case-analysis process compels the student to home in on making a definitive decision. It inserts the student, in Bruner's words, "into the shoes, into the dilemma, into the predicament of the professional."[7]

The most effective cases paint a complex and compelling picture that reveals no easy answers. John Colley, the Almand R. Coleman Professor of Business Administration and a Darden veteran of nearly four decades, summarized the objective of a well-crafted case:

Darden's Team Fiero. Darden students, participating in a 1987 General Motors competition, developed a marketing campaign for the Pontiac Fiero. Behind vehicle (left to right): Gerald Strauss, Professors James Clawson, Christopher Gale, and John Norton, Nancy McLean; (in front): Mary Hickey, Karen Strain, William Tonetti, James Gelly.

"My definition of a great case is a case that involves a decision.... There's something that I've learned to call 'constructive ambiguity.' And constructive ambiguity is when a case is just right. It leaves the uncertainty. It leaves you with the feeling that whatever I do could be wrong, but I've got to make the best of it and tomorrow's another day. And for those kinds of cases, the eyes of the students light up. They get interested. They argue with each other. They have honest differences of opinion.... They get to see that reasonable people could think differently about the same situation. So a great case to me has this character of constructive ambiguity, which is a balance between not being able to know everything, but realizing you have to move on."[8]

The key to the success of the case method, however, Darden faculty agree, is not just outstanding case materials, but also the instructor's ability to orchestrate lively and penetrating discussions. Paul Hammaker shared the secret of effective case teaching: "The function of the case-method teacher is *not* to come to a preconclusion.... All you want is discussion.... You are at ease and you try to put them [the students] at ease and you do that by a very simple device—by sincerely wanting to learn what they have to say. You say in good conscience, 'I'm de-

Student boxes. Each week students receive case-study packets in their individual mailboxes. The School developed an in-house publication service to accommodate just-in-time production and delivery of course materials.

answer. Just keep asking questions.'"[10]

Dedication to excellence in case-method teaching has endured as a shared value of the Darden faculty since the School's inception. Regardless of the generational cohort of which they were a member, Darden instructors came to realize that student-centered learning promoted by the case-method approach effectively prepared students for their future challenges as managers. The words of Paul Farris, Landmark Communications Professor of Business Administration and a renowned author of marketing cases, convey the consensus of Darden faculty across the School's 50-year history: "The case method for the Darden School has been absolutely critical. I love not only the case method; I love Darden's spin on the case method. And what I see in that is a concern for a general-management point of view and a love for cases that present students with decisions, but decisions that come in the context of a snapshot of reality, not some construction that we have hopped up to illustrate a favorite theory. And as long as Darden remains true to that, I think we'll have a place in the world of business."[11]

Edward Davis, the Oliver Wight Professor of Business Administration and a well-regarded writer of operations cases, agreed: "The case method is intertwined, in my view, with the success of Darden. You can't separate the two. To me, you can't talk about Darden without talking about the case method."[12]

lighted to be here, I respect you, I think what you're trying to do here at the University is just great and that will just delight me. So let's just say we have a mutual interest. You want to learn and I want to teach.'"[9]

Professor Leslie Grayson arrived at Darden in 1971 as a novice instructor with a PhD in economics from the University of Michigan but without an MBA or any case-method experience. He later recalled Paul Hammaker's wise words on the art of case-method teaching: "Hammaker's advice was to never answer a question; just ask another question. And I said to him, 'When I was brought up, I was told that answering a question with a question is not polite.' And he said, 'This is not about etiquette, this is about teaching. Just don't

Falls River ropes course.
For many years, Darden
students visited a nearby
experiential learning
facility for outdoor team-
building activities.

THE COLGATE DARDEN SCHOOL OF BUSINESS ADMINISTRATION

The Darden School's second home. In 1975, the School moved to a new concrete and brick building on the University's recently developed North Grounds.

THREE ❈ *TAKING ROOT*

Dean C. Stewart Sheppard

C. Stewart Sheppard served as the second dean of the Darden School. Assuming the School's leadership from Charles Abbott in 1972, Sheppard zealously cultivated the seed that his predecessor had so sagaciously planted during the School's first decade and a half. Under Sheppard, the School firmly took root and the stage was set for its leap to national prominence.

Sheppard's selection as dean represented a natural evolution. He had been present at the Graduate Business School's creation, having served as an adviser to the Snavely Committee, which studied the need for a graduate business school at the University of Virginia. Then dean at Cornell University's graduate business school, Sheppard advised the committee to move forward boldly. Sheppard became personally invested in the vision of creating the first graduate business school in the South. He eagerly joined the faculty of Virginia's nascent business school in 1961, when he received an invitation from Dean Abbott.

C. Stewart Sheppard, Darden's second dean. Sheppard oversaw the School's move to the North Grounds and its expansion to four MBA sections.

As a faculty member, Sheppard became the founding executive director of a new organization dedicated to training and certifying professional investment analysts, the Institute of Chartered Financial Analysts (ICFA). He was also a founder of the Olsson Center for Applied Ethics and a lifelong promoter of the importance of ethics in both business and the academy.

Born in Wales and naturalized while serving in the United States Army during World War II, Dean Sheppard was extremely personable and, as C. Ray Smith observed, was always "proud to let people know that he was a Virginian and that Mr. Jefferson was the son of a Welshman."[1]

Sheppard's accomplishments as dean were legion. His most important achievements sprang directly from the core strategy of a maturing school. First, Sheppard engineered the School's move from Monroe Hall, on the University of Virginia's Main Grounds, to a new, significantly larger structure on the University's recently developed Duke tract. He insisted that the Duke tract, a wooded area about a mile from the Rotunda, must be named the "North Grounds" of the University of Virginia to provide it with at least some connection to Mr. Jefferson's Academical Village.

Second, with a new, larger faculty in place, Dean Sheppard orchestrated the growth of the MBA student body from 240 to 480, from two sections to four, a figure that would hold steady for the next quarter century.

Third, Sheppard was instrumental in attracting some of the School's most effective and beloved faculty to Charlottesville—the School's Second Faculty Generation. Sheppard cast a wide net to secure young, intellectually vibrant faculty members whose passion was teaching from a practitioner-oriented perspective. This group of faculty continues to provide a major impetus for the School's progress.

Finally, Sheppard was the person most responsible for naming the School after Colgate Darden. The School had been known as the Graduate School of Business Administration (GSBA) since its founding, but Sheppard grasped the strategic importance of distinctively naming the School

to allow it to develop a unique and readily recognizable brand. What name could be more fitting, he believed, than the Colgate Darden Graduate School of Business Administration, in honor of the Virginia statesman who both fathered the institution and personally provided it with the critical wherewithal to take its first intrepid steps.

In 1980, anticipating his retirement, Sheppard summarized the central elements of his deanship: "I have … seen many changes—indeed, initiated quite a few. But certain things remain unchanged: the mission of the School; camaraderie of students and faculty; the loyalty of alumni and Sponsors. Don't think the fine building facades are the School image. It's what goes on inside that counts."[2]

Honoring Colgate Darden

In May 1974, the University's Board of Visitors officially named Virginia's graduate business school the Colgate Darden Graduate School of Business Administration, in honor of the University's third president and the School's early champion, Colgate W. Darden, Jr. President Edgar F. Shannon expressed the consensus of the School's faculty, staff, students, and alumni, as well as the Sponsor Trustees, in his announcement: "It is very fitting that the graduate business school bear the name of the man who has had the greatest influence on improving the quality of education in the Commonwealth during this century. Mr. Darden's special interest in the University and its grad-

uate business school has contributed significantly to the excellence of the institution."[3]

Shannon's announcement was greeted enthusiastically throughout the Commonwealth. The major newspapers in Norfolk, Lynchburg, and Newport News all praised the University of Virginia for taking this very fitting step in Mr. Darden's honor. The *Richmond Times-Dispatch*, in an editorial, best summed up the unanimity of opinion: "No more appropriate or gratifying action could have been taken by the University of Virginia's Board of Visitors than the recent renaming of its graduate business school as The Colgate Darden Graduate School of Business Administration.... Those who think Dr. Shannon got carried away with Cavalier pride in the accomplishments of his predecessor ought to be challenged to name another Virginian whose contributions to education have surpassed Mr. Darden's. The constructive influence of Colgate Whitehead Darden,

Jr., has been felt everywhere from the tiniest rural grade-school to the most advanced collegiate scholarship in Virginia.... The most immediate reason this particular school should proudly carry the Darden name is, of course, that former Governor Darden was instrumental in founding the School during his 12-year presidency of the University.... The School has been a force for wise and principled leadership in private enterprise."[4]

Colgate Darden accepted the naming of the School in his honor with his usual modesty and grace. When informed by Raymond C. Bice, secretary to the Board of Visitors, of the Board's action, he expressed his gratitude to Bice in a handwritten letter, observing that "no one knows better than I that without the help of many persons—alumni and nonalumni alike—we could not have succeeded.... I regard myself as a representative of this energetic and valiant company to which the Commonwealth owes so much."[5]

Deans Abbott and Sheppard discuss the state of the economy on Sponsors Day, 1978.

Opposite: **Dean Sheppard and his wife, Maria.** The Sheppards graciously opened their home in Pavilion IV to Darden students, faculty, and staff and fostered Darden's connection to the central University.

The 20th Anniversary

The year 1975 was a momentous one for the University of Virginia Graduate Business School. It had attained its 20th year—a benchmark of academic adulthood—and had, just a year earlier, adopted the proud name of

Dedication of the North Grounds building. Colgate Darden, University President Frank Hereford, and Professor Alexander Horniman gather in 1975 for the building dedication.

Jefferson on the North Grounds. Sited in the plaza between the Darden and Law Schools, this bronze casting was sculpted by Lloyd Lillie and dedicated by President Frank Hereford on April 13, 1978. The first bronze casting is located in the Jefferson National Expansion Memorial in St. Louis.

the Darden School. Moreover, 1975 witnessed the School's move from Monroe Hall, on the University's Main Grounds, to its modern new home on the University's recently developed North Grounds.

To mark these landmark events, the School hosted a very special Sponsors Weekend from October 10 through October 12. The celebration began with a "Symposium on Business in the Next Twenty Years," held at University Hall. The panel comprised four distinguished corporate leaders: Charles B. McCoy, president of the DuPont Company; James L. Ferguson, chairman and president of the General Foods Corporation; John E. Swearingen,

chairman of Standard Oil of Indiana; and John R. Bunting, chairman and CEO of First Pennsylvania Bank. The four speakers unveiled their crystal balls and shared thoughts on how the business environment and the role of business leaders would likely change over the next two decades.

The highlight of the weekend was the dedication of the School's newly constructed building on the North Grounds. Colgate Darden delivered the keynote address. With the School having completed its first two decades of operation, Darden proclaimed that "on this important birthday we can say with confidence and pardonable pride" that the dynamic, maturing graduate business school "shows evidence of being well able to hold its own in the brilliant constellation that is, in fact, the University."

In his address, Darden declared his personal devotion to the School, and connected its mission to Mr. Jefferson's vision for the University of Virginia: "Nor would the third President of the United States, with his keen interest in that which is useful as well as enlightening, be disappointed in what we are accomplishing. I suspect he would be pleased to see this addition to the distinguished institution of learning which was, I think, the crowning achievement of his long and eventful life. As for my feeling about the School, I like the words of Daniel Webster in the Dartmouth College Case. Mr. Webster, in his closing remarks before the Supreme Court in the case, which he won and which constituted a landmark in our early law, said, 'It is, sirs, as I have said, a small college, but there are those who love it.' This, I think, expresses the feeling of many of us who belong to an era which is closing."[6]

The dedication of the North Grounds building was followed by tours of the new facilities, including the library, which was named in honor of the Camp family in recognition of the Union Camp Corporation's donation to the Sponsors Hall building fund.

Sponsors Weekend in 1975 witnessed an additional milestone. The Sponsors Board of Trustees elected a Darden School alumnus as its president for the first time. The election of Richard Sullivan—a member of the second graduating MBA class, in 1958, and president of Easco Corporation, a Baltimore hand-tool manufacturer—to a leadership role as president of the Sponsors organization symbolized the coming of age of the Darden School's alumni.[7] It heralded the immensely important and active role that the Darden School's graduates have played in its development ever since.

The North Grounds Building

In August 1975, just two decades after the School's birth, the University of Virginia Graduate Business School migrated lock, stock, and barrel from the Main Grounds to its new abode on the North Grounds. Designed by Hugh Stubbins and Associates of Cambridge, Massachusetts, the $3.4-million, 90,000-gross-square-foot,

Ground breaking. University President Edgar F. Shannon, with Dean Sheppard and Darden faculty looking on, leads the ground-breaking ceremony for the North Grounds building.

Artist's rendering of Darden's second home.

Packing up. Faculty and staff celebrate the move from Monroe Hall to the North Grounds.

Henry Wingate (MBA 1973), longtime Darden School librarian.

Right: Plaza linking the Darden School and the Law School on the North Grounds.

brick-and-concrete contemporary structure housed 8 tiered amphitheater-style classrooms, accommodating 60 students each, and one similar 120-seat classroom. These classrooms were perfectly designed to support case-method instruction. The building also included 4 seminar rooms, 18 study-group rooms, 3 conference rooms, 90 faculty and staff offices, and the School's Camp Library. The new facility would permit the Darden School to increase its MBA enrollment to more than 480 students, twice the number in Monroe Hall. In the design process for the new facility, the School endeavored to ensure that growth would not undermine the intimate sense of community enjoyed at Monroe Hall. The new structure included a large, double-high lobby and a central

outdoor courtyard designed to support and preserve the traditional coffee hour and encourage close student and faculty interaction.

The new building was part of a three-school complex constructed on the North Grounds that included the Law School and the Judge Advocate General's School, an academic program housed at the University of Virginia that trained military attorneys and jurists. Hugh Stubbins developed the master plan for the entire North Grounds complex.[8]

The School's North Grounds structure never received a formal name. Initially listed simply as the GSBA (the Graduate School of Business Administration building), it gradually became known as the Darden building once the School itself was named for Colgate Darden.

Expansion of the Student Body

In accommodating student-enrollment increases—whether in the growth from one MBA section to two in the early 1960s, from two sections to three in 1971, from three sections to four in 1979, or from four sections to five in 2002—the faculty always kept at the forefront three basic principles upon which the academic program was founded, principles that have withstood the test of a half century. First, the MBA Program must be rigorously demanding. Second, the curriculum must integrate the functional fields of business study to reflect the complexity of managerial decision making in the real world. Third, the School must retain the case method as the most effective approach to preparing students for the challenges they will inevitably encounter as leaders grappling with difficult problems in complicated environments, confronting incomplete data, ambiguity, and time pressure.[9]

With the migration of the Darden School to its spacious new quarters on the North Grounds in 1975, the opportunity to expand the size of the School's student body became a reality. Virginia's graduate business school had never graduated more than 125 MBA candidates in a single year owing to its limited space in Monroe Hall. The opening of the North Grounds building meant that Darden could now accommodate a substantial increase in the size of its student body.

Dean Sheppard's posture toward growth was favorable, but cautious. Recognizing that enhancement of the School's reputation required growth and eager to take advantage of the vastly improved classroom availability the School now enjoyed, Sheppard nevertheless believed that growth in the size of the student body must be carefully managed to ensure the quality of the applicant pool. In no way, Sheppard believed, should expansion be

permitted to undermine the exemplary closeness—what Sheppard termed "the feeling of intimacy"—that the School had achieved in its Monroe Hall locale. The dean's sentiment was shared ardently by the faculty.[10]

Incremental growth in MBA-student enrollment offered the Darden School two important benefits. First, a larger student body in the mid-1970s and in the following decade afforded the School an opportunity to increase its demographic heterogeneity. Initially, Virginians composed a major share of the student body. More than 60 percent of

Professors fly high. Students loft Professors Frederick S. Morton and William E. Zierden across the lobby of the North Grounds building at a pre-exam coffee break on "Jeans Day" in 1980.

the early MBA students hailed from the Old Dominion. Within 20 years, however, the proportion of Virginians had fallen to 43 percent, a downward trend that has continued to the present day.[11] In addition to enhanced geographical diversity, the larger student body encouraged demographic diversity, as women and minority students and, later, international students began to view an expanding Darden School as an attractive option for an MBA education. Simultaneously, the School began to put greater emphasis on recruiting students who demonstrated solid work experience between receiving their bachelor's degree and their entry into the MBA Program.[12]

As a second benefit of enrollment growth, the Darden School enjoyed the freedom to

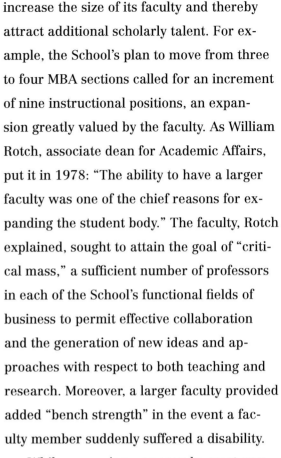

increase the size of its faculty and thereby attract additional scholarly talent. For example, the School's plan to move from three to four MBA sections called for an increment of nine instructional positions, an expansion greatly valued by the faculty. As William Rotch, associate dean for Academic Affairs, put it in 1978: "The ability to have a larger faculty was one of the chief reasons for expanding the student body." The faculty, Rotch explained, sought to attain the goal of "critical mass," a sufficient number of professors in each of the School's functional fields of business to permit effective collaboration and the generation of new ideas and approaches with respect to both teaching and research. Moreover, a larger faculty provided added "bench strength" in the event a faculty member suddenly suffered a disability.

While expansion was seen by most as a step forward for the Darden School as it approached its second quarter century, there were strong countervailing opinions holding that modest growth would be sufficient to achieve a proper balance for the institution. Observed Rotch in 1978: "Some years ago, when we examined the question of the optimal size for a school like Darden, with its integrated, general-management approach to management education, we concluded that a faculty size of around 50 and a student body of around 480 was about right."[13]

Rotch's observation held true for 25 years. The Darden School remained at a steady-state size of four MBA sections—

approximately 480 students—until the move into its second home on the North Grounds opened up further possibilities.

The Darden Case:
Strategic Self-Examination

As the newly named Darden School completed its modern facilities on the North Grounds, launched its initial capital campaign to raise funds for an executive conference center to be named Sponsors Hall, and expanded its enrollment to four MBA sections with a student body approaching 500, it became apparent that, while impressive progress had been accomplished over the course of its first two decades, the School needed to pause to define the aspirations required to guide its future development. What paths should this developing institution pursue in the years ahead?

What priorities should the Darden School set in regard to raising and allocating resources? With a firm foundation now in place, the School's future was auspicious, but only if it could coalesce around a common vision.

What better way for an institution dedicated to case-method pedagogy to explore its future than to analyze its current situation from a case perspective? To ignite a process of institutional introspection, Dean Sheppard appointed an ad hoc committee in early 1977 to write the "Darden Case." Led by Fred Morton, an enthusiastic faculty group consisting of C. Ray Smith, Brandt Allen, Neil Borden, John Colley, Robert Landel, Charles Meiburg, Dan Newton, William Rotch, John Snook, and Robert Vandell prepared the Darden Case.

The case was written in the context of the warm glow of the Darden School's initial success, but also with the realization that Darden faced numerous challenges if it wished to advance to the next level of prestigious graduate business institutions. Perhaps foremost among the challenges was the School's lack of recognition beyond Virginia. With a relatively small number of alumni and a location far from the financial and industrial heartland of America, the Darden School remained a well-kept secret. Moreover, Darden's unswerving emphasis on teaching, casewriting, and course development meant that the faculty's research time and scholarly output appearing in prestigious academic journals were limited. In addition, the School required augmented resources to sustain its intensive case-method instructional approach, to bolster its research efforts, and to underwrite its fledgling doctoral program.

With these issues as a backdrop, on April 1, 1977, in a unique, spirited three-hour joint session, the Darden School faculty, the Sponsor Trustees, and the Darden School Alumni Board all came together to dissect and discuss the Darden Case and to examine the Darden School's future. The discussion and analysis were lively, indeed. From the session, a consensus emerged that the School should undertake a formal, comprehensive strategic analysis. Initially slated for completion by April 1978, the strategic analysis was intended to, first, consider the School's current programs and their resource base; second, identify future strategic paths for the School and their resource requirements; third, evaluate the market for Darden's

current and potential new programs; and, fourth, define the probable strategies of Darden's competitors. The strategic analysis would surface alternatives for the School to consider. Darden would then flesh out priorities in a long-range plan designed to commit the School to specific teaching and research programs as well as to the acquisition of the resources to support them. According to Dean Sheppard, the analysis "constituted an essential reappraisal of where the Darden School has come from, where it is going, and how it will achieve its chosen objectives."[14]

The dean established a coordinating group to oversee the School's strategic analysis. Chaired by Fred Morton, the group visited other schools, solicited position papers from individual Darden faculty members, and commissioned a number of task forces, consisting of faculty, students, deans, alumni, Trustees, and outside business representatives, to tackle significant issues. The thorough process, which included the production of several internal reports, stretched the initial study time by an additional year. In December 1978, while the process was still unfolding, Morton predicted, "There should be few surprises in our report concerning the objectives of the School. The founders' objective for a school providing education in professional management, in a pragmatic context, of service to the Commonwealth, the South, and the Nation, and of recognized national excellence, will certainly be reaffirmed."[15]

Morton's prediction was not off the mark. Dean Sheppard, in early 1980, reported the major findings of the strategic analysis. First and foremost, the School would "reinforce" its "current position as a national institution" that "fosters practical application more than theory building" and that "directs its resources chiefly to its students and teaching programs." Second, the faculty would "capitalize" on its "distinctive competence in case-method teaching" and emphasize casewriting, while facilitating the "application of theory to practice." In addition, the Darden School would retain and strengthen its Doctoral Program and "reaffirm the valued position of executive education as an integral part of the School," while mapping out its future directions. Finally, for at least the next five years, the Darden School would maintain its size at a steady state in order to "consolidate its growth" and continue "the close relationship among students and between students and faculty."[16]

Women at Darden

The University of Virginia Graduate School of Business Administration was a decade old before it granted a degree to a woman. In 1965, Betty Sue Hamner Peabody received her MBA, becoming the School's first female graduate. Initially, the School's progress in recruiting women was slow. From 1966 through 1968, no women graduated, while only one woman graduated each year from 1969 through 1972. As the 1970s unfolded, however, the entry of women into Darden, as well as other business schools, slowly began to accelerate. Darden conferred the MBA degree on 39 women in 1978. By that

Betty Sue Peabody (MBA 1965), Darden's first female graduate.

Above: Professor John L. Colley gathers with some of Darden's increasing number of female students in 1985.

year, Betty Sue Hamner Peabody had been named president of Citibank (New York State) N.A. in Rochester, New York. Five years later, she was featured in the *Wall Street Journal* as a successful career woman.[17]

The mid-1970s witnessed the Darden School's first efforts to recruit female applicants on a priority basis. The admissions office, under the leadership of Walter J. Camp (MBA 1974), undertook vigorous recruiting at such women's colleges as Hollins and Sweet Briar, in Virginia, and Smith, Radcliffe, Vassar, Mt. Holyoke, and Wellesley, in the Northeast.

Margret Furman unfurls her Virginia MBA diploma at Final Exercises, 1980.

The Darden Women's Association, a group of students' wives that originally focused solely on providing "things to do for student spouses who have to do without their ever-studying husbands," expanded its mission in 1975 to involve female students, faculty, and staff actively in the organization. With a Darden student population in that year that was 15 percent female, the association sponsored an array of activities that went far beyond the original orientation of the group.[18]

By 1977, 25 percent of Darden's first-year class and 24 percent of its second-year class were female. These percentages matched the proportion of female students in other leading MBA schools, including Harvard, Dartmouth, Wharton, Stanford, and Chicago, but trailed the two graduate business institutions with the highest percentage of women, Columbia and MIT (35 percent). Darden's placement office reported that year that the starting salaries and positions of responsibility of the School's female graduates were "indistinguishable" from those of their male counterparts.[19]

As the number of female students at Darden increased, the School initiated activities to provide them with an enhanced support structure. For example, on Career Day in 1977, a special panel on "Women in Business," consisting of female executives from Booz Allen and Hamilton, INA, and Ogilvy and Mather, discussed issues concerning the simultaneous management of career and married life.

In the area of scholarship, Darden Professor Derek "Dan" Newton published a book titled *Think Like a Man, Act Like a Lady, Work Like a Dog* in 1979. Newton's book offered guidance to female MBAs who wished to pursue corporate careers, and reflected his belief that business schools, including Darden, needed to provide women with relevant professional training and advising. Newton followed this book with a study on the successful mentoring of female managers by senior corporate executives. Assisted by Lawton Fitt, a second-year Darden MBA student, Newton included interviews with 30

Lawton Fitt (left) and Diana Romney join Professor Ralph Biggadike (MBA 1972) for a laugh at the postgraduation reception in 1979.

Darden's first two African American graduates.
David L. Epps and Lemuel E. Lewis (both MBA 1972) were honored in 1999 by the Black Business Student Forum with the inaugural Pioneer Award.

pairs of female managers and their mentors. Newton also authored a number of cases with female protagonists in an effort to diversify the School's teaching materials and curriculum.[20]

In his preface to a 1979 issue of the *Darden Report* that focused on women in management, Dean Stewart Sheppard put forth this prediction: "In all probability, it will be another ten years before women in any large numbers will acquire dominant positions in senior management. But their rise up the ladder is inevitable. The next ten years foreshadow highly significant changes in organizational attitudes to the hiring and advancement of professional women—and minorities.... Women have indeed come a long way, and it is safe to predict that they are not going to stop short of the beautiful views of the executive suite."[21]

Minority Students

The first MBA class at the University of Virginia Graduate Business School was all male and all white. It was not until the early 1970s that a small number of African American students began to attend Darden. The School's first two African American students, David L. Epps and Lemuel E. Lewis, graduated in 1972. By the middle of that decade, the

School began to realize the importance and value of attracting a more heterogeneous student body. A report to the Admissions Committee and Dean Sheppard on minority-student enrollment at Darden, compiled by Professor William E. Zierden in April 1977, observed that "applicants tend to view UVA as a white, aristocratic school and Charlottesville as a place which is not socially attractive to black students. Darden suffers in its association with this view." The report recommended that the Darden School initiate an aggressive minority-student-recruitment program aimed at identifying potential black applicants.[22]

To this end, the admissions office, under the supervision of Assistant Dean of Student Affairs John L. Snook, Jr., and Admissions Director Walter Camp, actively recruited at predominantly black colleges. The admissions office also developed a series of programs for college-placement and career advisers designed to encourage them to recommend Darden to minority students. One such program invited advisers from Hampton Institute, Fisk University, Alabama A&M, Cornell, the University of North Carolina, North Carolina State, Penn State, and the University of Pennsylvania to visit Darden, attend classes, and meet with current black students. The efforts of the admissions office were greatly assisted by three of the School's early African American alumni: Lemuel E. Lewis (MBA 1972), Roland M. Lynch (MBA 1975), and William J. Harvey (MBA 1977), who

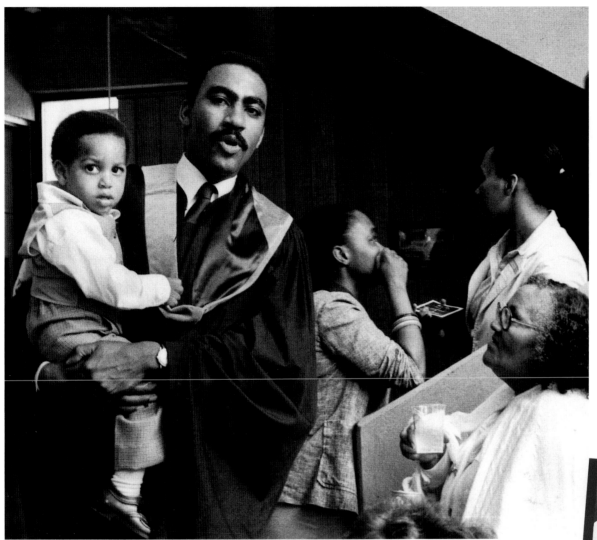

The celebration of graduation is a family affair for Kenneth Hill (MBA 1980).

Below: Brochure produced by the Darden Association of Black Business Students to promote the School.

MBA . . .
Plan for your Future
Darden
Association of
Black
Business
Students

made extensive personal contacts with minority applicants to help promote Darden.[23]

During the 1979–80 academic year, Darden's growing contingent of African American students formed the Darden Association of Black Business Students (DABBS). The founders of the organization, Rodney E. Cheek (MBA 1980) and Leroy E. "Gene" Hambrick (MBA 1980), cited four purposes for the group. First, the new organization would work to heighten the awareness among Darden students and faculty of the concerns of African Americans, both at the School and in the business world. Second, said Hambrick, "DABBS can also play a key role in exposing black applicants to the benefits of attending Darden. Overall, DABBS seeks to promote a very positive, educational, and social input in the Darden community that will benefit all—students, faculty, and alumni." Third, DABBS would actively assist the School in the recruitment of black students. Finally, DABBS would work to enhance Darden's interaction with black business people and black enterprises and to promote a continuing relationship between the Darden School and its black

alumni. Alumni Harvey, Lewis, Lynch, and Anne Shirley (MBA 1979) provided support and advice to Hambrick and Cheek.[24]

The members of DABBS elected Professor Leslie E. Grayson as their faculty adviser. Cheek credits Grayson with helping "us get DABBS off the ground. Without Les Grayson serving as our link to the faculty, I don't think we could have made it." The group's first meeting was held at Grayson's home. Like Grayson, Dean Sheppard strongly supported the new organi-

zation and its efforts. The benefits to the School were clear. Said Grayson: "We should continue to increase the number of black students at Darden in order to provide our nonblack students with a meaningful educational experience. In short, we at Darden are here to prepare students for the real world and the real world includes blacks."[25]

With the help of DABBS, the Darden School accelerated its minority-recruiting efforts in the 1980s. The acquisition of resources to enhance minority-student recruitment and financial aid became a major focus of the School's fundraising efforts. In 1981, the Marriott Corporation donated $100,000 to help Darden bring minority candidates to Charlottesville and to support the efforts of the admissions office in actively recruiting at predominantly black colleges. For the past 25 years, the Darden School has continued its efforts to attract minority candidates. Its most effective allies have been the School's African American students and alumni, who have energetically assisted in identifying candidates, played key roles in minority-recruitment events in Charlottesville, and provided ongoing advice and counsel.

DABBS also became active in other areas of the School, sponsoring speakers, holding orientation sessions for first-year African American students, and participating in national conferences. In 1986, reflecting an organizational scope that had expanded from providing support to minority students to participating integrally in the

School's activities, DABBS renamed itself the Black Business Student Forum (BBSF).

In 1982, Sherwood Frey succeeded Grayson as the organization's faculty adviser, a role he has played with unwavering enthusiasm for more than two decades. In

Future business leaders.
The Darden School has participated in the national LEAD Program for minority high school students each summer since 1983. The program encourages participants to consider careers in business.

1988, with Frey's encouragement, the BBSF sponsored its first annual Black Alumni Conference. This event, which has grown larger year by year, links Darden's African American alumni with current students while considering significant topics, ranging from the challenges facing black business professionals to urban development. In 1995, the BBSF expanded the Black Alumni Conference by inviting prospective minority-student applicants to attend a companion conference designed to inform them about the Darden

School and its attractions for minority students. At the 1999 Black Alumni Conference, David Epps and Lemuel Lewis received the first-ever Pioneer Award in honor of their accomplishments. Epps and Lewis had entered the MBA Program in 1970. Their pathbreaking achievements, the critical organizational work of the founders of DABBS, and the continuing commitment of their BBSF successors reflect the important role that African American students and alumni have played in the Darden School's history.[26]

Globalization

To be sure, the original focus of the University of Virginia Graduate Business School was local and regional. After all, an important impetus for its founding as the first exclusively graduate business institution in the South was to stem the brain drain to the North and to produce managers who could help modernize the economies of the states below the Mason-Dixon Line. Virginia businesses had ponied up the money to make the School a reality, and had envisioned the School as a vital instrument of local and regional economic development.

Certainly, Charles Abbott was sensitive to the motivation behind the School's creation and to the need to produce graduates who would serve the best interests of the Commonwealth and the South. Nevertheless, Abbott and the founding fathers who had selected him as dean—Colgate Darden,

Tipton Snavely, J. Harvie Wilkinson, and the other early Sponsor Trustees—were by no means parochial in their outlook. Abbott, the son of an eminent scholar of European history, had done a stint as a banker in London. Darden had served in France during World War I, studied at Oxford, and later served as a member of the U.S. delegation to the United Nations. These men were cosmopolitan individuals, keenly aware of the larger world and its economic and political importance.

It is not surprising, therefore, that in the spring of 1958, in just the second academic year in which the School offered electives, the course Management of Foreign Operations was introduced. As the School began to mature, Abbott recognized the need to add to his faculty a respected champion of the proposition that knowledge of the international economy was essential to the education of

a general manager. In 1962, Abbott invited John A. Purinton, Jr., to join the faculty as a lecturer in international management and to carry the School's global banner. Purinton had recently retired to a farm in nearby Ivy from his post of vice president at Searle and Company. Purinton brought with him a wealth of international business experience— he had been responsible for overseas production at Searle—which he fashioned into a second-year elective, Management of International Operations, a course he taught until his retirement from the faculty, in 1976.[27]

In 1971, Dean Abbott appointed Leslie Grayson as Professor of International Business Economics. Grayson joined Purinton in encouraging the School's international momentum. Born in Hungary and educated at Oberlin and the University of Michigan, Grayson had taught at the Fletcher School

International students. As the Darden School became more well known, it began to attract students from abroad. International students (left to right) Charles Edwards, Anne Shirley, Frederick Guyonneau, Huntington Hobbs, and Gary Pearson graduated in 1979.

of Diplomacy at Tufts and at Harvard, and had worked for the Caltex Oil Corporation abroad before coming to Virginia. A Fulbright Scholar in Japan in 1988–89 and now the Horween Research Professor Emeritus, Grayson championed Darden's globalization activities for more than three decades, both in Charlottesville and in countless trips abroad to develop opportunities for Darden students. His elective courses in international business were immensely popular and benefited generations of Darden students.

In 1976, with the encouragement of Grayson and others and in recognition of the growing importance of the world economy, Dean Sheppard forged an agreement with a leading European business school, IMEDE Management Development Institute in Lausanne, Switzerland (now known as IMD),

that established a cooperative casewriting venture. The objective of the effort, led by Professor Neil Borden, was to develop international cases with an emphasis on marketing.[28] This partnership reflected the growing ties Darden faculty had begun to develop with foreign business schools. Borden, Robert Vandell, William Rotch, Fred Morton, Dan Newton, and Christopher Gale had all spent time on leave in Lausanne teaching at IMEDE and deepening their appreciation of global business issues and the world economy. Lee Johnston exemplified the global orientation of the early faculty. He served as a visiting professor at the North European Institute in Oslo, Norway, the Finnish Management School in Helsinki, and Lahore University of Management Science in Pakistan. In addition, he was an adviser in South Africa to the University of Witswatersrand's graduate business school.

International students' interest in the Darden School took some time to develop. While the School's first foreign student, Theo Herbert of Belgium, received his MBA in 1959, international students were few and far between in the early years. It is not surprising that a brand-new, small graduate school in the South did not initially appear on the radar screens of foreign students. As the Darden School grew and became better known, however, international students began to take notice. In 1979, the School awarded MBA degrees to its first small cluster of international students, a

Globalization leader. Professor Leslie Grayson championed the Darden School's globalization activities for more than three decades.

Opposite: **John A. Purinton, Jr.** After a successful career in business abroad, Purinton joined Darden's faculty to teach international business.

group of five: Anne Shirley of Jamaica, Frederick Guyonneau of France, Gary Pearson of Australia, Huntington Hobbs of Mexico, and Charles Edwards of Canada.[29]

Interest in Darden from abroad quickened in the 1980s, particularly from Asia. Candidates from Japan, Singapore, Indonesia, Hong Kong, China, and India made their way to Charlottesville to pursue their MBA studies. They were soon joined by students from Latin America, Africa, and Europe. By 1987, 10 percent of Darden's entering class was international. As the School moved into the twenty-first century, international students composed almost 29 percent of the entering class. The presence of non-American students greatly enhanced the learning environment by injecting greater breadth of experience into classroom case discussions. So, too, did it enrich the School's cultural and social environments. The growing number of international flags in the classroom building's entry hall representing the home countries of Darden students, the always-enjoyable Darden School International Food Festival, the various country presentations and cooking demonstrations offered by international students—all pointed up the global flavor that Darden began to acquire.[30]

Professor Sherwood Frey explained the origin of the International Food Festival: "We started it because a student came to me one time and said, 'You know, all the guys get to go out and play basketball with the faculty. What about the people who don't play basketball?' And I thought, 'Hey, we all cook and eat so why don't we do something along these lines,' and so we started something that we can do for international students."[31] The International Food Festival was started in 1988, and has been an overwhelmingly popular annual highlight of life at Darden ever since, drawing hundreds of hungry attendees. Such student organizations as the International Business Society, the European Society, the African Business Organization, the Asian Business Club, and the Latin American Student Association—reflecting Darden's increasing globalization—began to flourish and often joined forces to present world-culture programs to which they invited the Darden, University, and Charlottesville communities to experience the richness of the School's diverse cultures.[32]

In terms of curriculum and educational opportunities, the Darden School also expanded its global horizons significantly,

beginning in the mid-1980s. The growing importance of Japan and China in the world economy inspired Dean John Rosenblum to initiate a joint graduate-degree program with the Graduate School of Arts and Sciences in 1985 that enabled students to pursue a joint MBA/MA in East Asian studies over the course of three years, including internships with companies in Asia. Students received their Darden management training while also doing course work in Asian history, culture, politics, religion, and language in the Graduate School of Arts and Sciences. Professor Les Grayson coordinated the program, and served as Darden's ambassador to Asian companies. The *New York Times* featured the first four graduates of the

Scandinavian students at Darden highlight their home countries on Virginia license plates in 1993.

program—John A. Bernas, Lori J. Goodell, Steven R. Horen, and Walter E. Shill—in its careers column. The *Times* noted that all the students had learned Japanese and were sought after by leading firms in the banking, consulting, and manufacturing industries.[33]

So important had the world economy become to the education of an MBA student that the Darden faculty developed a number of avenues to encourage students to participate directly in an educational experience abroad. The boldest attempt to expose Darden students to foreign businesses took place in January 1991, when the entire second-year class, as part of a new required course in leadership, was divided into multiple research teams and invited to visit 14 European cities for a weeklong experience. The School enlisted six multinational corporate sponsors—British Petroleum, General Motors, Digital Equipment, Hercules, PepsiCo, and Salomon Brothers—to host the student groups, which functioned as consultants who helped analyze a particular business problem under the guidance of Darden faculty advisers. Despite the threat and ultimate onset of the Gulf War, which inhibited travel plans in some cases, most of the class of 1991 participated in this memorable overseas activity.[34]

While students gained much insight from this experience, it became apparent that such a large and complex experiment could not be sustained effectively in future years owing to the dual challenges of cost and logistics. Still committed to the value of

International students enrich the School's cultural environment as well as case discussions in the classroom.

encouraging student learning abroad, however, the faculty put in place other opportunities. One promising avenue was the development of exchange programs with leading overseas business schools that permitted Darden students to experience another culture while taking courses at a foreign institution. Beginning in the early 1990s, Darden established student-exchange programs with a growing number of universities abroad. These exchange programs made it possible for Darden students to study at institutions in China, Hong Kong, Japan, Singapore, India, Australia, Spain, Sweden, Belgium, Holland, Great Britain, Argentina, Chile, and Mexico.

For students who were unable to spend a semester abroad as an exchange student or did not desire to do so, Darden developed the concept of the one-week elective course abroad. For example, during spring break in 1997, a group of Darden students took the

one-and-a-half-credit course Doing Business
in Mexico, led by Professor Robert L. Carraway. Aimed at exposing students to both
Mexican business and culture, the course
allowed students to spend an action-packed
five days taking classes at the Instituto Tech-
nologico de Estudios Superiores de Monter-
rey and visiting Mexican companies.[35] The
concept of offering intensive courses abroad
evolved into a series of such opportunities
at the Darden School known as the Global
Business Experience courses. By 2004, both
second- and first-year Darden students could
choose among spring-break global courses in
such countries as Spain, Slovenia, Bahrain,
Mexico, China, Sweden, and Argentina.

Still other avenues for students to learn
firsthand about business abroad were internships and international business projects. As
successive directors of the Tayloe Murphy
Center, William Rotch, Les Grayson, Brandt
Allen, Mark Eaker, and Robert Conroy all
worked to develop summer student internships that placed Darden students with host
companies overseas, where they served
as consultants on particular projects. In
most cases, these internships lasted two
months or so, and provided interns with
the chance to spend a third month travel-
ing or studying abroad. Likewise, the international field projects enabled students to
gain on-site experience working with such
multinational companies as United Technologies on a challenging business issue.[36]

As Darden students expanded their

horizons abroad and as the student body
took on a more international flavor, so
too did the Darden School faculty become
more international. A number of professors who were born abroad have joined the
faculty since the 1990s, including Sankaran
Venkataraman, Kamalini Ramdas, Wei Li,
Tihamér von Ghyczy, Matthias Hild, Yiorgos Allayannis, Ming-Jer Chen, and Saras
Sarasvathy. At the same time, many Darden
faculty who were born in the United States
have served abroad as visiting professors and returned to Darden to share with
students their expanded global view.

As it reaches the half-century mark, the
first graduate business school in the South
has assumed a global perspective. It encourages its students not only to study abroad,
but also to compete for positions abroad in
a world economy that knows no boundaries. At the same time, the Darden School
welcomes students from across the globe
to study in Charlottesville and to contribute to a student body that truly reflects the
world economy of the twenty-first century.

MBA Tournament, 1979

From 1960 on, Darden student teams
competed successfully with students from the country's top MBA
institutions in national case competitions. A major triumph came in June
1979, when a Darden team won the National
MBA Tournament held at New York University. The tournament was sponsored by

Victorious Darden School
MBA Tournament team
(left to right): Kirby Adams,
Peter Kiernan, Lawton Fitt,
and Michael Graham.

American Express, Bankers Trust, Chase Manhattan Bank, the Continental Group, Exxon, and IBM. Only seven schools—NYU, Northwestern, Cornell, the University of Rochester, the University of North Carolina, the University of Washington, and the University of Virginia—were invited to participate in this pressure-filled case competition requiring preparation of an analytical report, exhibits, and an oral defense under cross-examination by a panel of experts.

The Darden team consisted of Kirby Adams, Lawton Fitt, Michael Graham, Peter Kiernan, and Bertram Ellis (alternate). The team members represented a mix of strengths in finance, marketing, quantitative analysis, and organizational behavior. The Darden team members were dedicated, indeed. They practiced vigorously by preparing competition-like cases under tournament conditions during which Darden faculty served as judges. The students even returned early from their winter holiday break to attend special case-preparation classes and study strategic developments in a number of industries.

At the competition in June, the Darden team performed masterfully. Over the course of a grueling 23 hours, they digested a 41-page case on the Joseph Schlitz Brewing Company and a 46-page background paper on the brewing industry, wrote an extensive case analysis and recommendations, prepared an oral defense of their recommendations, and churned out five-year pro forma statements with the aid of a programmable Texas Instruments Model 59 calculator. Seated in the audience to demonstrate their support were several Darden students, as well as Professors William Rotch and Edward Davis.

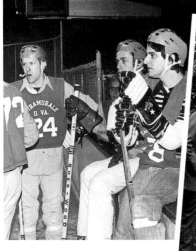

Darden's undefeated intramural ice-hockey team, 1977; Darden marathon runners (left to right) Alexander Horniman, Landis Gabel, Sarah Finlayson, Jack Weber, Richard Levering, and Scott Coleman, 1979; Darden Student Association President William Cahill, flanked by Philip Comerford and Steven Edwards, holds the Darden Cup, won by the first-year class in 1984–85.

In recognizing the Darden team's outstanding performance, the New York University Business School's newspaper, *Opportunity*, described the Darden students' oral presentation as "very polished and awesome…. It was obvious that Virginia was more adept at working on strategy." A very gratified Charles Abbott, Darden's former dean, remarked about the victory, "I can't remember when anything has pleased me as much."[37]

Student Activities

While at times the rubric "boot camp" may have had an element of truth in describing the Darden MBA experience, in reality, life for students at the University of Virginia Graduate Business School has never been all work and no play. From the outset, MBA students became involved in activities that went well beyond the classroom, activities ranging from interest clubs and organizations, which facilitated exploration of potential career paths, to athletics, music, and community service.

At one end of the activity spectrum were the myriad clubs that brought together students with interests in particular functional areas of business or specific industries. Beginning in the early 1970s, students formed clubs focusing on core functional areas, such as finance, marketing, and operations. Later, they established clubs for a growing number of newer fields, such as technology, health care, consulting, and entrepreneurship. The Entrepreneurs Club, for example, was founded in the fall of 1979, and had 50 members by the winter of 1980. The club's early objectives included assembling a student-résumé book for entrepreneurial firms, bringing representatives of small businesses to Darden as panelists for a Career Day public forum, developing a speakers program, and maintaining files on entrepreneurial companies. True to their interest, the incipient entrepreneurs raised money for their club by selling T-shirts and polo shirts.[38]

A particularly outstanding example of a "hands-on" student-interest organization is the Darden Capital Management Club. Consisting of students who wish to prepare themselves for positions in investment management and financial markets, members of this group have enjoyed an unparalleled opportunity to manage a piece of the Darden School's endowment. In 1990, the Darden School Foundation Board of Trustees allocated $250,000 of the Foundation's unrestricted endowment to a fund actively managed by Darden students. This activity has been enormously successful in terms of both investment results and student-learning opportunities in research analysis and portfolio management. By 2004, Darden Capital Management had grown to encompass three student-managed funds—the Darden, Monticello, and Jefferson Funds—totaling $3 million in endowment assets overseen by Darden students.

In addition to career-oriented clubs, Darden students established organizations to promote recreational and social activities. Some of these organizations, such as the a cappella singing group the Cold Call Chorus and its predecessors, had a cultural focus. Others, such as the Darden yearbook, *10K*, founded in 1977, and Darden's student newspaper, the *Darden News* (later renamed the *Cold Call Chronicle*), founded in 1984, attracted students with a journalistic bent. A major highlight of student life each spring has been the Darden Follies. This annual student-produced and -written comedy show pulls no punches in spoofing Darden faculty, administrators, and students alike, all in good fun.

Darden students—both men and women—have always been passionate about athletics. There is probably not a team sport in existence that has not been played by a group of Darden students at one time or another. By the late 1970s, participation in Darden's intramural sports was booming. In one year alone, Darden fielded 18 softball teams—softball, particularly in intense North Grounds competitions with rival Law

Darden student teams A and B were the fastest to run the annual spring Charlottesville 10-mile race in 1989; Darden Christmas-in-April volunteers repair a home in 1992; students present Korean cuisine in 2003 at the International Food Festival.

The International Food Festival, one of Darden's most popular annual events. Portuguese students display their culinary delights at the 2003 International Food Festival.

School teams, has been a perennial Darden favorite—and 4 basketball and volleyball teams, as well as field-hockey, water-polo, and soccer teams. Endurance sports have also attracted members of the Darden Community. Over the years, Darden has produced a number of fine marathon runners, not the least of whom were such faculty "ironmen" as Alec Horniman, Jack Weber, and Landis Gabel. Darden students and faculty have run in the Boston Marathon and the Marine Corps Marathon, as well as in regional marathons in Richmond and Waynesboro.

During the 1983–84 academic year, the Darden Student Association, led by its president, Stuart Frantz, initiated the Darden Cup, a series of competitive athletic

events held throughout the year designed to promote greater interaction among students, faculty, and staff. The events ranged from a 5-K run to golf outings. Competing groups earned points based on both participation and athletic prowess. The Darden Cup represented an important means not only of providing an exciting athletic experience, but also of building a sense of community throughout the institution.

Darden students' passion for athletics has been exceeded only by their devotion to community service. Despite their formidable workload, Darden students, year after year, have committed themselves to an impressive array of service activities. Some of these service initiatives were Darden School–focused, such as participation in the Darden Student Association (DSA), the School's student government, or in the University's Honor Committee. The DSA, in turn, encouraged a number of service ventures, including an annual student-run, multiple-day orientation program for entering Darden students and the Big Siblings Program, an effort by second-year Darden students to mentor the School's new first-year students. Students also organized and coordinated the Business Forum, a student initiative dating back to the 1970s that brought outstanding business speakers to Darden before the establishment of the Dean's Distinguished Speaker Series in the 1990s.

Many of Darden's service activities have been outward looking. The students' strong public-service orientation has served as a magnet for many prospective applicants. "I've had students come to me," reported Sherwood Frey, a stalwart supporter of student service, "and tell me that the reason they're here at Darden and not some other place is because of Darden Outreach."[39]

Among the most impressive and long-lived student-outreach projects has been Opportunity Consultants, Inc. (OCI). A student-managed nonprofit corporation, OCI was founded in 1969 by a group of MBA students and faculty for the purpose of providing volunteer managerial advice to local small businesses and agencies lacking the resources to acquire professional expertise. In its first decade of operation, some 400

MBA students participated in real-life learning experiences by contributing consulting time to more than 200 clients, many of whom were referred by the Small Business Administration and the Charlottesville-Albemarle Chamber of Commerce. OCI has proved itself to be an important local resource for stimulating economic development in the region.

Darden students have also been active in helping local residents in a number of ways, including tutoring schoolchildren through the University's Madison House programs and energetic fundraising, led by the Graduate Women in Business, for the local Shelter for Help in Emergency, an agency that assists families in crisis.

Perhaps the most visible and far-reaching community-service contribution by Darden students has been their leadership of the local Christmas-in-April venture. In 1991, Darden students established a chapter of Christmas-in-April, a volunteer organization that repairs the homes of people in need. Darden students coordinate this charitable event, which has leveraged the enthusiasm, commitment, and managerial talent of Darden students many times over by drawing in other organizations in the Charlottesville area to participate each year. Every April, Darden students lead a cadre of student and community volunteers—often as many as 300—in a concerted effort to renovate the homes of the elderly, disabled, and disadvantaged who lack sufficient resources of their own.

Sponsors Hall

The School's move to the North Grounds served as a catalyst for the development of its own conference center. As the School's residential executive-education programs expanded in the 1970s, the need for a proper facility to house and feed visiting participants became evident. Land adjacent to the School's new building was perfectly suited for a hotel and dining facility that could support executive-education students attending Darden classes.

Unlike the funding for its new academic building, however, the Darden School could not look to the University or the state to underwrite housing and dining facilities for executives taking courses under the auspices of the Sponsors organization. Consequently, philanthropy was the sole means of funding an executive-education conference center at Darden. A campaign to raise $1.1 million for the dining and office components of the conference center, later named Sponsors Hall, constituted the Darden School's first

major foray into fundraising since Colgate Darden had solicited the seed money for the School in the early 1950s. In addition, about $800,000 was needed for the hotel component of the project, which included 36 guest rooms and 6 study-group rooms. The hotel could be supported by state revenue bonds, the debt service on which would be the obligation of the Sponsors organization.

The School targeted several groups in the fundraising campaign for Sponsors Hall. First, Darden's small but growing group of alumni was tasked with raising $100,000, a goal they readily accomplished. Second, alumni from the School's TEP (The Executive Program) contributed $30,000. Third, the School asked Virginia banks to contribute

Above: **Early model of Sponsors Hall.** The construction of Sponsors Hall allowed the Darden School to provide outstanding lodging and dining facilities for executive-education participants.

Below: **Sponsors Hall**. The original dining (right) and housing (left) structures opened in 1979.

$150,000, offering the incentive of naming the attractive, central outdoor space in the new academic facility "Bankers Courtyard." To stimulate this effort, Mr. Darden himself donated $25,000, which was then augmented by a match from a University fund. Finally, the School asked corporate friends for donations. Several corporations, including Burlington, Chesapeake, Continental, Hazelton, and Massey, contributed and, in return, the Darden School named classrooms in their honor. Finally, the Camp family and the Union Camp Corporation contributed $300,000 to the cause. This donation represented the largest single corporate gift ever made to the University of Virginia up to that time. In recognition of this generosity, the School's library was officially named the Camp Library.

Ground for the Sponsors Hall conference center was broken on April 1, 1977. Designed by Carlo Pelliccia, a professor at the University of Virginia School of Architecture, Sponsors Hall provided convenient lodging and dining for executive-education participants and other guests of the School. The hotel and dining center were managed directly by personnel of the Sponsors organization, rather than by outsourced employees, to ensure the highest-quality, personalized service and seamless support of Darden Executive Programs' academic objectives. The facility was a huge success. To meet burgeoning continuing-education demand, 24 additional hotel rooms, recreation and meeting rooms,

a small health club, and an expansion of the dining room and kitchen were constructed in 1984. Later, wings were added to the hotel as part of the Darden Grounds Phase I and Phase II projects. By 2002, Darden's hotel, which was renamed the Sponsors Executive Residence, contained 180 guest rooms and 38 study-group rooms. In addition, a gatehouse, built at the entrance to the School's complex, functioned as a lobby and registration area, and Darden Exchange, a satellite of the University of Virginia Bookstore, conveniently offered hotel patrons, as well as Darden students, faculty, and staff, a variety of merchandise and Darden memorabilia.[40]

Dean Robert Haigh

Following Stewart Sheppard's announcement that he would step down as dean in 1980, a search committee chaired by Professor Neil "Pete" Borden went to work to seek a replacement. The committee did not have to look far. It recommended the appointment of Robert W. Haigh, who was serving as a visiting professor at Darden, to University of Virginia President Frank Hereford and Provost David Shannon. Haigh assumed the Darden deanship in September 1980.

Possessing a background that combined

The art and science of deaning. Upon his selection as dean, Robert Haigh received the mock book *All I Know About Deaning* by "Abbott Sheppard." It contained blank pages.

experience in both academia and industry, Haigh was viewed as an ideal candidate—a "dream dean," as a *Washington Post* reporter put it—to move the School forward.[41] Haigh received his MBA and doctorate from the Harvard Business School, and joined its faculty in 1956. After teaching and researching at Harvard for six years and authoring a book on the growth of integrated oil companies, he left academia to pursue a distinguished career in industry, which included serving first as a vice president at Standard Oil of Ohio and then as president of Standard Oil's Chemicals and Plastics Group, and later as president of Xerox Educational Publishing and Information Services. In 1978, the University of Pennsylvania's Wharton School drew Haigh back to academia, appointing him director of its Applied Research Center. Haigh, however, had longstanding ties to a number of Darden School faculty, including William Rotch, Pete Borden, Bill Sihler, and Fred Morton, from his Harvard days. Desiring to teach more than his position at Wharton allowed, Haigh jumped at an offer from Rotch, then Darden's associate dean for Academic Affairs, to come to Charlottesville as a visiting professor in 1979.

Upon becoming dean, Haigh was quick to appreciate Darden's excellence in teaching. To make the School better known, however, Haigh believed that it had to focus more on research productivity. To accomplish this goal, Haigh set an agenda designed to bolster the School's research efforts and permit it to compete with the top graduate business schools in the nation.

First, to boost vitality and enthusiasm in the School, Haigh restructured the Dean's Office by appointing John W. Rosenblum and Sherwood C. Frey, both recently arrived former Harvard professors, as associate dean for Academic Affairs and associate dean for Administration (and, shortly thereafter, associate dean for Academic Programs), respectively. Many joked that, with Haigh's appointment as dean and Rosenblum's and Frey's elevation to significant associate deanships—combined, they had a total of only three years of experience at Darden—the School had been taken over by the "Harvard Mafia." But Haigh was cognizant of the need for Darden's leadership to remain in touch with the School's roots and to cultivate its growing body of alumni. Thus, he also elevated Robert Fair, Darden's longtime director of Executive Education, to the newly created post of associate dean for External Affairs, giving him responsibility for alumni affairs, development activities, and public relations in addition to executive education. Fair's appointment, with its focus on Darden's external constituencies, reflected Haigh's awareness that Darden needed to augment its capitalization substantially if it were to enhance its research productivity. The new dean believed that Darden had major fundraising potential and thus had to set far more ambitious goals for annual giving as well as for Darden's share of the University of Virginia's upcoming capital campaign. Greater resources, Haigh recognized, were essential to accomplish his objective that the Darden School "become widely recognized by the business community as one of the very best graduate schools of business administration in the world."[42]

A second element of Haigh's agenda was enhancement of the Doctoral Program. Established in the mid-1960s, Darden's Doctoral Program had remained small and, in many ways, tangential to the School's core activities. Haigh believed that Darden's tiny Doctoral Program needed to be revitalized and expanded to at least 30 students if the School were to have any hope of approaching Har-

vard, Stanford, or Wharton in research output. Doctoral students, he believed, would inspire faculty research, stimulate intellectual collegiality, and attract additional top-notch faculty to Charlottesville. Moreover, as Haigh observed, "As a leading graduate school, we have an obligation to provide practitioner-oriented teachers and researchers for the Darden School, for other universities, and for industry and the government."[43] In an effort to promote doctoral-program growth, Haigh worked to establish a joint doctoral degree offered by both Darden and the University of Virginia's undergraduate business school, the McIntire School of Commerce. While

Dean Robert Haigh and C. Ray Smith chat with Tipton Snavely in 1980.

Lawn residents. Dean John Rosenblum, wife Carolyn, and son Nicholas lived in Pavilion III and became favorites of student Lawn residents.

the University favored the concept of a joint doctoral program in business and some faculty members at both Darden and McIntire supported the notion, others at both schools expressed concerns that a joint program might constitute a first step toward a merger of the two schools. No additional resources for doctoral education were forthcoming from the University, however, and the joint doctoral program never came to fruition.

The final element of Haigh's agenda was the creation of more space for the Darden School. Although the School had moved into its new North Grounds building only five years earlier, Haigh believed that Darden's ambition to expand its research program and its executive-education activities would require more offices and classrooms. In 1979, the initial phase of Sponsors Hall, Darden's executive-education lodging and dining facility, had been completed. Haigh saw this new construction as just the first step in building the facilities necessary to support Darden's ultimate needs. He appointed a committee, headed by Professor Louis Rader, to explore a number of options for expanding the School, including construction of an additional floor and a new wing on the Massie Road side of the building. This exercise produced the first of several studies on expanding Darden's facilities in the 1980s, driven by the School's increasing dynamism and potential for growth.

Haigh made special efforts to gain the University's support for Darden's growth plans. While additional funding for construction projects was not forthcoming from the University, Haigh was successful in obtaining University funding for 10 additional Darden faculty slots as well as for some faculty-salary raises.

Bob Haigh's agenda for the Darden School was cut short, however. Ill health compelled him to resign the deanship in early 1982, after serving for just a year and a half. Provost Edwin Floyd then appointed John Rosenblum, the associate dean for Academic Affairs, as interim dean.

Dean John Rosenblum

When he was appointed interim dean, in November 1982, John Rosenblum expected this assignment to be temporary. He had come to Darden in 1979, attracted by the School's dedication to the case method and excellence in teaching. Rosenblum, who received his bachelor's degree from Brown and his MBA and doctoral degrees from Harvard, had spent 10 years on the Harvard faculty before moving to Charlottesville. A master teacher of business policy and strategy, Rosenblum viewed Darden as the perfect place to practice his craft as a teacher as well as actively pursue his love of casewriting and consulting. He never imagined that the Darden School would suddenly call him into permanent administrative service and divert him to a career path of academic management.

As interim dean, Rosenblum recognized

immediately that his prime objective must be to restore the School's morale and equilibrium after the brief tenure and abrupt resignation of Robert Haigh. This he set out to do through a series of personal interactions with students, faculty, staff, and alumni. A consummate public speaker who exuded warmth, charm, and intellect, Rosenblum skillfully reassured Darden's key stakeholders that the School remained steadfastly on a path devoted to its core values. Aware that a graduate business school is beholden to a diverse group of stakeholders—students, faculty, staff, alumni, corporate recruiters, university officials, donors—Rosenblum articulated the concept that Darden was a very special institution because of its unique sense of community. He coined and widely used the term "Darden Community," defining it inclusively as the set of all individuals who cared deeply about Darden and shared its values.

Both in Charlottesville and with constituents throughout the country, Rosenblum successfully conveyed the reassuring message that Darden remained confidently on course with the interim dean at the helm. It is not surprising, therefore, that the search committee tasked with finding a new dean, chaired by Professor Charles Meiburg, director of the Tayloe Murphy Institute, and aided by an executive search firm, after an exhaustive process, concluded that the 39-year-old Rosenblum was the best person to lead the School to the next level. On July 1, 1983, President Frank L. Hereford, Jr., appointed

Rosenblum Darden's fourth dean. Observed Hereford, "I cannot recall a recommendation on which I have received such enthusiastic support from students, faculty, and alumni."[44]

With morale restored and enthusiasm rekindled, John Rosenblum embarked upon a decade as dean that further accelerated Darden's movement into the top echelon of graduate business institutions. Rosenblum's program for Darden was broad and ambitious: to attract and develop the best faculty, to link Darden more closely to the University of Virginia, to develop a global presence for Darden, and to envision a bold new home for the School.

Rosenblum keenly appreciated that the School had been founded firmly on ethical principles that had been articulated by President Darden, promoted by Deans Abbott, Sheppard, and Haigh, and introduced into the academic realm through the Olsson Center for Applied Ethics. While the Olsson Center had undertaken studies and sponsored seminars for more than a decade, Rosenblum believed that its true importance to Darden lay in its ability to integrate ethics directly into the MBA curriculum. To facilitate the migration of ethics from the library to the classroom and to build upon the pioneering ethics work that Alexander Horniman, Louis Rader, and Henry Tulloch had accomplished in the Olsson Center, Rosenblum recruited two of the nation's leading business ethicists, Edward Freeman and Patricia Werhane. In 1989, at Rosenblum's strong urging, Darden

Dean John W. Rosenblum, pictured in *Fortune* magazine in 1989.

became the first leading graduate business school to offer a graded course in business ethics as a segment of its required MBA curriculum. Moreover, with the support of the Olsson Center, marked attention to the ethical dimensions of managerial decision making has pervaded the entire Darden curriculum.

Rosenblum also emphasized the importance of enhancing Darden's links to the University of Virginia and developing the

School's international presence in a rapidly evolving world economy. He supported the creation of four joint-degree programs with other schools at the University: a joint MBA/ MA in East Asian studies; a joint MBA/MA in government, foreign affairs, and public administration; a joint MBA/master's in engineering; and a joint MBA/MS in nursing. He also encouraged student- and faculty-ex-

change programs with other institutions in Europe, Asia, Australia, and Latin America.[45]

To further solidify Darden's links with the University, Rosenblum followed Abbott's and Sheppard's strategy of living on the Lawn. In the mid-1980s, when the opportunity presented itself, John and Carolyn Rosenblum and their children moved into Pavilion III. The Rosenblums, and particularly their young son, Nicholas, became highly visible residents in the daily life of Mr. Jefferson's Academical Village.

In addition to supporting Darden's faculty, curriculum, and globalization, Rosenblum saw the need for Darden to improve and expand its facilities on the University's North Grounds. After a number of planning and architectural studies in the 1980s explored the expansion of the Darden School but failed to identify a satisfactory solution, Rosenblum and William H. Goodwin, chair of the Darden School Foundation Board of Trustees, developed the audacious concept of building a brand-new, larger facility for the School that would be designed from scratch.

Facetiously calling it the "South Bronx" strategy, Dean Rosenblum proposed that

Darden abandon—for value—its current building to another University function that required space and build for itself a new facility. Rosenblum and Goodwin were able to convince Darden's supporters and senior University officials that construction of a new building for the School was a viable concept that would benefit both Darden and the University. In April 1993, Rosenblum officiated at the ground breaking for Phase I of what is now the William H. Goodwin, Jr., Grounds.

As the resource stakes for graduate business schools escalated in the 1980s and 1990s, all deans, including John Rosenblum, had to devote considerable time and attention to developing private resources. Darden's initial capital campaign was conceived and implemented under Rosenblum, and he was instrumental in raising private funding for both the School's new home and the formation of the precursor to the Batten

Institute, as well as for additional scholarships, chaired professorships, and research.

Throughout his deanship, Rosenblum was a strong supporter of enhancing the Darden School's diversity by encouraging the recruitment of African American, Hispanic, international, and female students and faculty. In the wake of concerns about the hospitableness of the School to female faculty, however, an outside committee, invited by the dean and the provost to examine the matter, issued a controversial report in 1992 that portrayed the Darden School as having an environment hostile to women. In response, the dean undertook a number of actions, including establishing a committee on women's concerns and strengthening the role of the School's ombudsman, but the gender issue, as it became known, cast a shadow over the final year of what had been Rosenblum's highly positive deanship.[46]

Dean John Rosenblum welcomes the TEP class of 1983.

While serving as dean, Rosenblum maintained his and the Darden School's close ties to the business community. The dean was invited to sit on the boards of a number of companies, including Dansk, T. Rowe Price, Chesapeake, and the Providence Journal. Perhaps even more noteworthy was the role that Rosenblum played as an articulate spokesman and creative thinker for graduate business and executive education. He served on the board of trustees of the Graduate Management Admissions Council and cochaired that organization's prestigious Commission on Admission to Graduate Management Education, thereby bringing recognition to the Darden School as an important source of creative thinking about effective business education.

The Second Faculty Generation

On many occasions, after hearing the dean's presentation to a group of alumni, parents, or students, questioners asked John Rosenblum how he could make the greatest possible impact on the future of the Darden School. Rosenblum's response was quick and to the point. The role of the dean, he observed, as compared with that of the fac- ulty, is quite modest in driving the School to further achievements. It is the faculty that has a powerful and enduring influence in setting an academic institution's direction and character. Thus, he contended, the greatest contribution a dean can make is to recruit and develop the finest faculty possible. Rosenblum's predecessors, Stewart Sheppard and Robert Haigh, shared this viewpoint. Sheppard, Haigh, and Rosenblum, as Darden's leaders in a period of growth and expansion, had the opportunity to seek out additional faculty members, who could join the burgeoning graduate business school at Virginia and add their talents and energy to the youthful academic enterprise that

Professor L. Jay Bourgeois

136

Professor Paul W. Farris

Left: **Professor Sherwood C. Frey, Jr., in action.** Frey, who joined the Darden faculty in 1979, exemplifies the Second Faculty Generation's dedication to excellence in teaching.

had become firmly rooted under Abbott.

During the Sheppard, Haigh, and Rosenblum years, from 1973 to 1993, Darden's Second Faculty Generation arrived and quickly made its mark on the School's development. In recruiting this new generation of faculty, the three deans searched for outstanding teachers with a pragmatic orientation toward solving business problems. In most cases, the School sought academics who had already demonstrated strong teaching ability—in both the MBA and executive-education settings—elsewhere, who were excited about working closely with colleagues to refine an integrated curriculum, and who were enthusiastic about case-method pedagogy. Often, the School's most sought-after candidates had business as well as academic experience. Dean Sheppard expressed the extreme care with which new faculty were hired. In reassuring alumni that newcomers would in no way degrade the teaching excellence of the School's Founding Faculty and First Faculty Generation, who combined both academic and practical experience, Sheppard noted that his new faculty appointees "possess outstanding academic and business qualifications as teachers, researchers, and 'institutional citizens.' All are committed to case-method pedagogy and display the necessary dynamism to excite and stimulate classroom discussion. These new faculty are by no means to be regarded as inexperienced and theoretical academicians."[47]

Darden's Second Faculty Generation included an impressive array of teachers and scholars, who were quick to imbibe the School's culture and to knit themselves, often seamlessly, into effective teaching teams in conjunction with the School's First Faculty Generation. The melding of these two generational sets of instructors, who shared a common vision and set of values, created the powerful and sustained faculty impetus that has inspired Darden students for five decades and launched Darden into the top echelon of global graduate business institutions.

There are no better examples of the intertwining of the two faculty generations than John Rosenblum himself and Sherwood Frey, both of whom were recruited by Sheppard from teaching posts at Harvard in 1979. Both Rosenblum, a business-policy teacher, and Frey, the leader of the School's newly structured quantitative-analysis area, were outstanding case-method instructors, who became instant student favorites, respected faculty colleagues, and unflagging supporters of the Darden School's mission and culture. Sheppard attracted other outstanding Second Faculty Generation recruits, including E. Richard Brownlee II (1975) in accounting, Samuel E. Bodily (1977) in quantitative analysis, Edward Davis (1978) in operations, and James R. Freeland (1979) in operations, who, while not products of the Harvard Business School, became enthusiastically wedded to and stalwart proponents

Professors Samuel E. Bodily, James R. Freeland, E. Richard Brownlee II, and Lynn A. Isabella.

Professor Robert M. Conroy, associate dean for MBA Education, engages students inside and outside the classroom.

Professors Robert E. Spekman, James G. Clawson, and
Robert L. Carraway.

of Darden's instructional programs.

The passing of the dean's baton from Sheppard to Haigh and from Haigh to Rosenblum did not impede the momentum of the creation of Darden's Second Faculty Generation. From 1980 through 1993, a corps of additional Second Faculty Generation members signed on to the growing academic enterprise in Charlottesville, and quickly became invested in sustaining the School's vision and values and in enhancing its achievements. Among this group were Paul W. Farris (1980) in marketing, Philip E. Pfeifer (1980) in quantitative analysis, James G. Clawson (1981) in organizational behavior, Robert F. Bruner (1982) in finance, Mark E. Haskins (1984) in accounting, Robert L. Carraway (1984) in quantitative analysis, Mark R. Eaker (1986) in finance, R. Edward Freeman (1986) in ethics, L. J. Bourgeois (1986) in strategy, Elliott N. Weiss (1987) in operations, Robert M. Conroy (1988) in finance, Kenneth M. Eades (1988) in finance, Mark E. Parry (1988) in marketing, Lynn A. Isabella (1990) in organizational behavior, Robert E. Spekman (1991) in marketing, Jeanne M. Liedtka (1992) in strategy, Dana R. Clyman (1992) in quantitative analysis, and Patricia H. Werhane (1993) in ethics. These faculty sank their roots deep into Charlottesville's soil during the 1980s and early 1990s, and have become pivotal to the School's progress.

Rosenblum considered the recruitment of outstanding classroom teachers a top priority. At the same time, with the active participation of Charles Meiburg, Edward Freeman, and Robert Harris, the series of associate deans for Academic Affairs who served as his colleagues in the Dean's Office,

Professors Philip E. Pfeifer, Mark E. Haskins, Sherwood C. Frey, and Jeanne M. Liedtka.

Rosenblum revised the School's standards for tenure and promotion to include a requirement of significant research productivity. This new standard ensured that Darden's faculty would continually bring new knowledge into the classroom to enrich the MBA and executive-education experiences. Moreover, it helped to foster the School's reputation as an intellectual center that generated exciting new ideas with a ready relevance to practical management. "I remember sitting in some promotion and tenure meetings with some senior faculty," recalled Meiburg, "and Dan Newton encouraging us to hire people who are better than we are. And that was the thrust I always used."[48]

Darden's Second Faculty Generation fused with the First Faculty Generation to serve as the backbone of the School's academic structure and to energize its continued progress. Together, they became a unified group dedicated to both excellence in the classroom and the development of research products and teaching materials that would have a strong impact on the business world.

The Center for International Banking Studies (CIBS)

In 1977, the Bankers' Association for Foreign Trade (BAFT), an organization of 150 U.S. banks with international departments and nearly 80 affiliated foreign banks headquartered in 22 countries, chose the Darden School as the home

Finance Professor William W. Sihler, director of the Center for International Banking Studies. Sihler was appointed to the Morris Chair in 1976 and later to the Trzcinski Chair. He is pictured here in a tangible "Morris" chair.

of its new Center for International Banking Studies (CIBS). The purpose of the Center was to provide bankers with educational programs designed to enhance their skills in international commercial lending. The Center would also conduct research on international transactions and transnational lending. BAFT was attracted by Darden's strong practical orientation and the experience and success it had achieved in executive education. Darden beat out the Wharton School and Northwestern University's Kellogg School for the honor of hosting the new center. Professor William W. Sihler assumed the executive directorship of CIBS, and ensured that the Center's educational programs would focus on the case method.

P. Henry Mueller, chairman of the Credit Policy Committee of Citibank of New York and a vice president of BAFT, who had chaired the committee to establish the organization's formal educational activities, wrote of CIBS: "It was a success from day one.... At its peak, it was offering four one-week programs in international lending a year, along with four or five major conferences and shorter seminars."

CIBS remained active for 14 years; in 1991, it curtailed its activities in response to a combination of bank mergers and a decline in international lending by regional American banks owing to greater fiscal instability abroad and consequent risk. Approximately 1,000 bankers studied at the Darden School during CIBS' existence.[49]

Interim Dean C. Ray Smith (MBA 1958). Smith was called upon three times to serve as Darden's interim dean.

C. Ray Smith

There is no single individual who has played a more central role in the Darden School's development and success than Clyde Ray Smith. A 1958 graduate of Darden's second MBA class, Smith served on the faculty for 42 years. In 2003, when he retired from Virginia's faculty with the apt title of Tipton R. Snavely Professor of Business Administration, Smith was the University's longest-serving active faculty member.

Not only was Smith an outstanding teacher for more than four decades—having progressed from the rank of instructor to chaired professor while teaching countless MBA students accounting, entrepreneurship, and real-estate finance, development, and

C. Ray Smith receives a tee shirt emblazoned with the nickname, "Cool Ray", bestowed upon him for his unflappable demeanor and sagacious advice.

management—but he also held just about every significant administrative post in the Darden School at one time or another.

A Bridgewater College graduate, Smith enrolled in Virginia's untested MBA Program in the fall of 1956. After receiving his degree, he served as a finance officer in the U.S. Army at Fort Knox, Kentucky, where he also taught evening courses in economics to military personnel at a University of Kentucky branch campus. In 1961, when Smith emerged from the army at the tender age of 26, he was enticed back to Charlottesville by Dean Abbott to teach accounting while simultaneously obtaining his CPA certification. Thus, Smith has been either a fellow student or a faculty member of every Darden MBA alumnus or alumna with the exception

of the classes of 1960 and 1961. Moreover, he has instructed hundreds of Darden executive-education participants, was instrumental in developing six executive-education offerings, and has taught in such programs as Financial Management for Non-Financial Managers, The Executive Program (TEP), Managing Corporate Resources, Commercial Lending, and Advanced Commercial Lending. Smith not only authored several dozen cases on subjects ranging from accounting to real estate, but also richly sprinkled his elective courses with "live" cases by inviting many alumni from his vast network of Darden graduates to participate in class as guests.

Stewart Sheppard, then executive director of the Institute of Chartered Financial Analysts, tapped Smith, during his early years at the School, for his first administrative post: administrative director of that new affiliate of the School. In 1972, after becoming dean, Sheppard appointed Smith as the School's initial associate dean for Administration. This was the first of several associate deanships Smith has held. In 1991, Dean John Rosenblum appointed Smith to the post of associate dean for MBA Education, and Dean Lee Higdon appointed him to the position of associate dean for Executive Education in 1994.

But Smith's administrative service to Darden and to the University of Virginia has been even more remarkable. President John Casteen turned to Smith on three different occasions to assume the critical responsibility of serving as interim dean after the resignations of John Rosenblum in 1993, Lee Higdon in 1997, and Ted Snyder in 2001. Each time, Smith took the helm of the School and maintained its steady course in a progressive direction as a search for a new dean unfolded. Smith's calm and unflappable presence and his unparalleled appreciation of Darden's vision and values have meant that the Darden School has never missed a beat during its transitions in leadership.

At the university level, Smith served as chair of the University of Virginia's Faculty Senate and, in 1990, chaired the Faculty Senate's presidential search committee, which recommended John Casteen. He was also a member of the University's Accreditation Committee and chair of its Compliance Committee. In addition, he has served as

a trustee of Bridgewater College and the University of Virginia School of Medicine Alumni Foundation. He also served as executive director of the Darden School Foundation from 1996 until his retirement, in 2003.[50]

Relatively early in his career, Smith was dubbed "Cool Ray." While the origin of this sobriquet remains obscure—some claim it stems from an identification of Smith with

the popular Ray-Ban sunglasses that became the rage after being worn by Peter Fonda in the film *Easy Rider*, while others maintain that the description "cool" simply fits Smith's personality and demeanor like a glove—it has been used with affection by generations of Darden students who have known Smith as an instructor, as a dispenser of sage advice, and in his myriad administrative roles at the School throughout more than four decades of dedicated service.

C. Ray Smith not only taught thousands of MBA and executive-education students over the course of his 42 years on Darden's faculty, but he also held almost every significant administrative post at the School.

MBA Program RIGOR

Throughout the Darden School's history, its faculty has delivered an MBA Program characterized by intensity and rigor. In part, the Program's rigor stemmed from the School's dedication to the case method of instruction. This pedagogical approach compelled the student to become an active learner, always prepared to participate in class. From the mid-1950s on, most Darden students have harbored more than a little anxiety about being a potential victim of the dreaded "cold call," the instructor's selection of a nonvolunteering student to explain his or her approach to a case. Lem Lewis (MBA 1972), from his position as a Darden School Foundation Trustee three decades after his graduation, recalled vividly the impact of the feared cold call on his fellow students: "But whether it was the actual time spent with the case or whether you got the key talking points from your study group, you absolutely did not show up to class with-

"Thank you. I had a harder time getting into the Darden Graduate Business School."

Opposite: **Faculty commitment to curriculum integration**. Professors Edward Davis, Brandt Allen, and Alan Beckenstein (left to right) in intense discussion.

out having a fairly good feel for the case in case you were called on as the first participant. It's a very daunting experience."[1]

For Darden students, the cases came fast and they came in volume. The result was a heavy workload and a daily lesson in balancing competing demands under time constraints. Professor John Snook, a former assistant dean of Student Affairs, explained that making students nervous was not the faculty's intent: "We recognize that with all of the things the Program tries to do in two years—in its rigor, its fast pace, and the ambiguity implicit in the case method—we will induce anxieties and frustration among some of our students. We don't strive to create them, but we don't shy away from them, because we believe that the real world demands that they be faced and dealt with."[2]

In part, too, the MBA Program's rigor was the result of the School's newness and its sense of urgency to define its place as a respected graduate business institution. Professor James Dunstan candidly explained the challenge Virginia's new and unknown graduate business school faced during its first two decades: "The atmosphere at Darden in those days was completely different. The problem was that we were not attracting top students. So to make sure that our students

Voices

"While at times, the boot camp may be difficult, I am always impressed by the fact that Darden grads tell surveys that they have the heaviest workload *and* the best professors. Darden students are respectful of the workload because it comes from an incomparable faculty in so many disciplines."

— *Jeremy Shinewald,*
Graduation speech, 2003

147

"... and we offer a choice between purgatory and the first-year program at the Darden Business School."

were in demand, we had an extremely rigorous program. We went to class on Saturday, we had three cases a day and were known as the boot camp of business schools.... We also eliminated 10 to 15 percent of the students each class and this, of course, put a lot of stress on the students.... We had to keep the program very rigorous so that our students would be in demand. I mean, nobody ever heard of Darden in those days."[3]

Despite the intensity of the School's curriculum and the high expectations of its faculty, the relationship between faculty and students was close and cordial. Darden's faculty relished the time they spent with students, both inside and outside of class. Founding faculty member John Forbes described the School's earliest students: "The students were wonderful.... The simple fact is that the students we had at the start were the best

students we had because they had the courage to attempt an untried venture. They took a chance. They had large sums of money involved, and they had large chunks of their lives involved.... They were men who had real guts; they were men who were prepared to work hard at what they were doing. They were delighted to be admitted and took every advantage of it; knocked themselves out with work, and they were just wonderful people."[4]

Interviewed at the age of 97 in 2000, Paul Hammaker corroborated Forbes's opinion of the fortitude and amiability of the School's early generation of students: "They were young, of course. They struck me as being enthusiastic and upbeat. They certainly were hard workers because you couldn't stay in these courses without putting in 50, 60, 70 hours a week. So I did respect them, and I found them to be absolutely great. In fact, I kept a diary at the time, and I wrote, 'Those kids are wonderful; it's just like going out into the sunshine; it's a great time.'"[5]

While the faculty has set a high bar for student performance since the founding of the institution, it has done so to ensure the soundest possible preparation for students' future careers as business leaders. It has done so from a deep-seated belief in the ability of dedicated students to succeed and to represent the Darden School with distinction. Professor Almand Coleman spoke for all generations of Darden faculty when he wrote, in 1976: "I like to be in the classroom. I like the students. They are all."[6]

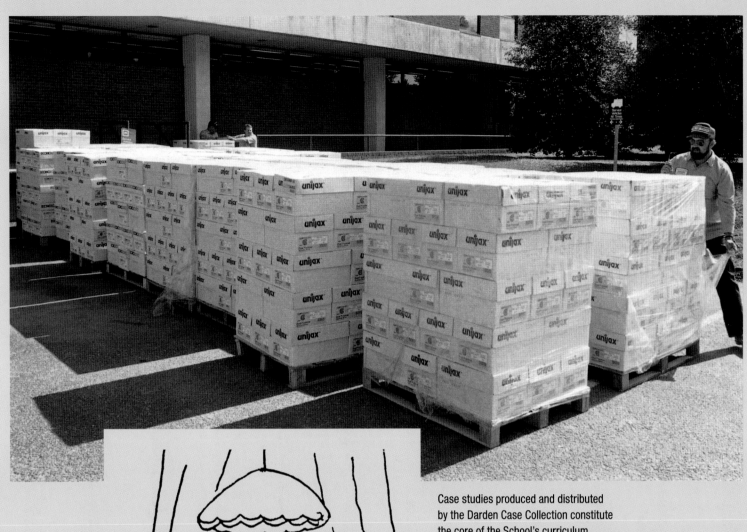

Case studies produced and distributed
by the Darden Case Collection constitute
the core of the School's curriculum.

Left: "The good news is the job of your dreams
awaits you. The bad news is you have to
graduate from the Darden School to get it."

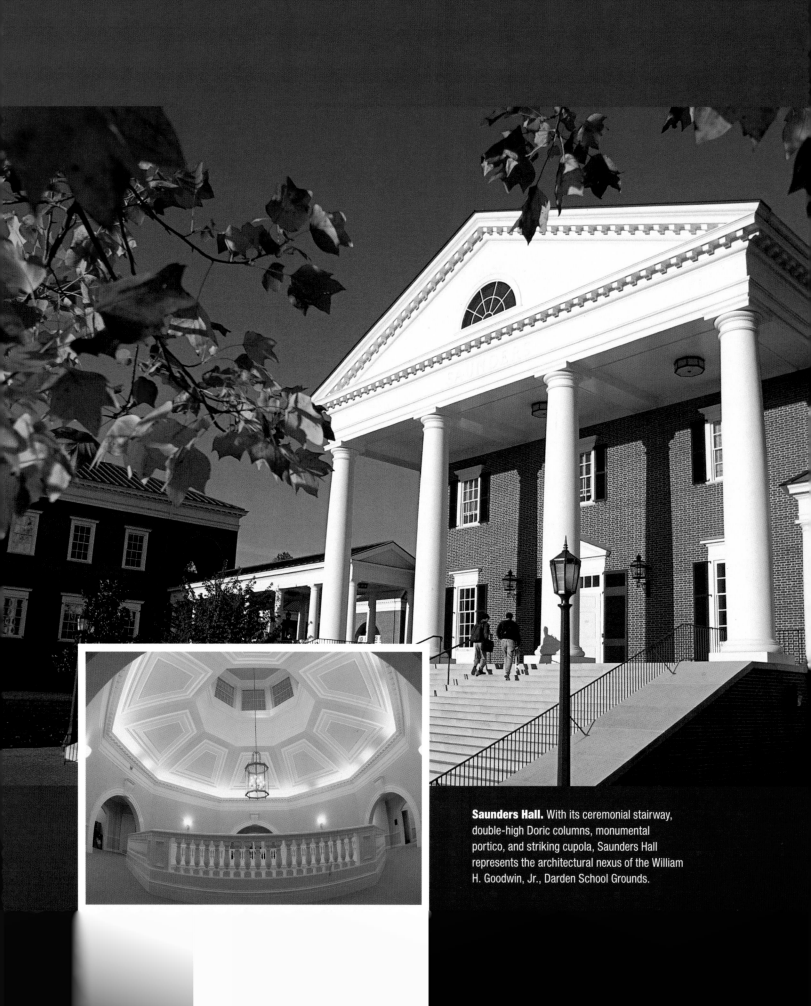

Saunders Hall. With its ceremonial stairway, double-high Doric columns, monumental portico, and striking cupola, Saunders Hall represents the architectural nexus of the William H. Goodwin, Jr., Darden School Grounds.

F O U R ❀ *F L O W E R I N G*

The Darden School Mission Statement

For many organizations, mission statements are little more than window dressing mounted on a plaque to simulate a semblance of institutional purpose. For the Darden School, however, the mission statement is an enduring reflection of the School's vision and values, which date back to its founding. In 1959, the Founding Faculty established the young School's original objectives: preparing students to learn to think, to make decisions, and to take action. In 1970, the faculty approved the following overriding objective for the MBA Program: "To prepare men and women of high promise to act with determination, judgment, and integrity in increasingly responsible positions of leadership in the world of practical affairs."[1]

The Governor as professor. Virginia Governor Mark R. Warner visits a Darden finance class to share his experience as a venture capitalist and entrepreneur shortly before winning the governorship.

In 1991, Dean John Rosenblum appointed a faculty committee to draft a formal mission statement designed to expand this well-accepted objective and to codify what had become, over time, the Darden School's raison d'être. The committee, composed of Brandt Allen, Sherwood Frey, Robert Harris, Robert Landel, John Rosenblum, and Ray Smith, brought its thoughts back to the faculty for a series of detailed discussions. The result was a unanimous faculty vote, in December 1992, to adopt and promulgate a formal mission statement for the School. As a corollary, the faculty stipulated that each and every year it would discuss and affirm or modify the mission statement. Every September since 1993, the faculty, at its initial meeting of the academic year, has voted to affirm that "the Darden Graduate School of Business Administration is a professional school that seeks to better society by developing leaders in the world of practical affairs."[2] The School's emphasis on educating practical, action-oriented leaders for the purpose of improving society has never wavered.

The William H. Goodwin, Jr., Darden School Grounds

While the School's first building on the North Grounds offered much more space than cramped Monroe Hall—enough space, in fact, for several offices to lie fallow for a few years after the move from the University's Main Grounds—it was not long before facilities-planning issues once again sprang to the forefront. The School's growth to four MBA sections, its acquisition of additional faculty and support staff, and the flowering of its affiliated organizations (the Tayloe Murphy Center, the Center for the Study of Applied Ethics, the Center for International Banking Studies, and the Financial Analysts Research Foundation) soon consumed all available square footage in the new building. Consequently, when Robert Haigh became dean, in 1980, just five years after Darden moved to its first North Grounds building, he commissioned an internal study on how best to expand the new building to prepare for further growth.

The study, led by Professor Louis Rader, called for construction of a new office wing, mirroring the existing building, to be erected on the flat, grassy area between the School and Massie Road. Although this approach would yield additional offices, it failed to capture the Darden Community's imagination as an inviting solution to future space needs. This study, whose recommendation was never implemented, was the first of several expansion plans devised in the 1980s by local and national architectural firms. These plans

Dean John Rosenblum explains the Darden master plan. The plan provided for two phases of construction to accommodate the School's growing space needs.

Opposite: **A dedication to remember**. A ceremonial procession from the School's former home, led by Grand Marshal of the University Donald E. Dougald, accompanied by the Colonial Williamsburg Fife and Drum Corps, celebrated the dedication of the new Darden Grounds in 1996.

were intended to offer creative ways to capture more square footage while remedying some of the new building's evident deficiencies. Not the least of the facility's shortcomings was the unintended outcome that its original back door, located adjacent to trash dumpsters and leading directly to rest rooms, had become the School's de facto front door. This situation arose owing to the location of parking—guests, faculty, and staff all beat a path to the building's entrance closest to their cars—and to the opening of Sponsors Hall in 1979, which shifted Darden's physical center of gravity from the School's formal front entrance, on a landscaped terrace opposite the Law School, to the rear of the building, where Sponsors Hall was sited.

A final attempt to provide additional space and correct the building's shortcomings was made by the respected New York City architectural firm Hardy Holzman Pfeiffer. This plan called for a major addition projecting from the side of the building into the parking lot and the construction of an additional access road leading to a new front entrance. While imaginative, this scheme entailed a large amount of site work that dramatically elevated its potential cost. The upshot was an expensive project that would yield only a limited gain in net square footage.

As Darden entered the 1990s, it appeared that the School was stymied in finding a viable solution to its space needs through an expansion of its existing building. Rather than settle for an unsatisfactory addition,

Jeffersonian influence.
The new Darden buildings, with their sand-struck Virginia brick, white Chippendale balustrades, and red metal standing-seam roofs, bring elements of the University's Academical Village to the North Grounds.

however, Dean John Rosenblum crafted a bold alternative approach: Darden would abandon its inadequate building and start fresh. If the School could find an acceptable "greenfield" site, Rosenblum believed, it could design and construct a highly functional new facility sufficiently large to meet Darden's dynamic aspirations for years to come. William H. Goodwin, Jr., chair of the Darden School Foundation Board of Trustees, was intrigued by this radical new direction. He and the Board encouraged Rosenblum to seek the required land from the University. If the University of Virginia would allocate land to Darden, Goodwin pledged to lead the Foundation in raising the private funds necessary to build a new facility for the School.

After inspecting three possible green-field building sites, Rosenblum, preferring to remain on the North Grounds rather than move even farther away from the core of the University, selected an open parcel of land between Sponsors Hall and the University's North Grounds Recreation Center that had been earmarked for intramural softball and soccer fields. President John Casteen supported Darden's plan to build a new facility. The University then reserved Darden's chosen parcel in its Master Plan, and found an alternative site elsewhere on the North Grounds for the proposed intramural athletic fields.

With the land identified, the School's next step was to define the project's funding and development models. In regard to funding, three potential sources became the center of attention—major gifts to a Darden capital campaign, executive-education net revenue, and the "sale" of Darden's existing building. As the fundraising campaign began in earnest, the Darden School let it be known to the University's other academic units that its current building would be available to them in return for a "contribution" to the Darden School's new-building project. After considerable negotiation and with critical eleventh-hour brokering from Leonard W. Sandridge, the University's executive vice president, Dean Rosenblum struck a deal with Law School Dean Thomas H. Jackson. The Law School would take over Darden's current building—which it later renovated and linked via new construction to its existing building as a component of the David Harrison Law Grounds—in return for a contribution to Darden's fundraising campaign.

The arrangement constituted a triple win. Darden gained a new home. The Law School gained a significantly expanded and attractively integrated multiple-building complex. The University of Virginia gained greatly enhanced facilities for two of its outstanding professional schools without the need to contribute University or state funds.

As the dream of a new facility for Darden became more real, the issue of how the large and complicated project should most efficaciously be implemented came to the forefront. Ordinarily, the University's Department of Facilities Management developed all capital projects at the institution. In 1990, however, the Virginia General Assembly had, for the first time, passed legislation permitting private firms to develop projects on land owned by state colleges and universities. Although the law's primary intent was to encourage private development of dormitories, the Darden School Foundation stepped forward, under the umbrella of this legislation, to serve as developer of the new Darden Grounds. The Trustees of the Darden School Foundation believed strongly that, because the project would be funded totally by private resources, it made sense to privatize the project to the extent possible within the constraints of state regulations and requirements. Moreover, the Trustees believed that the project could be implemented more rapidly and more economically with the Foundation as its developer.

President John Casteen and Executive Vice President Leonard Sandridge supported the concept of the Darden Foundation as developer, and sought and received the Virginia General Assembly's blessing for the Darden project to proceed on this basis. In addition, Casteen and Sandridge, with the help and guidance of University of Virginia Treasurer Alice Handy, backed the project

Saunders Hall's octagonal cupola and clock in pediment.

with a University bond issue, the debt service on which the Darden School Foundation pledged its full responsibility. The University and the Foundation entered into a formal agreement setting forth the terms of the project's development parameters and the Foundation's financial obligations to the University. Thus, the stage was set for creation of the new Darden Grounds, the first major academic capital project at a state institution to be developed by a private entity.

In 1991, the Darden School began detailed planning for its new facilities. An important step in this process was the selection of an architectural firm that could, on the parcel of land allotted, design a captivating and enduring vision for the School's physical presence that embodied both the core values and the functional requirements of a vibrant institution in a highly competitive academic environment.

In an effort to identify the ideal architect for this assignment, the Darden School Foundation, with the help of University Architect and Architecture School Dean Harry Porter, devised a painstaking architect-selection process. The Darden School Building Committee invited 20 firms, prequalified on the basis of institutional experience and stature, to submit proposals and credentials. After reviewing these proposals, the committee asked seven firms to visit Charlottesville for presentations and interviews. As an outcome of this process, the committee narrowed the field to three firms, which it then invited to participate in an architectural competition. The three architectural firms—Kallmann McKinnell and Wood of Boston, Allan Greenberg of New Haven, and Robert A. M. Stern of New York—were given six weeks to develop conceptual approaches to Darden's new facilities based on actual site conditions. Each firm submitted a series of architectural drawings and models, which it then presented in a public forum open to all members of the Darden Community.

After close examination of the submissions, the Darden School Foundation selected Robert A. M. Stern Architects to develop a master plan for the new Darden Grounds and to design the new facilities. Stern and his associates set forth a vision of Darden as an interconnected community of buildings constructed on a human scale in the architectural vernacular of Thomas Jefferson. A Columbia University architectural historian as well as a notable and prolific practicing architect, Stern drew inspiration for his Darden concept from Mr. Jefferson's Academical Village. Stern's careful, historically respectful approach resonated with the Darden School Foundation Board of Trustees and with the University of Virginia's Board of Visitors. Both boards believed that, for far too long, the architectural style of many University buildings had strayed from

As (left to right) William H. Goodwin, former chair of the Darden School Foundation Trustees, and associate dean for Administration Mark Reisler and Professor Neil H. Borden, co-chairs of the Building Project Work Group, look on, Henry J. Faison, chair of the Trustee Building Committee, breaks ground for Phase I of Darden's new home in 1993.

the tradition of excellence that Jefferson had
initiated when he designed his University.

As the Darden School advanced its
detailed internal program planning, it became evident that the School's long-term
physical needs would significantly outstrip
the project's limited budget. The School
then prioritized its program needs, which
Stern translated into a design for Phase I
of the new Darden Grounds. The Building
Committee commissioned a second architectural firm, Ayers Saint Gross of Baltimore,
to produce the construction documents for
Phase I and serve as the architect of record,
while working cooperatively with Stern, the
design architect. Cognizant of the School's

needs beyond Phase I, Stern included in his
master plan for Darden the identification
and preservation of specific building sites
for a future second phase of construction.

Excitement abounded as Darden broke
ground for its new home on April 3, 1993.
Phase I—which included a classroom building, a faculty-office building, a library/stu-
dent-services building, a "commons" building
(later named Saunders Hall), and a 60–guest
room wing of the Sponsors hotel, accompanied by a freestanding reception and check-
in building known as the Gatehouse—comprised a total of 210,000 gross square feet.

Construction of the project was completed in December 1995, just in time for

the entire Darden School to move from its existing building to the new complex over the 1995–96 holiday break, a mammoth task. On January 8, 1996, a major blizzard, bringing 22 inches of snow propelled by 35-mile-per-hour winds, delayed the new facilities' opening ceremony and the start of classes. But as soon as the storm abated and the snow was plowed, the School's students, faculty, and staff began to enjoy their new quarters.

Completion of Darden's five-building Phase I project in late 1995 represented the culmination of the initial portion of a planning process that began in 1991. It accomplished the objective of producing a facility—inspired by the University founder's architectural vision—that constituted the first major step in Darden's quest for unparalleled facilities.

The facilities-planning process, foresightedly, allowed for future similarly designed structures that would meet the needs of a growing and dynamic institution. Some needs identified in the planning process, such as an auditorium and a new dining center, which could not be accommodated in Phase I, were immediately apparent. It was not long, however, before other space needs came to the forefront as well.

Since the inception of planning for the new Darden Grounds, the School had experienced substantial expansion in a number of its programs that necessitated additional space. During the 1990s, for example, the School significantly enriched the depth and

breadth of its MBA Program's elective offerings through the creation of 40 new elective courses. As the School gained prominence in the media in the mid-1990s, it received a record-breaking number of applications, increasing the need for more space for the Admissions Office. Likewise, intensified demand by corporate recruiters for Darden's graduates put increased pressure for additional space on the Career Development Center. Finally, Executive Programs experienced unprecedented customer interest. Between 1991, when planning for the Darden complex began, and 1998, the number of executive-education participants at Darden more than doubled. At the same time, the School expanded its international dimensions and attracted more MBA students and executive-education participants from around the world. This coincided with growth in the activities of the Tayloe Murphy Center. Similarly, the School's Olsson Center for Applied Ethics and its new Batten Center for Entrepreneurial Leadership accelerated their activities in the mid-1990s.

In short, Darden's dynamism over the course of the 1990s was impressive. This growth, coupled with the reality that the initial phase of the Darden Grounds had

Darden students take advantage of the snow for a bit of fun.

Robert A. M. Stern. The noted architect received the commission to design the new Darden School Grounds upon winning an architectural competition.

Opposite: **Wilkinson Courtyard**. Located between the Abbott Center and the Darden Library building, Wilkinson Courtyard offers an inviting outdoor space for both individual contemplation and social gatherings.

been unable to accommodate key identified needs, triggered planning for Phase II of the Darden Grounds. Again serving as project developer, the Darden School Foundation commissioned the architectural firm Ayers Saint Gross to extend its work as the architect of record for Phase I by, first, revisiting and refreshing the School's master plan and, second, designing a major Phase II expansion. This project, like the initial phase, was supported fully by private funds donated by friends of the Darden School.

Ground breaking for Phase II took place after the graduation ceremony in May 2000. Phase II consisted of significant additions to the classroom and faculty-office buildings. It also included an expansion of the Sponsors Executive Residence, bringing Darden's hotel capacity to 180 guest rooms, supported by 38 group-study rooms and a satellite of the University of Virginia Bookstore, dubbed Darden Exchange. The signature building of Phase II

was the Abbott Center, a multipurpose structure containing a beautifully appointed 470-seat auditorium, designed for teaching purposes as well as for distinguished speakers, conferences, and cultural events; a breathtaking 400-seat double-high dining room with skylight; and staff offices. Finally, Phase II included a 500-space parking garage for both student parking and the new conference facilities. With the completion of the final elements of Phase II at the end of 2002, Darden had attained its objective: creation of a highly functional and aesthetically pleasing set of facilities second to none among graduate business schools, facilities that will ensure the support of Darden's academic aspirations well into the twenty-first century.[3]

Robert A. M. Stern

Darden's second home on the North Grounds was designed by Robert A. M. Stern Architects of New York. Founder and Senior Partner Robert A. M. Stern, with his colleagues Graham Wyatt and Gary Brewer, led the effort to create a highly functional and technologically state-of-the-art facility aesthetically compatible with Jefferson's architectural vocabulary. Stern, a Fellow of the American Institute of Architects, received the Medal of Honor from the Institute's New York chapter, and served as a professor at Columbia University's Graduate School of Architecture. He was appointed dean of the School of Architecture at Yale University in 1998.[4]

Dean Leo Higdon

Leo I. "Lee" Higdon, Jr., was the first Darden School dean to assume the leadership of the School directly from a post in the business sector. Although a nonacademic, Higdon had always possessed a strong affinity for academia. A Georgetown University graduate who served two years as a Peace Corps volunteer teaching and advising on community development in Malawi before receiving his MBA degree from the University of Chicago in 1972, Higdon had considered pursuing a doctorate in business at Harvard. Instead, after completing his studies at Chicago, he joined Salomon Brothers, where he enjoyed an extremely successful 20-year career as an investment banker.

At Salomon, Higdon rose rapidly through the ranks, and negotiated many noteworthy deals involving such companies as IBM, Time-Warner, and CPC International. The periodical *Institutional Investor* cited Higdon for overseeing "Deals of the Year" on four occasions, including the 1987 merger of American Motors and Chrysler. On October 1, 1993, when Higdon became Darden's dean, he was cohead of Salomon's Global Investment Banking Division and a member of the firm's executive committee. He was also a member of Georgetown University's board of trustees and a member of the Georgetown Business School's advisory board. In addition, Higdon served on the board of directors of Africare, a nonprofit organization that assisted in economic, agricultural, and health-

Darden's close connection to business. Dean Lee Higdon and Darden School Foundation Trustees (right to left) Thomas A. Saunders (MBA 1967), E. Thayer Bigelow (MBA 1967), George A. L. David (MBA 1967), and H. Eugene Lockhart (MBA 1974) prepare to board a Sikorsky helicopter at the Wall Street heliport.

Opposite: The Abbott Center dining room seats 400 for major banquets.

The Darden Garage.
The convenient 500-space garage blends seamlessly with the architectural style of the Goodwin Grounds.

care development in many African nations.

Noted at Salomon Brothers for his skill in consensus building and for his thoroughness and thoughtfulness, Higdon impressed the search committee, chaired by C. Ray Smith, as a respected and seasoned executive. The committee believed that Higdon could set an agenda for excellence and at the same time ensure stability at Darden in the wake of a study that concluded that the School's climate for female faculty was less than welcoming. In announcing his appointment, University of Virginia President John Casteen observed that Higdon "comes to Darden uniquely sensitive to its requirements for leadership, which, while distinct from those of the marketplace, ultimately draw on the same exemplary personal and intellectual qualities."

Vice Provost Barbara Nolan, a University of Virginia professor of English and a member of the search committee, observed, to a *New York Times* reporter, that "it was very clear to all members of the committee that Mr. Higdon will regard women and minorities as equal players on the Darden team. He impressed us as a man of impeccable integrity and directness who will pay close attention to integrating individual concerns into a compelling vision for the School's future."[5]

In addition to Higdon's crisp management style and tested leadership ability, his close ties to business in general and to the financial community in particular appealed to the search committee at a time when the Commonwealth of Virginia's funding for the University of Virginia was declining.

In this fiscal environment, it was becoming clear that Darden would have to augment its private resources significantly.

Upon his appointment as Darden's fifth dean, Higdon told the *Virginian-Pilot and Ledger-Star* that "my game plan is very much oriented toward questioning, listening, and learning." He observed that Darden "is a School that has a very strong culture, a real sense of itself. From my standpoint, it's a situation of building on strengths and considerable competencies."[6] True to his word, even before arriving in Charlottesville, Higdon began to make the rounds of several top business schools, meeting one-on-one with their deans to gain a more comprehensive understanding of the challenges facing the best of the nation's graduate business schools as well as to solicit the deans' perceptions of the Darden School. In addition to this carefully planned intelligence operation, Higdon plunged into a series of meetings with Darden's key constituencies—students, faculty, alumni—with his characteristic energy, optimism, and focus. His aim was to learn as much as possible about the institution as rapidly as possible.

Although a newcomer, Higdon was quick to discern Darden's strengths and to acknowledge that a major repositioning of the institution was not in order. Instead, he moved forward quickly, first, to assure the community that diversity concerns would be addressed as a priority and, second, to initiate a planning process designed to identify how the School could best build upon its

Voices

"Dean Higdon worked tirelessly to improve our pubic relations and our visibility ... in the business community.... He had lots of energy and enthusiasm and there was a feeling the engines had been revved up while he was here."

— *James Clawson*

existing areas of excellence. Higdon established a clear goal: to ensure that Darden became recognized *indisputably* as one of the world's best graduate business schools.

In regard to tackling the issue of diversity, much had already been done by Dean Rosenblum and Interim Dean C. Ray Smith. Since the appearance of the report on gender issues, the School had conducted a survey on its climate, revised its mission statement to emphasize its dedication to diversity, and hired its first chaired female professor, Patricia Werhane. Higdon moved with dispatch to assert his and Darden's commitment to gender equity. He established an Equity Council, consisting of faculty, staff, and student representatives, to consider ways to make Darden a more welcoming environment for women and minorities. He made it clear to faculty search committees that the recruitment of a more diverse faculty was a nonnegotiable priority for the School.

In June 1994, as Higdon concluded his initial year as dean, he published a "Strategic Overview" document for Darden that set forth his vision for Darden and the initiatives and priorities that the School needed to pursue to meet the demands of the future. In the document, the dean posed the challenge at hand: "Darden must expand its capabilities and build further upon its core competencies if it is to enhance its standing globally and establish its position—indisputably—in the very top tier of graduate business schools." Future managers, Higdon asserted, would

have to cope with a more global economy, a more pluralistic workforce, and new corporate organizational models reflecting flexible designs and decentralized decision making. Darden had to be ready to prepare such managers by adopting a number of important educational initiatives.

To ensure that Darden MBA graduates would be well positioned to meet the challenges of the twenty-first century, Higdon commissioned the School's Required Curriculum Committee to undertake an intensive study of the required portion of the MBA Program. The goal of this process was to identify any curriculum modifications necessary to provide a focused, responsive, and integrated MBA education second to none in both design and delivery.

In addition to general curriculum improvement in response to changes in the business environment, Higdon identified leadership and entrepreneurship, globalization, and information technology as areas of strategic importance for Darden. In the realm of leadership and entrepreneurship, in particular, Higdon believed Darden could develop distinction. "Given the Darden School's traditional general management orientation and its commitment to pedagogy that stresses decision making, further concentration on leadership and entrepreneurship represents not only a close fit with the School's

Trustee Chair Thomas Saunders, architect Robert Stern, and Dean Lee Higdon grace the cover of *Albemarle* magazine in a 1996 issue featuring the architecture of the School's new facilities.

Opposite: **The South Lounge.** A quiet place for study and reflection is the beautifully appointed South Lounge in Saunders Hall.

Saunders Hall, main entrance to the new Darden facilities. With its three-story PepsiCo Forum atrium, comfortable lounges, and inviting café, Saunders Hall serves as the social "commons" for the Darden Community.

Inset: President John T. Casteen speaking at the dedication of the new Darden School Grounds in 1996.

heritage, but also an opportunity for Darden to distinguish itself as a preeminent graduate business institution," he asserted in his June 1994 Strategic Overview document.[7]

In regard to globalization, Higdon's meetings with the deans of peer schools revealed a perception that, in Higdon's words, "Darden was not a very global institution." As a result, globalization became one of his priorities. During Higdon's deanship, Darden increased its number of international MBA students and developed exchange programs with a number of business schools abroad, including the Richard Ivey School at the University of Western Ontario, in Canada, and IPADE, in Mexico.

To undergird his ambitious and focused aspirations for Darden, Higdon realized that resource enhancement and major investments in critical areas like technology would be essential. He therefore moved to strengthen the School's development and alumni efforts as well as its Office of Career Services. Annual giving

and major gifts to Darden reached record levels. By 1996, the Darden School had become increasingly recognized as a major player in graduate business education. It was ranked fifth in the *BusinessWeek* survey of MBA programs that year.[8]

In January 1997, Lee Higdon surprised the School by announcing that he would be leaving Darden at the end of the academic year to assume the presidency of Babson College. University of Virginia Provost Peter Low asked C. Ray Smith to serve once again as the Darden School's interim dean.

Philanthropy

From the original conceptualization of a graduate business school at the University of Virginia, in the early 1950s, to the present, philanthropy has been a bulwark for the Darden School. In the years following World War II, Colgate Darden challenged the Virginia business community to generate the private seed money necessary to make the School

a reality. The business community met the challenge, and has continued its close ties to the School as the latter has progressed over the course of five decades.

The Sponsors organization, later named the Darden School Foundation, has been at the forefront of Darden's fundraising efforts. From the mid-1950s to the mid-1970s, the Sponsors organization received annual donations from companies and individuals who became supporters of Virginia's Graduate Business School. At the same time, the School garnered incremental increases in its budget allocation from the University as it expanded its enrollment and prepared to move to the North Grounds. By fiscal year 1976–77, however, it became evident that reliance on a combination of modest annual donations from the private sector and University funding would be inadequate to meet the School's long-term goals. In that year, the Darden School faced an operating-budget cut of 5 percent from the University owing to Virginia's overestimation of revenue from bicentennial tourists. To Dean Stewart Sheppard, the message of constricted public funding was an ominous warning for the School. "Our only recourse," he advised, "is to rely more heavily on private fund sources if we expect to keep the same standards with which we have lived since the School's beginnings."[9]

Sheppard recognized the importance of enhanced philanthropy not only to meet the

operating needs of the School through annual giving, but also to underwrite Darden's strategic capital needs. In 1976, Sheppard and the leadership of the Sponsors organization launched the first capital campaign since the School's founding. A major goal of the campaign was to raise $1 million toward the construction of Sponsors Hall, Darden's proposed executive-education conference facility. Significantly, in this campaign, the School's alumni, for the first time, began to play what was to become a central philanthropic role for the School. The 1976 campaign established a $100,000 fundraising goal for Darden's growing Alumni Association, then 20 years old. Sheppard observed that this goal "represents the first time the Association will have provided a significant financial contribution to the School's capital needs and consequently marks the entrance of the School into a new level of maturity."[10]

In 1976, 60 percent of Darden's alumni contributed to the Sponsors organization's fundraising efforts. This remarkable par-

ticipation rate signaled a future trend of high levels of alumni donations in support of the Darden School's private-resource needs. In addition to contributions toward the construction of Sponsors Hall, donations from alumni and friends flowed in for endowed chairs, casewriting and research, student loans, and student events, such as field trips and the annual postgraduation reception. By 1980, the School's endowment reached $5 million.[11]

As Darden's alumni matured and began to achieve remarkable success in business, they soon stepped forward to demonstrate their commitment and loyalty to the School through significant leadership gifts. This generosity originated in the early 1980s, when Darden played a key role in the University of Virginia's first major fundraising effort, a $90-million capital campaign led by President Frank L. Hereford, Jr. The Darden School raised $8 million in that campaign for endowed chairs, scholarships, and research and course development.[12]

Within a few years, this figure seemed modest as new needs jumped to the forefront. In 1991, Darden unveiled the Campaign for Darden, the School's major effort to fund construction of the new Darden Grounds and to endow professorships and scholarships. With an original goal of $40 million, unparalleled generosity on the part of alumni, friends, and corporations encouraged the School to reevaluate the campaign's goal as the decade unfolded. In 1996, the Darden School Foundation Board of Trustees elevated the goal to $100 million. By the conclusion of the Campaign for Darden, in 2001, the Foundation had raised in excess of $204 million, and had assured funding not only for the construction of both phases of the new facilities, but also for several endowed chairs and scholarships as well as matching contributions to the Olsson and Batten family challenges. Darden had become one of only three business schools at that time to surpass $200 million in donations.[13]

Darden has benefited from the philanthropy of a number of close friends of the School who have made exemplary donations. The Darden School has memorialized these leadership gifts in the Rosenblum Entrance Hall in Saunders Hall with the inscription of the following names on the room's crown molding: Armstrong, Batten, Bigelow, Daniels, Darden, David, Duffy, Fitt, Genovese, Goodwin, Jones, Killgallon, Lewis, Lockhart, Macfarlane, Mayo, McCullough, Saunders, Siegel, Termeer, Todd, Wilkinson, and Worrell.

These leadership gifts represent a deep commitment to the Darden School's vision and values. That same commitment has been manifested by Darden's recent students, who annually spearhead a class-gift campaign whose aim is to maximize student participation. Since 1996, more than 90 percent of the graduating MBA students have contributed to the class gift. The level of devotion of recent MBA students to the School has best been exemplified by the Class of 1999. In a class-gift campaign led by student volunteers Dean W. Krehmeyer and Vera S. Liapunov, the 242 members of the Class of 1999 achieved an unprecedented 100 percent participation rate while raising nearly $320,000.[14] Thus, the growing tradition of giving initiated by the School's earliest graduates has been passed on to its most recent generation of alumni.

William H. Goodwin, Jr.

As Dean Ted Snyder stated in nominating him for the Colgate Darden Leadership Award, "Simply put, without Bill Goodwin's generosity and dedication, we would not have the new Darden Grounds." William H. Goodwin, Jr., as chair of the Darden School Foundation Board of Trustees from 1990 to 1992 and as principal donor, "supplied the vision and means to make the School's new grounds a reality." Goodwin discerned that an uninspired expansion of Darden's original North Grounds building—a concept put to the architectural test a number of times during the 1980s and found wanting—would not provide the essential space and infrastructure necessary to support a top graduate business institution in the twenty-first century. He shared Dean John Rosenblum's bold vision of starting fresh and constructing an entirely new graduate business complex rather than trying to graft a less-than-adequate addition onto an existing structure that carried with it substantial shortcomings.

As chair of the Darden School Foundation Board of Trustees, Goodwin, together with his wife, Alice, not only made a personal gift to the School unprecedented in its magnitude, but also championed the strategy of building extensive new facilities, fully

William H. Goodwin, Jr., (MBA 1966) speaks at the May 2000 groundbreaking ceremony for Phase II of the Darden School Grounds. Goodwin's leadership and generosity were instrumental in bringing Darden's current home to fruition.

privately funded, with the Darden School Foundation functioning as project developer. He envisioned a beautiful, new, technologically sophisticated home for the Darden School that could be built in the Jeffersonian architectural tradition with maximum efficiency and minimum bureaucracy. As Goodwin recalled, many Darden and University of Virginia graduates were "somewhat disappointed with the architectural styles that had been used [by the University] over the last 10 or 15 years." Consequently, he, together with the Darden School Foundation Board of Trustees and the University of Virginia Board of Visitors, decided "that we would try to go back to where we came from with architecture. So one of the guiding forces to the School was that it had to be something that was architecturally designed in a Jeffersonian type of architecture."[15]

Bill Goodwin's catalytic role in the planning and execution of the new Darden Grounds mirrored his unflagging record of service to Darden and the University of Virginia. A mechanical-engineering graduate of Virginia Polytechnic Institute and State University, Goodwin entered Darden in 1964, after serving as a first lieutenant with the U.S. Army Ordnance Corps. As he recalled, "I hadn't even thought about going to school 30 days before I enrolled. It was all because of Dean Abbott. Dean Abbott let me in as a dean admit. Back in those years, Dean Abbott took some people that might not have gotten in through the normal process and let them in the School. So I got in the School—purely by accident."[16] Thus began a lifelong relationship between

Bill Goodwin and the Darden School.

Goodwin's experience at Darden was one he would never forget as his business career blossomed. Upon receiving his MBA, in 1966, Goodwin joined IBM as a marketing representative. In 1971, recognizing the entrepreneurial opportunity made possible by the escalating demand for computing hardware, Goodwin formed his own enterprise, CCA Industries, which leased computers to businesses. The company proved to be a great success, acquiring a number of other businesses, including AMF, Pompanette, the Jefferson Hotel in Richmond, Virginia, and Kiawah Island Resort near Charleston, South Carolina.

Goodwin has remained involved in Darden alumni activities, and has served as both a member and chair of the Darden School Foundation Board of Trustees, a member of the University of Virginia's Board of Visitors, and chair of the University's investment-management company. In 1994, he became the first recipient of the Charles C. Abbott Award, an honor bestowed by the Darden Alumni Association on the alumnus or alumna whose contribution of time, energy, and talent to the Darden School has been exemplary. In addition, he has been active with a number of other educational institutions, including the Virginia Commonwealth University School of Engineering Foundation, the Medical College of Virginia Foundation, the Collegiate School of Richmond, and the Virginia Business

Higher Education Council. In 2001, the Darden School awarded Goodwin its highest honor, the Colgate Darden Leadership Award, "in recognition of his significant contributions to society through distinguished leadership and generosity of spirit."

In all he has done in his business career and in all he has done for Darden, Bill Goodwin has taken a common-sense approach rooted in individual integrity and enduring values, principles he appreciated as fundamental to the Darden School's culture since his impromptu interview with Dean Charles Abbott, in 1964. Wallace Stettinius (MBA 1959), Goodwin's successor as chair of the Darden School Foundation Board of Trustees, summed up Goodwin's contributions to Darden: "Bill is one of a very select number of people that you could genuinely call a force for change."[17] In April 2004, in recognition of Goodwin as

William H. Goodwin, Jr., chair of the Darden Foundation Trustees when the concept of the new Darden School Grounds was conceived, confers with Wallace Stettinius, his successor as chair of the Trustees.

an outstanding force for change at Darden, the University's Board of Visitors voted to dedicate formally the new Darden Grounds as the William H. Goodwin, Jr., Grounds.

George David

In January 2004, *BusinessWeek* recognized George A. L. David (MBA 1967), chairman and CEO of United Technologies Corporation (UTC), as one of the world's best managers in 2003. The magazine noted that, while David "almost takes pride in avoiding the headlines," under his steady and firm leadership, UTC had, over the past decade, "quietly outperformed rival General Electric Co. in total shareholder return" while averaging double-digit earnings growth.[18] Ten months later, *BusinessWeek* featured David on its cover, praising his achievement and "cerebral approach" in leading the $31-billion conglomerate for more than a decade.[19] Almost two decades earlier, in 1986, *Fortune* named David to its "A" list of 20 up-and-coming executives, and predicted his success in the corporate world. At the time, David was executive vice president and chief operating officer of Otis Elevator. *Fortune* listed David's attributes: "Superbright management star. Good with people despite computer-like mind. Candidate for a bigger job. Should go far at UTC or elsewhere."[20]

Eighteen years later, *BusinessWeek* commended David's performance as UTC's CEO. In particular, it cited his initiation at UTC of a

George A. L. David, CEO of United Technologies, speaking at the Phase II ground-breaking ceremony. David served as chair of the Trustees when Phase II was initiated.

program that generously supported employee education, including guaranteeing a college education for every employee who wished to pursue one. David shared with *BusinessWeek* his straightforward prescription for success as a CEO: "You put your head down, do good work, and good things will happen."[21]

David has applied this dictum to his relationship with the Darden School as well as with UTC. Since receiving his MBA, in 1967, David has remained closely connected to his alma mater, doing good work for the Darden School. Good things have resulted. David's service to and support of the School have been outstanding. Joining the Darden School Foundation Board of Trustees in 1990, David served as its chair during the planning and fundraising for Phase II of the Darden School Grounds. His incisive and effective leadership of the Board ensured the success of Darden's building campaign. On a personal level, he generously supported the Campaign for Darden, providing not only critical endowment resources to help the School construct the Abbott Center, but also funds to help match the Batten family's challenge gift. He also encouraged UTC to endow the United Technologies Professorship in Business Administration, and delivered the Darden School's commencement address in 1994. Tireless in his support of the School, George David fondly recalled his time at Darden: "Those were the best two years of my life."[22] "I think, for many of us," David asserted, "it was a truly life-forming experience."[23]

Dean Edward Snyder

Edward A. "Ted" Snyder's tenure as dean was relatively brief—July 1998 through June 2001—but it witnessed a number of significant steps for the School, not the least of which was preparation for growth in both the size of the MBA student body and Darden's physical plant.

Selected by a search committee, chaired by Robert Harris, that reviewed the credentials of more than 150 candidates, Snyder seemed a perfect match for the Darden School. Ray Smith, a member of the search committee and interim dean, told the *Washington Post*: "It was like the moon shined bright one night and we fell in love. But no other person had all the attributes Snyder had."[24]

Snyder was senior associate dean at the University of Michigan's business school at the time of his nomination for Darden's deanship. A member of the Michigan faculty for 15 years, Snyder received his MA in public policy and his PhD in economics, both from the University of Chicago. Specializing in antitrust and financial-institution-governance issues, he had taught applied economics and competitive tactics in the MBA program and chaired Michigan's Department of Business Economics and Public Policy. Prior to his academic career, Snyder served as an economist in the Antitrust Division of the U.S. Department of Justice. At Michigan, he became the founding director of the Davidson Institute, a privately funded academic center that focused on business and policy issues in transition economies and emerging markets. Upon his appointment as the business school's senior associate dean, Snyder assumed responsibility for Michigan's BBA, MBA, and Global MBA programs, as well as the business school's offices of faculty development, admissions, and career services.

Coming from a highly respected MBA program such as Michigan's, Snyder's experience as director of the Davidson Institute and as senior associate dean, especially in regard to internationalization of the business curriculum, was attractive to the search committee. In particular, Snyder had played

a key role in developing Michigan's MBA programs in Brazil, Hong Kong, and Korea and in fostering partnerships with foreign companies, which often involved the sponsorship of MBA student-project teams.

As dean, Snyder set an agenda that encompassed what he termed four "transitional opportunities" for the Darden School. First, he embraced Darden's aspiration to develop, in Snyder's words, "the best business-school facilities in the world," supporting initiation of the construction of the Phase II expansion of the new Darden Grounds, the planning for which was well under way when he arrived in Charlottesville.

Second, Snyder grasped the importance of achieving financial self-sufficiency for the Darden School. In order to increase the tuition revenue necessary to underwrite financial self-sufficiency, Snyder made the case for adding a fifth MBA section. He argued that expanding the total size of the MBA student body by approximately 120 students would not only generate revenue, but also—and more important—both attract more corporate recruiters to Charlottesville and permit Darden to increase the size of its faculty in important academic and research areas lacking critical mass.

A third transformational opportunity that Snyder set as a goal was to establish Darden as "a high-profile thought leader on major business issues." Here, Snyder's objective was to bring more focus and coherence to the faculty's wide array of scholarly interests. After orchestrating a series of faculty forums on research strategy, Snyder enumerated six "Issue-Based Initiatives"—areas "on which Darden will deliver world-class expertise"—as topics of focus for the Darden faculty: e-business, creating globally diverse senior-management teams, managing innovation, environmental management and sustainable business, postmerger integration, and strategic alliances and the extended firm. The dean appointed faculty leaders for each of the six initiatives, and urged the faculty to commit themselves to research and ancillary activities in these areas. Opined Snyder, in 1999, "We have to raise Darden's visibility and establish the School as a leader in what I call the broader knowledge industry. That means not just competing with other business schools, but positioning us with external audiences as a source of great knowledge and experience on major business issues."[25]

Finally, Snyder espoused "leveraging the Batten Center to equate Darden with creating, transforming, and building companies" as a fourth transformational opportunity for the School. He envisioned the Batten Center—restructured and renamed the Batten Institute in light of Frank Batten's unparalleled gift in December 1999—as playing "a foundational role" in the Issue-Based Initiatives. The work of the Batten Institute, as Snyder viewed it, would provide synergy for all the School's activities and enhance Darden's visibility and its ability to attract top-notch students, faculty, and corporate partners.

In May 2001, Snyder made a surprise announcement. He planned to leave Darden at the end of the academic year to accept the post of dean at his alma mater, the University of Chicago's graduate business school. In June 2001, just before his departure, the Darden School forged a formal financial self-sufficiency agreement with the University of Virginia, which was represented by Vice President and Provost Peter W. Low and Executive Vice President and Chief Operating Officer Leonard W. Sandridge. Despite Snyder's departure, the Darden School—first under C. Ray Smith, who was called upon by the University to serve as interim dean for the third time, and then under Snyder's permanent successor, Robert Harris—moved ahead vigorously, not only with implementation of

financial self-sufficiency, but also with construction of Phase II of the Darden Grounds and development of the Batten Institute. The research emphasis that Snyder had placed on specific issue-based initiatives, however, was replaced by a broader Batten Institute agenda that included providing seed capital for an array of research projects and activities geared to innovation and entrepreneurship.

Scale and Scope:
Expansion of the MBA Program

In December 1999, Dean Ted Snyder announced that the Darden School would expand its MBA student body from four to five sections, essentially a 25 percent increase in enrollment, beginning in the 2002–03 academic year. For the School, expansion represented a significant event. The School's MBA enrollment had been stable for about 25 years.

The decision to grow came after several months of discussion among faculty, staff, students, alumni, and Trustees. The discussion was triggered by "The Scale and Scope of Management Education Programs at the University of Virginia's Darden School," a paper Snyder prepared in which he explained the rationale for MBA-enrollment growth. Snyder argued that the addition of a fifth section made sense for Darden for a number of strategic reasons.

First, in the context of a booming economy in the late 1990s, Snyder highlighted a growing imbalance between the

School's steady-state MBA Program and rapidly expanding executive-education activities. Darden's relatively small faculty was stretched to capacity at a time of seemingly boundless opportunities to provide executive education. Increasing the size of the MBA Program would permit the faculty to grow and bring greater depth to critical areas in both the MBA and Executive Programs. It would also bolster the School's research relating to important business issues.

Second, Snyder argued that the School's "MBA pipeline"—the transformation of students from admissions candidates to students gaining value from Darden's curriculum to graduates seeking initial jobs—was too

narrow as compared with most competitor schools. The Darden School's small size limited both the demographic and career-path depth of its student body. Moreover, in a time of economic health, the School's limited number of graduates meant that many corporate recruiters were unable to attract one or more Darden students sufficiently to accept a job offer. A larger MBA talent pool would help nourish the School's relationships with diverse companies, avoid recruiter disappointment, and maintain a multitude of career options for students. Enhancing corporate relationships and partnerships along several dimensions, Snyder asserted, was "critical to maintaining a healthy portfolio of career options for Darden MBA students."

Developing increased visibility for Darden constituted another reason to grow. Snyder observed that, in the highly competitive and increasingly global graduate business industry, it was becoming increasingly difficult for smaller schools to obtain recognition in the media. Almost all of Darden's competitors were larger and better-known institutions. The growth in faculty size permitted by expansion of the MBA Program would, in turn, result in more research, casewriting, and executive-education innovation, all of which would raise Darden's profile as a dynamic institution that had much to say in regard to major business issues. At the same time, an expanded number of loyal alumni would make a positive contribution to a wider array of companies, thereby further enhancing the School's reputation.

Finally, the financial argument for growth was compelling. An additional section of students would mean that Darden could spread some of its substantial fixed costs more effectively and take advantage of the economies of scale enjoyed by its larger peers. Snyder noted that, although tuition by itself, even with enrollment expansion, would not nearly cover the cost of MBA education, growing the size of the program would "reduce the extent of losses from running the program." Moreover, the tuition generated from a larger student body would assist in Darden's movement toward financial self-sufficiency.

While emphasizing the positive reasons

Registrar Catherine "Kitty" Smiley. Kitty Smiley has guided and befriended Darden students and orchestrated annual Final Exercises for more than three decades.

for growth, Snyder acknowledged that there were potential negatives. The most important of these was the danger that growth could reduce the quality of Darden's stellar educational experience. Would expansion, for example, mean that the MBA Program would become "less personal, less intense, and less supportive"?[26]

Snyder encouraged all of Darden's key stakeholders—students, faculty, staff, alumni, recruiters, Trustees—to engage in an "active dialogue" on the question of the School's scale and scope. Over the course of the fall 1999 semester, considerable discussion of the issue took place in a variety of venues, including a faculty forum at which a student Darden Business Project team summarized the findings of its study of peer-school growth. While some stakeholders expressed concerns about how growth would affect Darden's sense of community and its intimate culture, many shared the

Faculty open-door policy.
Throughout its history, Darden's faculty have encouraged students to visit their offices. No appointment is necessary. Here Professor Elliott Weiss explains his innovative production-management exercise, "Gazogle," to students.

view that Professor Les Grayson, a 28-year veteran of the School at that point, articulated in a memo to the faculty that placed the growth decision in a historical context:

"I have lived, worked, and traveled all over the world for the last 45 years, and I have observed that one of the distinguishing characteristics of this country is that we manage to change well. Change sometimes does get bad press, but once a course of action is decided upon, Americans do implement it well. And so has Darden. We moved from Central Grounds to North Grounds (talk about a cultural impact!) and then to our present location.... My recollection is that the objections to growth in the '70s were the very same that the School hears now. Yet, in retrospect, the expansion went smoothly."[27]

In announcing the decision to add a fifth MBA section, Dean Snyder noted that careful planning would ensue over the next two and a half years in advance of the arrival of an expanded student body in the fall of 2002. He invited students, faculty, and staff to convey their ideas on how best to manage the expansion as the institu-

tion addressed the question, "How do you introduce change and still preserve what people treasure most about Darden?"[28]

Financial Self-Sufficiency

As Darden began to achieve recognition as one of the nation's premier graduate business schools, the matter of resource enhancement to sustain the School's progress became increasingly important. While private support generated from philanthropy and the success of executive education had become essential to maintain the School's momentum, the funding that Darden received from the University and the state remained vital. As the University of Virginia experienced state-imposed budget cuts in the early 1990s, however—and as the prospects for future significant infusions of state support for the University dimmed—the need for sustained, nonstate revenue sources became evident. This was true for the entire University, but it was particularly true for two of Virginia's leading professional schools, Darden and Law, both of which required substantial, sustained funding beyond state resources to compete with their well-endowed and primarily private peers.

By 1995, the Darden School, the Law School, and the University had reached the common conclusion that a new financial model was required if Darden and Law were to remain sparkling jewels in the University's crown. In that year, the Board of Visitors endorsed a concept to restructure the funding relationship between the two professional schools and the University that became known as "financial self-sufficiency." The concept called for an evolutionary period of five to eight years, during which Darden and Law would relinquish their state subsidies and become, in effect, tubs on their own financial bottoms.

The concept included a number of principles. First, in the case of the Darden School, MBA tuition for non-Virginians would be raised to a market level approximating the tuition charged by Darden's competitors. Second, a reasonable differential between in-state and out-of-state tuition would be retained "in recognition of the University's responsibility to the Commonwealth." Third, Darden and the University would share the cost of the differential between in-state and out-of-state tuition. Fourth, Darden would bear full responsibility for its direct costs and contribute an indirect-cost charge to the University. Fifth, Darden would be "granted increased say" over its operations and budgets.

Both the University's Board of Visitors and the Darden School Foundation's Board of Trustees were in agreement that Darden needed to compete "on a level playing field with the very best" graduate business schools in the country and that Darden was well positioned to assume "increased financial and operational responsibility" for its programs. The Foundation Trustees embraced the concept and pledged the supplemental private resources necessary to make financial self-sufficiency viable for Darden. An official memorandum of understanding was forged between the Darden School and the University of Virginia in 2001 to formalize the financial self-sufficiency arrangement.[29]

Thus began a phase-in period for Darden, during which the School gradually surrendered its financial subsidy from the University—resources thus freed up for use elsewhere at the University—as its MBA tuition rose to market levels. With the expansion of the MBA student body by 25 percent, beginning in 2002–03, the Darden School was able to attain full financial self-sufficiency.

Its future financial health now rested on a three-legged funding model: tuition, philanthropy, and executive-education revenue.

Batten Institute

The Darden School's approach to management education and its curriculum have been deeply rooted in a general-management perspective, with an emphasis on leadership and decision making, since the School's earliest days. It was, therefore, fitting that the transformational series of gifts bestowed on Darden by Frank Batten and his children, Frank Batten, Jr. (MBA 1984) and Dorothy Batten (MBA 1990), were intended to propel the School to a preeminent position in the areas of leadership, entrepreneurship, and innovation through the formation of a new center of intellectual activity, the Batten Institute.

The seeds of the Institute were sown in 1990, when Dean John Rosenblum and Frank Batten, Sr., engaged in a series of conversations regarding Darden's long-range aspirations. In particular, they defined the specific recent initiatives at Darden that might profoundly "make a difference" for the School. Rosenblum emphasized the School's pioneering curriculum changes then under way in the area of leadership and his desire to augment the School's teaching and research capabilities in leadership education. Rosenblum's vision for leadership education at the Darden School resonated with Frank Batten and his children, who, in 1991, pledged

an initial Batten family leadership challenge gift of $3.5 million for professorships, research, and curriculum development.

Rosenblum's successor, Lee Higdon, likewise appreciated the Darden School's strengths in the areas of leadership and entrepreneurship. In his Strategic Overview document of June 1994, he observed that the School "is well positioned to establish itself as a recognized center of excellence in these fields." Higdon highlighted as a priority the enhancement of resources to enable Darden to build on its existing strengths and "to promote recognition of Darden as a unique supplier of both out-

Informal student-faculty exchange. Despite growth in the size of its student body, the Darden School continues to value close student-faculty interaction. Here Professor Gregory B. Fairchild speaks informally with students in the Camp Library.

Chips and Quips

Year after year, Darden's student newspaper, first named the *Darden News* and later the *Cold Call Chronicle*, published its most popular section, "Chips and Quips," which contained a sample of the most humorous classroom exchanges between faculty and students that had transpired over the previous two weeks or so. Both students and faculty anxiously awaited each issue to see if either their wittiest remark or their most embarrassing faux pas might have been captured for posterity. A few examples of classic chips and quips:

Professor Pfeifer to student: "You can finish your analysis, and then we'll crucify you."

Student: "We could argue this point forever."
Professor Freeman: "Well, at least until the end of class."

Professor Davis: "So, what is the next question?"
Student: "You mean the next question in the assignment?"
Professor Davis: "Well, I could get real philosophical here and ask what the next question of life is, but let's just start right here."

Professor Spekman: "What did the company learn from their previous experience in Europe?"

(class remains silent)

Professor Spekman: "I'm patient. I get paid by the year."

"I know you guys are here. I can hear breathing."

Professor McBrady (to a student whose hand is raised): "Yes?"
Student: "Oh, I don't know the answer. I didn't think you were actually going to call on me."[30]

Professor Horniman: "What's the name of the seventh dwarf?"
Student: "Well, that depends on where you start the list."[31]

Professor Grayson to student: "What you said is both true and not very helpful."

Professor Carraway: "What I've said hasn't made sense, has it?"
Student: "You're the teacher. I assume what you say is right."

standing educational programs and creative thought in leadership and entrepreneurship."[32] This path would "help assure the School's stature as a top-tier institution."[33]

Higdon shared his plan for Darden's development and priorities with Frank Batten, Sr., and, in 1995, discussed with him the concept of establishing the Batten Center for Entrepreneurial Leadership at the University of Virginia. The Center, Higdon contended, would set Darden apart from other schools by means of a distinctive focus on leadership, entrepreneurship, innovation, and sound values.

Batten was convinced that Higdon's ambitious concept had great potential. He supported the plan "to establish Darden as a leader in stimulating entrepreneurship and innovation."[34] As evidence of that support, in the fall of 1995, Batten pledged an additional $10 million to establish the Center for Entrepreneurial Leadership, with the stipulation that his gift be matched by others. The Batten funding was geared to attracting outstanding faculty and students; supporting research, curriculum, and case development; and underwriting outreach programs.

Following the announcement of this gift, the Darden School proposed to the University of Virginia the formal establishment of the Batten Center for Entrepreneurial Leadership. Provost Peter W. Low endorsed the Darden School's proposal and forwarded it to the State Council of Higher Education for its blessing. In January 1996,

the Council officially approved the creation of the Batten Center for Entrepreneurial Leadership at the Darden School.[35]

Professor Wendell Dunn joined the Darden faculty in the spring of 1996 as executive director of the Batten Center. Dunn had previously served as academic director of the Sol C. Snyder Entrepreneurial Center at the Wharton School. Dunn formulated the Batten Center's activities within the framework of a three-pronged approach encompassing teaching, research, and outreach. The Center stimulated the creation of new second-year elective courses in the MBA Program that emphasized entrepreneurially related topics, such as Managing the Growing Enterprise and Entrepreneurship and Venture Capital.

In the area of research, the Center was instrumental in attracting Sankaran Venkataraman to the Darden faculty. Venkataraman was editor of the *Journal of Business Venturing*, the leading academic journal on entrepreneurship, and brought the journal with him to Darden. He was soon named the research director of the Batten Center, and worked to encourage research and casewriting relevant to the Center's mission. In regard to outreach, Dunn strongly favored collaboration with other segments of the University as well as with the local business community. The Center became a sponsor of and active participant in the Charlottesville Venture Forum. It also cosponsored events with the Virginia Center for Innovative Technology, such as a

biotechnology-financing conference designed to help the Commonwealth's biotechnology and biomedical companies attract capital.

In December 1999, Frank Batten, Sr.—pleased with the progress made by the Batten Center and, after discussions with Higdon's successor, Ted Snyder, mindful of the even greater strides that Darden might make in the domains of influential scholarship and outreach—made an unprecedented additional endowment gift of $60 million to the Darden School to take its entrepreneurship and innovation program to the highest level.

Recognizing this gift—the largest single donation to a U.S. business school up to that time—as transformational, Dean Snyder reconfigured the Batten Center for Entrepreneurial Leadership into the Batten Institute. Snyder appointed Robert Bruner, Distinguished Professor of Business Administration and a member of Darden's finance faculty, executive director of the Batten Institute. Bruner explained the new, wider scope of the Batten initiative: "Significantly, we dropped the words 'entrepreneurial leadership,' and the reason is that Frank Batten wanted to broaden the scope of the activities of the Center because he realized that entrepreneurship truly emanated throughout most of what we do in the world of business."[36]

The infusion of significant supplemental resources allowed the Batten Institute to initiate additional innovative programs. Among them was the Progressive Incubator, a multiphase program that offered resources to MBA and other University of Virginia students who wished to pursue an actual entrepreneurial venture while still in school. Students with a well-thought-out commercial concept could apply to participate in the Batten Institute's Progressive Incubator.

Jeanne Liedtka became executive director of the Batten Institute in 2004.

The Incubator provided office space, equipment, expert practitioner advisers, and a faculty mentor as students worked to implement their embryonic entrepreneurial business plans and develop them to the stage where venture capitalists would find them attractive. When the Progressive Incubator began, in 1999, it was located on West Main Street in downtown Charlottesville, an area that was attracting a number of high-tech start-up firms. In 2003, the Incubator moved to the Darden School, into new space made possible by the Phase II expansion project. This move strengthened the program's ties to the School's activities. The Progressive Incubator has encouraged collaborative ventures

between Darden students and students and faculty members from other University of Virginia schools, such as Engineering and Medicine. The Incubator's overriding purpose has been to provide students with the opportunity to test entrepreneurial ideas in real-world situations while simultaneously allowing them to continue their degree programs.

The concept of the Progressive Incubator fit nicely with the Batten Institute's broad, action-oriented mission, as articulated by Robert Bruner. He conceived of the Institute as a philanthropic "foundation of sorts, as an intellectual venture capitalist within Darden and the University communities."[37] The Institute's central purpose called for it to invest in applied-research and knowledge-transfer programs in the areas of innovation, entrepreneurship, and corporate transformation. "The Batten Institute sets a very high goal for itself," stated Bruner. "It's a goal focused around the idea of the entrepreneur as change agent."[38] The Institute developed a number of new programs. Its Batten Fellows Program brought several dozen high-profile entrepreneurial and innovative thinkers from varied disciplines and backgrounds, both academic and practitioner, to Charlottesville to work collaboratively with Darden faculty on specific research projects that have led to tangible scholarly output.

The Institute's Intellectual Capital Program has actively managed, funded, and supported scholarly interaction on cutting-edge topics, resulting in publication and dissemination of pathbreaking ideas. This facet of the Batten Institute initiated the *Batten Briefings*, a practitioner-oriented newsletter conveying state-of-the-art thinking on innovation. It also spearheaded a number of research conferences on relevant topics. Another important Batten Institute initiative, the Batten Business Innovation Speaker Series, sponsored a series of public presentations by distinguished thought-leading practitioners and scholars on topics relating to innovation. In short, the Batten Institute, under Bruner and his successor, Jeanne Liedtka, who assumed the executive directorship in 2004, has developed a number of programs that pervade the School, involving faculty, staff, and students alike in practical intellectual journeys that explore the criticality of innovation and risk taking in organizations, large and small.

Frank Batten

In 1999, Frank Batten, Sr., chairman of the Executive Committee of Landmark Communications, Inc., and leader of the philanthropic Landmark Foundation, contributed $60 million to the Darden School to establish the Batten Institute. This unparalleled gift catapulted the University of Virginia's Capital Campaign past the one-billion-dollar mark.[39]

Batten believed that "most entrepreneurs failed not because their ideas were bad, but because they did not manage the business well." His goal in founding the Batten Institute was "to make it possible for Darden to become a leader in developing entrepreneurs who are successful." He saw in Darden an institution devoted to producing graduates skilled in action-oriented problem solving in a context of ethical decision making, characteristics that he considered essential to the future of successful business leadership. In accepting the Batten gift, Dean Ted Snyder stated: "Batten has challenged the Darden School to become the world's leading center on innovation, value creation, entrepreneurship, and leadership. It is fitting that the great center of learning that is the University of Virginia—challenged five decades ago by a visionary whose name adorns this School—be challenged yet again, this time by a colleague of Colgate Darden who is among the most innovative leaders of the information age."[40]

Frank Batten's unprecedented gift represented the culmination of his long-term relationship with the University of Virginia's Darden School. Batten received his undergraduate degree from the University of Virginia in 1950. Interested in pursuing management education at the graduate level to acquire a body of knowledge he could apply to the *Virginian-Pilot* (the Norfolk-based newspaper owned by his uncle, Samuel L. Slover, for which he had worked summers as a copy boy, ad salesman, and reporter since high school), Batten enrolled at Harvard Business School. He received his MBA from Harvard in 1952, three years before the Darden School was founded, and assumed the post of publisher of the *Virginian-Pilot* at the age of 27, in 1954. When he learned of the University of Virginia's intention to start a graduate business school, Batten was enthusiastic. He wrote President Darden to recommend that the new school adopt the case method of instruction. A devotee of the case method, Batten believed it to be "the most effective way to teach because it requires students to confront a variety of problems and think through the best solutions."[41]

Batten became an important adviser to Virginia's fledgling business school, serving as an early member of the Sponsors Board of Trustees. His lifelong interest in higher education has been broad and deep. He has served on the boards of trustees of the College of William and Mary, Hollins University, and the Chrysler Museum. In 1962, he was appointed the first rector of Norfolk-based Old Dominion University, a post from which he often sought wisdom from Colgate Darden regarding how best to build a new state-affiliated university. "Whenever the School was faced with a difficult policy or political decision, I often went to Colgate for advice," Batten noted, while recalling his days as rector of Old Dominion University. In 1987, Batten, together with Joshua Darden, a Norfolk businessman and nephew of Colgate Darden, created the Tidewater Scholarship Program. Under Batten's and Joshua Darden's leadership, the program raised $1 million for a pilot effort to assist needy students from Tidewater Virginia who wished to attend college.[42]

Frank Batten's career in business exemplified entrepreneurship, integrity, and progressive thinking. As publisher of the *Virginian-Pilot*, he highlighted front-page editorials in the mid-1950s that supported the U.S. Supreme Court's landmark school-desegregation decisions at a time when many Virginia politicians and media were advocating a policy of massive resistance to federal rulings. The *Virginian-Pilot* was awarded a Pulitzer Prize for its courageous and influential stance. Likewise, as a manager, Batten actively pursued the promotion of a diverse workforce within his business by stressing goals for the recruitment of women and minorities. He provided similar progressive leadership to the newspaper industry while serving as chairman of the Associated Press, from 1982 to 1987, as a director of the Newspaper Association of America and the American Press Institute, and as chairman of the board of the Newspaper Advertising Bureau.

In 1966, Batten transformed his privately held newspaper company into Landmark Communications, an entrepreneurial enterprise that diversified into broadcasting, cable networks, specialty publications, and electronic publishing. Batten masterfully molded what was originally ridiculed by many as a fanciful, far-fetched notion—the concept of a 24-hour-a-day, 7-day-a-week broadcast of current local weather conditions in communities throughout the country—into the Weather Channel, one of the most successful ventures in cable-TV-programming history. Since its founding, in 1982, the Weather Channel has expanded its viewership to more than 75 million households in the United States.[43]

It is this entrepreneurial spirit, grounded in a strong set of values, that Frank Batten saw in the Darden School and which inspired him to create the Batten Institute. "I concluded," said Batten, "that a great opportunity to make a difference is to develop at Darden a world-class program in entrepreneurship." The Batten gift represented a truly transformational opportunity for Darden, and triggered a plethora of intellectually stimulating activities designed to sustain and to transmit to others Frank Batten's entrepreneurial vision and spirit.[44]

Dean Robert Harris

In 1997, when he chaired the search committee that recommended the selection of Ted Snyder as dean, Robert S. Harris had no inkling that just four years later he himself would be tapped to become Darden's leader. Upon receiving Snyder's resignation in early 2001, President John Casteen quickly sprang into action to find Snyder's successor. Casteen appointed C. Ray Smith to his third stint as interim dean and, at the same time, appointed a search committee, chaired by Smith, to identify replacement candidates without delay.

The committee did not have to look far. After reviewing the credentials of dozens of outside candidates, it became evident that one of Darden's own faculty, Robert Harris, perfectly fit the School's criteria for its dean. Said Adam P. Carter, a student member of the search committee: "Bob Harris emerged head and shoulders above the rest of a very impressive field."[45]

Harris combined noteworthy accomplishments in the classroom and in research with outstanding achievements in administration, both in academia and at the senior-executive level in the private sector. Holder of a PhD in economics from Princeton, he had taught at the Wharton School and the University of North Carolina, as well as at the London Business School as a visiting professor, before John Rosenblum recruited him to Darden, in 1988. An expert on corporate finance, mergers and acquisitions, and financial markets, Harris published extensively in leading finance journals while excelling in the classroom. In 1990, Harris was appointed the C. Stewart Sheppard Professor of Business Administration in recognition of his scholarship and teaching.

Although an accomplished academic, Harris, throughout his career, stayed in close contact with business through consulting assignments and casewriting. In 1998, when the Darden School and the United Technologies Corporation (UTC) formed a partnership to promote the development of managerial talent within UTC, the company appointed Harris its chief learning officer. In that capacity, he led UTC's educational programs and was responsible for educational technology. Said Ray Smith of Harris: "Being involved with United Technologies as a vice president for three years just before he took the School's leadership certainly helped him get the perspective of management education from a corporate viewpoint…. He knows the business world and the academic world."[46] Possessing a rare combination of academic and corporate experience, Harris, in the eyes of the search committee, was an excellent choice for Darden's deanship. President Casteen accepted the committee's recommendation, and Harris was appointed Darden's seventh dean, in October 2001.

Harris assumed his position at a difficult time. With the country in the midst of an economic recession, intensified by the aftermath of the recent tragedy of 9/11, the Darden School faced a number of challenges. The poor economy and the bursting of the Internet bubble significantly affected the job prospects of MBA graduates and caused employment instability for some alumni. Likewise, the market for executive education was severely impacted by corporate downsizing, cutbacks in training budgets, and travel restrictions driven by international political uncertainty.

As dean, Harris worked to bolster the efforts of Darden's Career Development Center to help MBA students find jobs in a very difficult market. Likewise, Darden's Alumni Career Services Office, directed by W. Herbert Crowder (MBA 1967), marshaled all available resources to assist Darden alumni whose job situations had become tenuous.

At the same time that Harris sought to maintain the Darden School's steady course in the midst of troubled economic waters, he appointed a faculty committee, chaired by Professor Marian Moore, to study a potential new executive MBA program. An additional degree program would benefit Darden by expanding the School's portfolio and, consequently, its revenue base. Even more important, however, an MBA for executives offered the opportunity to energize the faculty to create an innovative, market-driven academic experience beyond the traditionally structured MBA that would provide midcareer enterprise leaders with the skills required to meet the multifaceted challenges of business in the twenty-first century. Harris emphasized, however, that any new Darden degree program had to be fully consistent with the School's deepest

values and deliver the highest possible quality. The faculty agreed. In 2004, it voted to move forward with the planning of a Darden School MBA for executives, designed to enhance their leadership skills and their contributions to their sponsoring companies.[47]

While considering an additional Darden School academic program, Harris also put in motion major initiatives in communications and fundraising. In regard to communications, Harris accelerated implementation of a centralized strategy designed to enhance Darden's brand recognition globally. The launch of Darden Business Publishing was an important component of this strategy. This communications and marketing initiative was inextricably tied to Harris's effort to set the stage for a major new Darden School Capital Campaign, destined to become part of the University's Capital Campaign, which was slated to begin in 2006.

In September 2004, however, Harris decided not to seek a second term as dean. With the University of Virginia's Capital Campaign on the horizon, he stepped down at the end of the 2004–05 academic year in order to give the School sufficient time to identify a new dean who could lead a critical, sustained fundraising effort that would continue through 2011.

The Third Faculty Generation

James Freeland was appointed associate dean for Faculty in 1993. Throughout his tenure in this critical position, which spanned the deanships of Higdon, Snyder, and Harris, Freeland's primary objective was to build a Third Faculty Generation to carry the Darden School's vision and values forward into the twenty-first century. In coordinating the recruitment of new faculty for the School, Freeland and his faculty colleagues searched for people who harbored an

intense interest in teaching both MBA students and executives and who also were proponents of maintaining a close relationship with business. Candidates with such views, who also possessed strong instructional and scholarly credentials, were often scarce.

Freeland and Darden faculty members who served on search committees worked diligently to court, often over a period of years, candidates who seemed to fit a profile consistent with the Darden School's culture. That diligence paid off with the addition, over the past decade and a half, of a Third Faculty Generation, which has accepted the torch from previous faculty generations. This newest group of outstanding teachers and scholars has continued to sustain the School's mission while initiating curriculum modifications in response to changes in the business environment. Among those coming to Charlottesville as part of Darden's Third Faculty Generation were Susan Chaplinsky

(1994) in finance, Yiorgos Allayannis (1996) in finance, Kamalini Ramdas (1996) in operations, Elizabeth O. Teisberg (1996) in operations and innovation, Martin N. Davidson (1998) in organizational behavior, Joseph W. Harder (1998) in organizational behavior, Luann J. Lynch (1998) in accounting, Sankaran Venkataraman (1998) in entrepreneurship, Wei Li (2000) in business and the political economy, Gregory B. Fairchild (2000) in strategy, Erika H. James (2001) in organizational behavior, Ming-Jer Chen (2001) in strategy, Michael J. Moore (2001) in business and the political economy, Michael J. Schill (2001) in finance, Ronald T. Wilcox (2001) in marketing, Mary Margaret Frank (2002) in accounting, Timothy M. Laseter (2002) in operations, Marian C. Moore (2002) in marketing, Matthias Hild (2002) in quantitative analysis, Paul J. Simko (2002) in accounting, Andrew C. Wicks (2002) in ethics, Matthew R. McBrady (2003) in finance, Peter Rodriguez

(2003) in business and the political economy, and Saras D. Sarasvathy (2004) in entrepreneurship.

Darden's Third Faculty Generation also included a core group of full-time faculty members in management communications. These faculty—James R. Rubin (1991), Elizabeth A. Powell (1994), June A. West (1997), and Marc W. Modica (1998)—continued the School's tradition of providing quality instruction in written and oral communications that Charles Abbott carried with him from Boston, instruction and skill development that, for almost five decades, have helped Darden students achieve excellence in conveying ideas and generating effective team efforts in organizational settings.[48]

Instructional Technology

To say that instructional technology was almost nonexistent in 1955, when the Graduate Business School's first students matriculated, is to state the obvious. The School's early crop of students had little more than slide rules at their disposal. The Founding Faculty's use of instructional technology was largely confined to chalk, chalkboard, and ditto machine. The chalkboard, in fact, from the School's earliest days in Monroe Hall, has served as a prime teaching focal point. Instructors today, just as they did in the 1950s, jot down, often with breathtaking speed, a torrent of ideas expressed by students eagerly participating in an animated case

Computing pioneers.
Professor James R. Freeland instructs students (left to right) Eric Schmitz, John Ford, Craig Anderson, and John Mattson (all MBA 1983) in the use of Apple microcomputers in 1982. Freeland, an ardent proponent of integrating technology into Darden's curriculum, served as associate dean for Faculty under Deans Higdon, Snyder, and Harris.

discussion. Throughout its 50-year history in three different buildings, the School's multiple, massive, movable classroom chalkboards have remained, if not king, at least an important device for teaching purposes despite their supplementation by exciting advances in instructional technology.

Data processing arrived at the Graduate Business School in the early 1960s. The School installed terminals in Monroe Hall to permit time-sharing access to the University's central computer-science center. By 1970, the School had added a time-sharing system linked to four commercial vendors. Students were required to learn the BASIC computer programming language, and used programs in statistics, finance, and accounting; they also participated in a one-day business-game simulation developed by the faculty. A small room in Monroe Hall containing eight teletype terminals, supplemented later by CRT video terminals and an IBM card sorter, constituted the School's technology hub. With the move to the North Grounds, in 1975, a room outfitted as a computer-terminal lab provided more space for students and greater access to the University's mainframe computers, but little additional technological functionality.[49]

In the early 1980s, however, the advent of the personal computer had an impact of major proportions on the Darden School. It soon became apparent that the personal computer would become a ubiquitous tool in the business world and, as a consequence, emerging managers needed to possess a

thorough understanding of the personal computer's capabilities and appreciate its potency as an agent of organizational and process change. In 1982, the School purchased two dozen Apple II computers, and installed them in a newly created student computer lab. Even before the lab opened, personal computers had begun to infiltrate individual faculty and staff offices. In the same year, the School also hired its first fulltime technology-support-staff member to assist both students and faculty in their use of computer hardware and software.

The computer invasion.
Mary McCall (MBA 1985) presents her new personal computer.

Faculty interest in integrating this exciting new technology into the School's academic programs spread quickly. In the spring of 1982, a faculty committee—comprising Darden faculty computer pioneers Brandt Allen, as chair, and James Freeland, James Clawson, Christopher Gale, and Sherwood Frey—developed a new course, Computer Fundamentals for Managers, which became a required part of the first year of the MBA Program in the fall of 1983. The course included a number of topics designed to ensure computer literacy: system implementation, word processing, financial modeling, and introductory programming. The School also offered the course as an elective to provide second-year

The Darden School is a leader in video technology. A professional-quality broadcast studio in the School's new facilities enables production of state-of-the-art curriculum materials. Video producer Christina Seale is at the controls.

MBA students an opportunity to acquire computer savvy before they graduated.[50]

The use of technology at Darden for both academic and administrative purposes ballooned in the 1980s. In 1982, in the MBA Program, first- and second-year courses began to use the new Apple II microcomputers as well as VisiCalc spreadsheet models. Students quickly became adept at using Screenwriter, an early word processor; PFS, a presentation-graphics package; and BASIC for microcomputers. Microcomputers and ceiling-mounted video projectors were installed in classrooms to permit the projection on large screens of data prepared by students. These were exciting years, observed Brandt Allen: "Apple IIs blossomed all over the building like flowers in the spring." Within two years, however, the Apple II machines were gone, replaced by more powerful IBM personal computers driven by a variety of more sophisticated programs that allowed technology to expand further into the curriculum on a daily basis.[51]

By 1987, Allen, the James C. Wheat Professor of Business Administration, who also served as the School's director of Computing, reported that more than a million dollars' worth of computer equipment had been installed at Darden. This equipment included more than 150 personal computers, three minicomputers, a central word-processing system, and five local area networks. Advanced IBM personal computers were located in an enlarged student lab, as well as in each of the classrooms, where students could demonstrate "live" their case-analysis calculations.[52]

In recognition of the important role that information technology was playing in business, the faculty voted to expand the first-year curriculum, beginning in the fall of 1990, to include a required course on information technology. Its purpose, Allen observed, was to provide MBA students with "what every general manager needs to know about information resources." Utilizing cases and stressing decision making, the new course covered such topics as information-resource management, systems development, project-risk analysis, and building effective information systems.[53]

By the mid-1990s, personal computers had become pervasive at Darden. Sophisticated computer-based analytical tools and simulations, as well as frequent consideration of technology issues, were integrated into a wide variety of Darden School courses to such an extent that a required first-year course on information systems became superfluous. Students particularly interested in this topic could elect to take one or more of a growing number of specialized technology-based electives to enhance their knowledge in this area.

In conjunction with the construction of Phase I of the Darden School Grounds, technology made additional important strides at the School. The new facilities included wiring for Internet access and electrical power at every seat in the new classrooms, in group-study rooms, at all carrels and tables in the Camp Library, and even at the tables in Café '67, the main student eatery. Thus, student access to the rich resources of Darden's and the University's networks, as well as to the world beyond, became universal. At the same time, the School implemented a policy requiring entering MBA students to have an adequately configured laptop to ensure that they could take full advantage of the technology-related materials that had become prevalent throughout the curriculum. The microcomputer was heavily used both in and outside class. By the mid-1990s, the laptop had become far more widespread at Darden than the slide rule had been 40 years earlier, when the School was founded. To meet the computing needs of students (for example, the School annually purchased a pool of "loaners" that students whose laptops were being repaired could borrow), Darden established a permanently staffed technology service desk and beefed up its technology staff in both numbers and quality.

In 1997, Dean Higdon named Randall Smith the Darden School's first chief technology officer. The aim of this new position was to enhance the use and support of technology in all areas of the School. Darden's strategy in regard to technology was not, however, to introduce state-of-the-art

The School's very first piece of technology, an opaque projector, was acquired by Professor Lee Johnston in 1958.

equipment for its own sake. Rather, it was to consider how technology could most effectively augment the School's strengths in teaching and student development. Higdon and his successors concurred with the admonition of George David, CEO of United Technologies, a firm whose success has been predicated on implementation of advanced technologies: "What we must not lose sight of in the pursuit of technology are the core traditions of the School, which are case method and study group, which lead to critical thinking and to relationships. An awful lot of business is about exactly that. We need to make sure we weave technology into those two core values, which have been so important to Darden."[54]

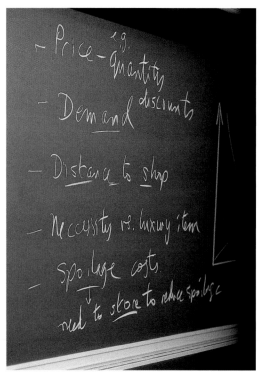

Chalkboards remain a constant classroom tool.

Smith's purview, as chief technology officer, included not only hardware and software support, but also three other important units, which, in aggregate, composed Darden Technology Services. The first area was Instructional Technology. As far back as the 1980s, Darden faculty began to experiment with the creation of video cases. The completion of the new Darden Grounds gave further impetus to the School's early interest in video. A full-scale professional-quality broadcast studio was constructed in the new facilities, as was a sophisticated video-delivery system in the classrooms, all of which were outfitted with powerful ceiling-mounted projectors and sound systems. At the same time that the School was further developing its technical video capabilities, it was also creating a multimedia and graphics staff group. This unit took advantage of the latest digital technology by applying the technical skills of its developers to the creative ideas of faculty members. The result was the crafting of intriguing new cutting-edge educational materials. Under the codirection of Cary Cheseldine (video) and Christian Lehmbeck (multimedia), Darden Instructional Technology—later renamed Darden Media—produced an array of multimedia case studies for use at Darden and for sale around the world.

Another technology support unit developed in the midst of the technology explosion of the late 1990s was Darden Web Services. This staff group, directed by Lauren Moriarty, spearheaded the creation and advancement of the School's external and internal Web sites. With the Darden Web site vaulting into prominence as the School's most widespread, timely, and efficient means of communication, Darden Web Services collaborated with all of the School's constituent groups to facilitate the presentation of Darden's message and the cross-fertilization of the Darden Community's emerging ideas.

Finally, Darden Technology Services included an Information Services unit. This

High-tech classes. Professors Philip E. Pfeifer and Paul W. Farris teach an experimental distance-learning course in which Darden partnered with the University of Michigan and the University of California–Berkeley.

group, in conjunction with key internal Darden clients, created and continues to enhance a series of state-of-the-art student administrative systems designed to support such functions as Darden's Admissions Office, its Career Development Center, its course-registration process, and its alumni network. So impressive were these Darden-developed systems that a number of the nation's top business schools sought them out for their own use. Beginning in 1997 on a small scale, Darden began to license to selected external clients its student-systems software, first under the banner of "EDU Link," later renamed "Darden Solutions." Darden Solutions counted among its customers such top-tier graduate business schools as Wharton,

Stanford, Duke, Chicago, Columbia, Cornell, Yale, Berkeley, MIT, Chicago, and UCLA, as well as the Kennedy School of Government at Harvard. In addition, the University of Virginia's undergraduate admissions office and the graduate programs at the McIntire School and the Engineering School adopted Darden's on-line admissions-application system.

In short, while maintaining its commitment to highly integrated and personally delivered educational programs emphasizing rigorous debate and decision making, the Darden School has embraced new developments in technology. It has adopted technological advancements to enhance the quality of Darden's instructional programs through the use of computers, multimedia cases, and simulations. It has also improved the quality of life for students, faculty, and staff through the creation of extremely useful administrative systems. Moreover, Darden has made its technological creativity available to other academic institutions across the globe.

Darden Business Publishing

During the School's formative years, the materials used in Darden's case-method curriculum consisted largely of case studies produced at the Harvard Business School. As devotees of case-method pedagogy, the Graduate Business School's young faculty soon began to generate cases of their own to ensure that the curriculum in an ever-changing business world remained relevant and current.

During Darden's initial three decades, its output of cases, while relatively modest in comparison to Harvard's owing to Darden's small size, grew steadily. Darden faculty authored cases to enrich the School's curriculum by adding new and important topics or treating enduring fundamental topics more effectively than did other available course materials. By 1987, more than half the materials used in Darden's academic programs were written by Darden faculty members.[55]

A number of Darden cases had their origin in the Supervised Business Study, the independent field-based business-analysis project required of all MBA students from the time of the School's founding through the 1980s. Written under the close supervision of a Darden faculty member, the Supervised Business Study, later broadened and renamed the Directed Study, required students to compile real-world case facts and data, weave them into an interesting narrative, and provide an analysis of managerial options. Faculty would often select the most instructive of the Supervised Business Studies and use them as a springboard to create polished case studies for future use at the School. Faculty would also develop a teaching note for each case—a carefully conceived instructional plan that set forth the most efficacious way to present the case's salient lessons to students.

By 1984, a sufficient number of worthwhile Darden cases had been written and tested in classrooms in Charlottesville for the School to begin offering them to other institutions. In that year, encouraged by William Rotch, chair of the Research and Course Development Committee, the Darden School published its first case bibliography. It listed 100 cases. By 1998, the bibliography of the Darden Case Collection contained more than 1,500 cases. Technology soon overtook the bibliography's traditional publication method. In the following year, the School abandoned the printed case bibliography in favor of a CD-ROM format that could provide more extensive and up-to-date information for prospective customers—including video testimonials from Darden faculty on the benefits of case-method pedagogy—at a fraction of the cost.[56]

Technology has affected the dissemination of Darden's cases in ways well beyond the bibliography's format. Advances in software have permitted Darden's talented Instructional Technology staff to work with professors to create an array of exciting multimedia cases that supplement the School's traditional text-based offerings. Likewise,

computer-based simulations have emerged as another Darden School product. Finally, technology has enabled Darden to move far beyond the modest sales of its cases to other institutions in the 1980s and 1990s. In 2003, Dean Harris announced the launch of Darden Business Publishing, an initiative dedicated to promoting the reputation of the Darden School through widespread distribution of Darden's intellectual property. Directed by Katherine Amato, a 1980 Darden MBA graduate whose earlier career spanned both marketing and publishing, Darden Business Publishing, with the help of a state-of-the-art storefront on the Web and customer-relationship-management software, aimed its sights at a major increase in the sales of Darden's management-education materials, including traditional text-based cases and technology-based products rang-

ing from multimedia cases on CD-ROM to Darden-hosted on-line business simulations.

Business Roundtable Institute for Corporate Ethics

The early years of the first decade of the twenty-first century witnessed a seemingly unending stream of high-profile corporate accounting scandals that undermined public trust in the leadership of American business. The scandals—several of which led to the prosecution and conviction of prominent corporate officials—revealed serious lapses in ethical behavior that dealt a major blow to the public's confidence in business institutions and their governance. In reaction to the questionable behavior of corporate leaders unearthed by a variety of investigative processes, both criminal and regulatory, the Business Roundtable, an association of 150 CEOs of the nation's leading corporations, decided to form an institute devoted to restoring public confidence in the marketplace and in the leaders of the business organizations that constitute the foundation of the free-enterprise system. In 2004, the Business Roundtable selected the Darden School as the home for that institute.[57]

The choice of Darden as the partner for the Business Roundtable's Institute for Corporate Ethics was a logical one for both parties. Rooted in the University of Virginia's Honor System and its strong Jeffersonian tradition of individual rights and responsibilities, the Darden School, since its founding, has manifested a well-articulated devotion to the promotion of ethical behavior in business. The School's namesake, President Colgate W. Darden, as well as its other founding fathers, placed ethics and integrity at the pinnacle of the list of values they cherished and wove into the fabric of the graduate business school they established. On almost every public occasion in which he spoke about the School, Colgate Darden made a special effort to stress the importance of ethics in business and to remind all those associated with the Graduate Business School and the University of Virginia of their obligation to fulfill the highest standards of honorable behavior.

In 1980, the final year of his life, Darden's message of greetings to the School on its twenty-fifth anniversary encapsulated the criticality of the School's dedication to ethics and to the importance of integrity to the success and survival of the free-enterprise system. While taking great pride in the accomplishments of the School and noting that "it had succeeded beyond my dreams and, I believe, the dreams of any of the others who were engaged in the quest," Darden reiterated that the School must continue to promote ethical behavior fervently. Said Darden:

On my honor as a student, I have neither given nor received aid on this assignment or exam.

The University of Virginia's honor pledge is posted in each Darden classroom. The Darden School's emphasis on ethics is deeply rooted in the University's Honor System.

"I am too old to advise, but I cannot resist a suggestion which embodies all of my hopes for the School. It is that nothing will ever induce us to lay aside instruction in the ethical foundations of American business. Without a firm attachment to unimpeachable integrity, in our business as well as in our personal affairs, we build on shifting sands and there can be no future for any of us."[58]

Consistent with Colgate Darden's counsel, the Olsson Center for Applied Ethics, founded in 1969, had become a living testament to the Virginia Graduate Business School's mission to promote ethics in business. The Center's prominence, and the esteem it achieved in the 1990s under the leadership of Professors R. Edward Freeman and Patricia Werhane, made it a leading candidate to nurture the Business Roundtable's vision. That vision included activities designed to achieve a triple impact: conducting

Alumni loyalty, a Darden School hallmark. No class has been more dedicated to the School than its first. Here (left to right) Stuart Quarngesser, Gene Crotty, and Harry Lewis of the Class of 1957 return for a 1995 reunion.

relevant seminars and programs in ethics for business leaders, developing curriculum materials to incorporate into the nation's leading MBA programs to strengthen the ethical awareness of future business leaders, and undertaking research in business ethics directly beneficial to practitioners. Observed Franklin Raines, cochairman of the Business Roundtable and chairman and CEO of Fannie Mae, upon establishment of the Institute: "Real people are facing real problems that are not always immediately recognizable as ethical issues. If the Institute can spot these challenges in advance and sensitize business leaders and business students, we are doing a great service."

Dean Harris and Olsson Center Codirector Freeman saw the Darden School's mission as fully congruent with the Business Roundtable's aspirations in regard to teaching and research in business ethics. Darden became the Institute's home base, with Freeman

serving as its academic director. Freeman recruited an impressive team of academic advisers for the Institute, which included many of the nation's leading business ethicists, representing such institutions as Harvard, Pennsylvania, Michigan, Texas, Notre Dame, Emory, Northwestern, Penn State, Minnesota, Rutgers, Georgetown, and the University of Washington. "We desperately need," stated Freeman, "a new conversation and new narrative about business. We must come to see business and ethics as going together." For the Darden School, throughout its first half century, business and ethics have always been in tandem. Darden's role in the Business Roundtable Institute for Corporate Ethics is to help spread this overriding principle throughout the business community.[59]

Alumni Showcase

For 50 years, the Darden School has enjoyed an exceedingly close relationship with its alumni. In 2004, in order to highlight the professional achievements of alumni and make those achievements better known to prospective and incoming students, executive-education participants, and corporate and other visitors to the School, a group of second-year Darden students launched the Darden Alumni Showcase project. Annually, the project asks the Darden Community for nominations of alumni who have exemplified leadership, vision, and determination in their professional careers. From the list of nominees, a group of about a dozen is selected. The showcase displays the selected nominees' photographs and biographies on plaques that are prominently displayed in the School's main classroom corridor. The Alumni Showcase serves as an evolving, organic link between today's and yesterday's Darden students and today's and tomorrow's Darden alumni.[60]

The Darden School has benefited from the service of a growing corps of dedicated alumni who provide support and advice. Alumni such as Thomas A. Saunders, Steven S. Reinemund, Lawton W. Fitt, and Warren M. Thompson exemplify the passion that Darden graduates feel for their alma mater.

THOMAS A. SAUNDERS III

After earning his MBA in 1967 from the Darden School, where he received the Hyde Award, Tom Saunders launched a successful career on Wall Street, rising to the post of managing director of Morgan Stanley and Company and chairman of its leveraged-buyout fund. At the helm of this fund, Saunders raised $2.3 billion in private equity from investors across the globe. In 1989, he left Morgan Stanley to found the private-equity firm Saunders, Karp & Megrue, which controls a portfolio of more than two dozen companies.

Throughout his career, Saunders has remained close to Darden and the University of Virginia. The Darden School recognized Saunders's generosity and his leadership of the Darden School Foundation Board of Trustees during completion of construction of Phase I of its new facilities by naming the "commons" building Saunders Hall in honor of him and his wife, Jordan.

Saunders inspired what he termed "the intellectual debate on taking Darden private" in a speech at the black-tie affair celebrating the dedication of the new Darden Grounds on April 12, 1996. His speech served as a springboard to discussions leading to Darden's attainment of financial self-sufficiency. Saunders also served as a member of the University's Board of Visitors and has co-chaired the University's Capital Campaign.[61]

Thomas A. Saunders chats with Cress Carter and Daniel Seats (both Class of 1992), student managers of Darden Tech.

Steven S. Reinemund.

STEVEN S. REINEMUND

A graduate of the U.S. Naval Academy, Steve Reinemund, after receiving his MBA from the Darden School in 1978, joined the Marriott Corporation, where he rose to the position of vice president and general manager of the Roy Rogers Restaurant Division. In 1984, he joined PepsiCo as senior vice president of Operations at Pizza Hut, the start of a successful career that led to the posts of president of Pizza Hut in 1986 and CEO of PepsiCo in 2001, when *BusinessWeek* termed him a "fierce competitor" and one of the nation's top-25 managers. The same magazine named Reinemund one of the world's best managers in 2004, citing his "constant innovation" and "savvy" acquisition moves. "But Reinemund's greatest achievement is in developing people," noted *BusinessWeek*, as it commended him for developing at PepsiCo "one of the deepest executive benches in Corporate America."

Always interested in the growth and development of his employees, Reinemund has likewise remained devoted to Darden's educational mission. In 1989, Reinemund was Darden's Sponsors Day speaker, an occasion at which he presented Dean Rosenblum with a $1-million donation from the PepsiCo Foundation, the initial major gift that helped underwrite the new Darden Grounds.[62]

LAWTON W. FITT

Turning down admission to Harvard Business School, which both her parents had attended, Lawton Fitt instead selected Darden for her MBA education. She graduated in 1979, and began an outstanding career of more than 20 years on Wall Street at Goldman Sachs, rising to the post of managing director.

An expert on raising capital for cutting-edge-technology companies, Fitt led many high-tech firms through initial public stock offerings in both New York and London. *BusinessWeek* named her one of the "e.biz 25" in 1999. In 2003, she became the first American and the first woman to be ap-

Lawton W. Fitt

pointed Secretary of the Royal Academy of Arts in London. She has served as a Darden School Foundation Trustee since 1998.[63]

Warren M. Thompson. Thompson was named "National Black MBA Entrepreneur of the Year" in 2002.

WARREN M. THOMPSON
A 1983 Darden graduate, Warren Thompson has served on both the Darden School Foundation Board of Trustees and the University of Virginia Board of Visitors. A tireless advocate for the Darden School, he received the Charles C. Abbott Award in 2004. Thompson joined Marriott after leaving Darden, and learned the restaurant business so well that, in 1992, at the age of 32, he purchased a number of Bob's Big Boy restaurants from Marriott. His entrepreneurial venture flourished into Thompson Hospitality Corporation, a food-service contractor and major restaurant operator that

is the largest minority-owned food-service company in the United States. The National Black MBA Association named Thompson Entrepreneur of the Year in 2002.[64]

The Darden Experience

Whether attending the Darden School during its first decade or its fifth, most Darden graduates would proudly agree that they had persevered through two unforgettable years during which they participated in an all-encompassing, life-altering experience. This special "Darden Experience," recalled by alumni of all ages, emanated from Darden's enduring dedication to the learning process.

The learning process has been the essence of Virginia's Graduate School of Business Administration since its establishment. The vision of the School's founders was to craft a graduate business institution noted for its distinctive instructional and learning experience. Today, this remains the vision of the School's faculty, staff, students, and alumni as Darden seeks to enhance its contribution to business and society as the twenty-first century unfolds.

The term "Darden Experience" is evocative of Darden's characteristic approach to management education. The Darden MBA Program, over the course of a half century, has not simply been a conglomeration of courses composing a loosely defined academic curriculum. Rather, it has been a carefully planned, unified series of inter-related activities and relationships, both inside and outside the classroom, focused on a single and singular purpose: the provision of learning that will better society by developing leaders in the world of practical affairs.

The Darden Experience has been fueled by the faculty's extraordinary commitment to teaching and to fostering close interaction with students. The Darden Experience

Student giving. MBA class gift co-chairs Carter Whisnand, Wendy Bolger, and Ransom James present the class of 2001 gift to Dean Snyder.

arose from the faculty's design of an intensive learning process that emphasized team building, effective communication, rigorous analysis, and creative and *decisive* decision making. The Darden Experience has also been characterized by a strong sense of shared ethical values firmly grounded in the University of Virginia's Jeffersonian tradition.

Those who have experienced Darden have been immersed in a very rigorous learning process. But they have studied and progressed within the context of the collective efforts of a talented mix of faculty, staff,

students, and alumni—an engaged community of people who have shared a personal dedication to participating in a unique, mutually supportive learning enterprise.

A strong sense of community, in fact, has served as the most important pillar of the Darden Experience for faculty, staff, and students alike. Whether manifested in the School's venerable morning-coffee tradition or in daily informal interaction between students and faculty at student-club events, Darden's community-oriented culture has been one of its most prominent features.

Ray Smith, who has lived the Darden School's half-century history more completely than all others, described this enduring feature of Darden's culture: "We've always been known as small and a close community and having easy access to faculty. The faculty, for the most part, even today, does not have posted office hours. If the faculty's here, they're available. And most faculty still keep their doors open. And that's always been sort of an unwritten policy. If you're there, you're in your office. Your door's open. If students come to see you, you see them."[65]

Professor Ed Davis observed the distinctiveness of this aspect of Darden's culture. Comparing Darden with other graduate business schools, he judged Darden "more congenial. It's more community here. There's more social interaction among students ... Darden is more like a family."[66] Professor Jim Clawson agreed: "Darden's distinctiveness lies in a number of areas. Number

one, there is a stronger sense of community here than I think one feels at many business schools…. The smaller scale and scope of the Darden School community means that people have a greater opportunity to get acquainted with each other, to be more involved in each other's lives, and to take a more well-rounded or realistic approach to their relationships rather than just dealing with people primarily as professionals in that narrow segment of life."[67]

Staff and faculty alike have valued the School's extraordinarily informal, even intimate, environment, which invites close contact with students. Catherine "Kitty" Smiley, who has been Darden's efficient registrar, orchestrator of Final Exercises, and friendly guide to thousands of Darden students for more than three decades, emphasized that "the beauty of being here at the Darden School is the fact of interacting with students. Darden is very much a community."[68] Professor Dick Brownlee agreed: "As I reflect on my 25-plus years here at Darden, one thing that stands out more than anything to me is the relationship that I have with all my former students. This is a very special place, and you form a closeness with the students whom you teach…. And they stay in touch…. That's been one thing that, as I reflect, has been really special to me."[69]

Throughout the School's history, as students have graduated from Darden after two years of personally transformational, intensive work, they have tended to perceive their labors in the context of the total Darden Experience. They have transitioned from students to alumni with an appreciation of the important roles that peers, faculty, and staff have played in their development and success.

In his address to his classmates and their families and guests at Darden Final Exercises in 2003, Jeremy Shinewald expressed this appreciation: "From the professors and learning teammates who stayed late to help with cases, to the classmates who worked all weekend long to lead exam reviews, Darden community members exhibit an intense dedication to each other. Darden is the rarest of places, where the generous thrive, where the most devoted receive the greatest return."[70]

E P I L O G U E

The Promise of the Future

On the twentieth anniversary of the founding of the University of Virginia's Graduate Business School, Tipton R. Snavely, the Darden School's intellectual father, reminisced about the expectations of those who were present at the creation: "It was felt that the University had a great opportunity to create a School that would have supremacy in the South and rank alongside the half-dozen best schools in the nation."[1]

As the Darden School celebrates its fiftieth anniversary, the University of Virginia may proclaim proudly that the School's founding fathers, as well as the faculty, staff, students, and alumni who followed them, seized this great opportunity and built an enduring institution whose influence extends not only throughout the Commonwealth of Virginia and the South, but also throughout the world. The clear vision set forth by Snavely, Darden, McWane, Wilkinson, Abbott, and their colleagues has stood Virginia's Graduate Business School in good stead for half a century and promises to continue to do so in the decades ahead.

Opposite: The MBA Class of 2000 celebrates graduation.

The vision of a graduate business school dedicated to preparing men and women of high promise to act with determination, judgment, and integrity as they lead organizations in the world of practical affairs is an enduring one. Likewise, the values that have come to sustain this vision—excellence in teaching, close faculty and student relationships, penetrating analysis, decisive decision making, focus on real-world managerial issues, and commitment to ethical behavior—continue to guide the students, faculty, staff, and alumni who compose the Darden Community.

Adhering to this firm basic vision and set of values, the Darden School, in the years ahead, will remain well positioned to adapt and refine its programs in response to the challenges of a constantly evolving business environment. The School will continue to prepare men and women to assume with confidence the responsibilities of leadership in a world confronting economic, social, political, and technological change and uncertainty. Through its academic programs as well as its satellite service and research organizations—the Batten Institute, the Olsson Center for Applied Ethics and its partnership with the Business Roundtable Institute for Corporate Ethics, the Tayloe Murphy Center, and Darden Business Publishing—the Darden School will continue to distinguish itself with innovative ideas that address practical problems from an action-oriented perspective.

In 1959, the young School's faculty determined that the overarching objective of the School's academic programs must be to help students learn the following core attributes: "To Think. To Make Decisions. To Take Action."[2] As the Darden School enters its second half century, these characteristics will remain as essential as ever for leaders in the world of practical affairs, leaders whom the Darden School will unfailingly continue to educate in order to better society.

S O U R C E S

An exceedingly rich mine of information for this volume has been a series of video interviews conducted by Elaine Ruggieri between 2000 and 2004 for the Darden School 50th Anniversary History Project. The following individuals graciously agreed to share their recollections and observations regarding the Darden School's history, culture, and programs:

Brandt R. Allen
25 February 2003

Alan Beckenstein
17 June 2003

Neil H. "Pete" Borden
3 October 2000

Barbara Brent
14 February 2002

E. Richard Brownlee II
24 September 2003

Robert F. Bruner
8 May 2003

James G. Clawson
24 September 2003

John L. Colley, Jr.
8 May 2003

A. Eugene Crotty
12 April 2002

Edward W. Davis
17 September 2003

James C. Dunstan
25 July 2001

Robert R. Fair
9 February 2001

Paul W. Farris
17 September 2003

John D. Forbes
1 June 2001

James R. Freeland
18 March 2003

R. Edward Freeman
17 June 2003

Sherwood C. Frey, Jr.
28 February 2003

Christopher Gale
8 May 2003

Leslie E. Grayson
25 October 2001

Robert W. Haigh
14 December 2000

Paul M. Hammaker
25 June 2000

Robert S. Harris
11 October 2002

Leo I. Higdon, Jr.
5 September 2001

Alexander B. Horniman
18 March 2003

Tyson L. Janney
12 April 2002

Robert D. Landel
18 March 2003

Harry N. Lewis
12 April 2002

Lemuel E. Lewis
18 October 2002

Eleanor G. May
15 May 2002

Ellen "Beth" McDermott
14 February 2002

Charles O. Meiburg
9 February 2001

John A. Purinton, Jr.
15 October 2000

E. Stuart Quarngesser, Jr.
12 April 2002

John W. Rosenblum
4 May 2001

C. Stewart Sheppard
13 April 2000

Maria Sheppard
13 April 2000

William W. Sihler
25 February 2003

Catherine H. "Kitty" Smiley
14 August 2002

C. Ray Smith
26 September 2002

Edward A. "Ted" Snyder
18 June 2001

R. Jack Weber
14 October 2003

Patricia H. Werhane
17 June 2003

J. Richard "Dick" Wilson
12 April 2002

Copies of the videotapes of these interviews and the accompanying transcripts are housed in the Darden School's Instructional Technology department. In 1996, the Darden School Foundation commissioned a video by Dennis Powers and Associates to document the celebration of the dedication of the new Darden School Grounds. This video and the transcripts of the source interviews conducted for it are also housed in the Darden School's Instructional Technology department.

Of great value in the research for this project were documents in the Darden School's administrative archives, including the minutes of the meetings of the Darden School Faculty, recorded by the School's Secretaries of the Faculty (John D. Forbes, 1955–80; Elaine Ruggieri, 1980–81; Mark Reisler, 1982–present). Immensely valuable also were the issues of Darden's alumni magazine since its inception (*Darden Report*, Fall 1974 through Summer 1994, and its successor, *Darden*, Fall 1994–present).

Transcripts of earlier oral interviews with Colgate W. Darden, Tipton R. Snavely, John D. Forbes, and Everard Meade, held by the University of Virginia Library's Manuscripts Division, were also helpful, as were clipping files on the Darden School and Deans Abbott and Sheppard maintained in the University of Virginia Library's Reference Division. The *University of Virginia Alumni News*, the Darden School's student newspapers (the *Darden News* and the *Cold Call Chronicle*), and the Darden School's student yearbooks (*10K*) were also helpful sources.

Published works and manuscripts consulted include the following:

Batten, Frank. *The Weather Channel*. Boston: Harvard Business School Press, 2002.

Byrne, John A. "The Best B-Schools." *BusinessWeek* (21 October 1996).

Crane, Courtney S. "Jefferson Interpreted: The New Darden Grounds." *Albemarle* (April–May 1996).

Cruikshank, Jeffrey L. *A Delicate Experiment: The Harvard Business School, 1908–1945*. Boston: Harvard Business School Press, 1987.

Dabney, Virginius. *Mr. Jefferson's University*. Charlottesville: University Press of Virginia, 1981.

Darden, Colgate W. *The Inauguration of Colgate Whitehead Darden, Jr., President of the University of Virginia*. Charlottesville: 1947.

Dunmaine, Brian. "What the Leaders of Tomorrow See." *Fortune* (3 July 1989).

Fair, Robert R. *Some Memories*. Charlottesville: 1997.

Friddell, Guy. *Colgate Darden: Conversations with Guy Friddell*. Charlottesville: University Press of Virginia, 1978.

Gleeson, Robert E., and Steven Schlossman. "The Many Faces of the New Look: The University of Virginia, Carnegie Tech, and the Reform of American Management Education in the Postwar Era." *Selections* (Winter 1992).

Grayson, Leslie E. "A Mission for Globalization at the Darden School, 1971–2004." Unpublished manuscript, 2004.

Hammaker, Paul A. *9.5 Decades*. Staunton, VA: 1998.

Hammaker, Paul A., and Louis T. Rader. *Plain Talk to Young Executives*. Homewood, IL: Richard D. Irwin, 1977.

Herndon, Booton. "Origins of the Graduate School of Business Administration." *Nation's Business* (August 1956).

Hitchcock, Susan T. *The University of Virginia: A Pictorial History*. Charlottesville: University Press of Virginia and University of Virginia Bookstore, 1999.

Main, Jeremy. "B-Schools Get a Global Vision." *Fortune* (17 July 1989).

Maurer, David. "A New Take on Classicism at the University of Virginia." *Colonial Homes* (September 1997).

May, Eleanor G. *Memoirs of My Life*. Charlottesville: 1997.

MBA Class of 1973 Looks at GSBA. Charlottesville: Darden Graduate School of Business Administration, 1973.

Mueller, Henry. *In a Nutshell: A Memoir*. New York: Vantage Press, 2002.

Newton, Derek A. *Think Like a Man, Act Like a Lady, Work Like a Dog*. Garden City, NY: Doubleday, 1979.

O'Reilly, Brian. "What's Killing the Business School Deans of America?" *Fortune* (8 August 1994).

Schmotter, James W. "An Interview with John Rosenblum." *Selections* (Autumn 1993).

Shannon, Edgar F., Jr. *The University of Virginia: A Century and a Half of Innovation*. New York: Newcomen Society, 1969.

Shenkir, William G., and William R. Wilkerson. *University of Virginia's McIntire School of Commerce: The First Seventy-Five Years, 1921–1996*. Charlottesville: McIntire School of Commerce, 1996.

Sheppard, C. Stewart, ed. *The First Twenty Years: The Darden School at Virginia*. Charlottesville: Colgate Darden Graduate Business School Sponsors, 1975.

Stein, Karen D. "Business School Connects to Distant Past." *Architectural Record* (July 1996).

Stern, Robert A. M. *Buildings and Projects, 1987–1992*. New York: Rizzoli, 1992.

Wilkerson, Elizabeth. "University of Virginia Plans to Restore 'Founder's Vision.'" *Richmond Times-Dispatch* (16 August 1992).

N O T E S

CHAPTER 1: PREPARING THE SOIL, 1946–1954

The Concept: A Graduate Business School at the University of Virginia
1. Tipton R. Snavely, "Typescript of Reminiscences," sent to Virginia GSBA faculty by Charles C. Abbott, 1 May 1972, Darden School Archives, p. 278.
2. Henry E. McWane, "Address at the First Meeting of the First Entering Class," 16 September 1955, Darden School Archives, p. 1.
3. J. Harvie Wilkinson, Jr., to Tipton R. Snavely, 19 February 1947, quoted in Snavely, "Reminiscences," p. 278.
4. C. Stewart Sheppard, ed., *The First Twenty Years: The Darden School at Virginia* (Charlottesville: Colgate Darden Graduate Business School Sponsors, 1975), p. 13.

Finding the Seed Money
5. *UVA Alumni News*, March 1948, pp. 2–3, 11–13.
6. McWane, "Address," p. 2.
7. Sheppard, *First Twenty Years*, p. 14.
8. McWane, "Address," p. 4.
9. Sheppard, *First Twenty Years*, pp. 16–18.

Colgate Whitehead Darden, Jr.: Political Father of the Graduate Business School
10. *Richmond Times-Dispatch*, quoted in *Darden Report* 7, no. 2 (Summer 1981): p. 9.
11. Guy Friddell, *Colgate Darden: Conversations with Guy Friddell* (Charlottesville: University Press of Virginia, 1978), p. 101.
12. Colgate W. Darden, interview by Ann Stauffenberg and Michael Plunkett, n.d., University of Virginia Library Manuscripts Division, p. 6.
13. Friddell, *Colgate Darden*, p. 96; Virginius Dabney, *Mr. Jefferson's University*, (Charlottesville: University Press of Virginia, 1981), pp. 271–73, 327–28, 340–41.

Organization of the Graduate Business School
14. T. R. Snavely, "Report of the Committee on the Organization of a Graduate School of Business Administration" (hereafter cited as Snavely Committee Report), 13 June 1953, p. 17.
15. Snavely Committee Report, p. 8.
16. Snavely Committee Report, pp. 9–13.
17. Snavely Committee Report, pp. 12–17.
18. Snavely Committee Report, p. 13.

Philosophical Approach to Virginia's Graduate Business School
19. J. Harvie Wilkinson, Jr., "Memorandum on a Philosophy of and an Approach to a Graduate School of Business at the University of Virginia with Some Comments on the Areas of Business to Be Studied within the School in Its Early Years," Darden School Archives, p. 1.
20. Wilkinson, "Memorandum," p. 6.
21. Wilkinson, "Memorandum," pp. 6–7.
22. Wilkinson, "Memorandum," p. 13.

Selection of Charles Abbott as Dean
23. Snavely Committee Report, p. 13.
24. Tipton R. Snavely to Charles C. Abbott, 9 April 1953, Darden School Archives.
25. Charles C. Abbott to Tipton R. Snavely, 12 April 1953, Darden School Archives.
26. Colgate W. Darden to Charles C. Abbott, 14 September 1953, Darden School Archives.
27. Friddell, *Colgate Darden*, p. 125.

The Sponsors Organization: "The Equivalent of a Body of Alumni"
28. J. Harvie Wilkinson, Jr., "Basic Preconceptions of the Need, Purpose, and General Plan of the University of Virginia Graduate Business School Sponsors," Statement to the Trustees, 5–6 November 1955, p. 1.
29. Wilkinson, "Basic Preconceptions," pp. 1–2.
30. Sheppard, *First Twenty Years*, pp. i–ii.

INTERLEAF: THE TRADITION OF COFFEE

1. C. Ray Smith, Darden School video interview, 26 September 2003.

CHAPTER 2: PLANTING THE SEED, 1955–1972

Virginia to Operate School of Business
1. *New York Times*, 2 December 1954.

Dean Charles Abbott
2. *UVA Alumni News*, May–June 1972, p. 12.
3. Jeffrey L. Cruikshank, *A Delicate Experiment: The Harvard Business School, 1908–1945* (Boston: Harvard Business School Press, 1987), p. 86.

Birth of the Curriculum
4. Charles C. Abbott, "Origins of the Graduate School of Business Administration," 1955, Darden School Archives, p. 2.
5. Booton Herndon, "What Future Executives Must Know," *Nation's Business* (August 1956, reprint): p. 1.
6. Charles C. Abbott, Annual Report to President Colgate W. Darden, 1955, p. 5.
7. Charles C. Abbott, "Education as a Resource," *UVA Alumni News*, December 1960, pp. 8–9.

The Founding Faculty
8. Abbott, Annual Report, 1955, p. 1.
9. Charles C. Abbott, "Statement on General Faculty," 20 December 1955, Darden School Archives.

John Forbes
10. John D. Forbes, interview by Theresa Carroll, 21 October 1996, University of Virginia Library Manuscripts Division; Forbes, Darden School video interview, 6 June 2000.
11. Herndon, "What Future Executives Must Know," p. 3.
12. *Darden Report* 6, no. 2 (Spring–Summer 1980): p. 33.
13. Paul M. Hammaker, Darden School video interview, 25 June 2000.
14. Forbes, interview by Theresa Carroll, pp. 8–9.
15. *Darden Report* 6, no. 2 (Spring–Summer 1980): p. 17.

Forrest Hyde
16. *Darden Report* 6, no. 2 (Spring–Summer 1980): p. 17.
17. J. Richard Wilson, Darden School video interview, 12 April 2002.

Lee Johnston
18. Sheppard, *First Twenty Years*, pp. 31–32.
19. *Darden Report* 24, no. 2 (Spring 1998): p. 2.
20. *Darden Report* 6, no. 2 (Spring–Summer 1980): p. 17.

Almand Coleman
21. *Darden Report* 2, no. 2 (Spring–Summer 1976): p. 7.
22. Herndon, "What Future Executives Must Know," p. 4.
23. Tyson L. Janney, Darden School video interview, 12 April 2002.
24. C. Stewart Sheppard to Robert M. MacLeod, 28 March 1975, Darden School Archives.

George Maverick
25. *Darden Report* 6, no. 2 (Spring–Summer 1980): p. 6; Darden School Archives.

Maurice Davier
26. *Darden Report* 6, no. 2 (Spring–Summer 1980): p. 29; Darden School Archives.

Abraham Zelomek
27. *Darden Report* 6, no. 2 (Spring–Summer 1980): pp. 7, 16; Darden School Archives.

Everard Meade
28. *Darden Report* 6, no. 2 (Spring–Summer 1980): p. 17; Darden School Archives.
29. *Darden* 26, no. 1 (special issue, 2002): p. 9.

William Rotch
30. *Darden* 29, no. 1 (Spring 2003): p. 12; *Darden* 23, no. 1 (Winter 1997): p. 6; *Darden* 25, no. 3 (Summer 1999): p. 11; Sheppard, *First Twenty Years*, pp. 28–29, 33, 45.

Paul Hammaker
31. Hammaker, Darden School video interview, 25 June 2000.
32. Sheppard, *First Twenty Years*, pp. 35, 43.
33. Hammaker, *9.5 Decades* (Staunton: 1998), p. 301.
34. Hammaker, *9.5 Decades*, pp. 212–14.

The Class of 1957
35. *Darden* 23, no. 2 (Spring 1997): p. 15.
36. Janney, Darden School video interview, 12 April 2002.
37. Abbott, Annual Report, 1955, p. 3.
38. *Darden* 23, no. 2 (Spring 1997): pp. 14–17.
39. *Darden Report* 6, no. 2 (Spring–Summer 1980): pp. 14–16.
40. *Darden Report* 6, no. 2 (Spring–Summer 1980): p. 16.
41. A. Eugene Crotty, Darden School video interview, 12 April 2002.
42. Wilson, Darden School video interview, 12 April 2002.
43. *Darden Report* 6, no. 2 (Spring–Summer 1980): p. 17.

The 1960 MBA "Business Bowl"
44. Darden School Archives.

Monroe Hall
45. *Darden Report* 6, no. 2 (Spring–Summer 1980): p. 22.
46. Sheppard, *First Twenty Years*, pp. 159–61.

The First Faculty Generation
47. Neil H. Borden, Darden School video interview, 3 October 2000.
48. Borden, Darden School video interview, 3 October 2000.
49. Sheppard, *First Twenty Years*, p. 119.
50. Faculty Meeting Minutes, 11 November 1970, p. 1; Minutes, 23 February 1971, p. 1; Minutes, 12 May 1971, p. 1.

Executive Education
51. McWane, "Address," 16 September 1955.
52. Sheppard, *First Twenty Years*, p. 157.
53. Sheppard, *First Twenty Years*, pp. 157–58.
54. Robert R. Fair, Darden School video interview, 9 February 2001.
55. Sheppard, *First Twenty Years*, pp. 178–83.
56. *Virginian-Pilot*, 13 July 1958.
57. Sheppard, *First Twenty Years*, pp. 183–85.
58. Sheppard, *First Twenty Years*, pp. 186–88.
59. Fair, *Some Memories* (Charlottesville: 1997), pp. 135–40.
60. Sheppard, *First Twenty Years*, pp. 188–93; *Darden Report* 6, no. 1 (Winter 1980): p. 13.
61. Sheppard, *First Twenty Years*, pp. 191–93.

62. *BusinessWeek*, 8 March 1976, quoted in *Darden Report* 6, no. 1 (Winter 1980): p. 11.
63. *Darden Report* 5, no. 2 (Spring–Summer 1979): p. 39.

The Doctoral Program
64. Sheppard, *First Twenty Years*, pp. 113–15, 127.

The Institute of Chartered Financial Analysts
65. *UVA Alumni News*, July–August 1961, p. 11; *Darden Report* 2, no. 2 (Spring–Summer 1976): pp. 21–22; *Darden Report* 6, no. 1 (Spring–Summer 1980): p. 45; *Darden Report* 7, no. 1 (Winter 1981): p. 29.
66. "C. Stewart Sheppard, a Founder of the Chartered Financial Analyst Program, Dies," *AIMR Press Room*, 12 March 2002.

The Tayloe Murphy Center
67. Sheppard, *First Twenty Years*, p. 205.
68. Sheppard, *First Twenty Years*, pp. 207–20.

The Olsson Center for Applied Ethics
69. Wilkinson, "Memorandum," p. 2.
70. Sheppard, *First Twenty Years*, p. 227.
71. *Darden Report* 6, no. 2 (Spring–Summer 1980): p. 43.
72. Sheppard, *First Twenty Years*, pp. 112, 228–30.
73. *Darden Report* 3, no. 2 (Spring–Summer 1977): p. 13.
74. *Darden Report* 6, no. 2 (Spring–Summer 1980): p. 1.
75. *Darden Report* 8, no. 1 (Winter 1982): p. 11.
76. *Ethics Digest* 2, no. 2 (September 1984): p. 1.
77. Alexander B. Horniman, Darden School video interview, 18 March 2003.
78. *Ethics Digest* 5, no. 2 (September 1987).
79. *Ethics Digest* 5, no. 2 (September 1987); *Darden Report* 13, no. 3 (Summer 1987): p. 2; *Darden Report* 14, no. 3 (Summer 1988): pp. 20–27.
80. *Ethics Digest* 6, no. 5 (September 1989).
81. *Darden Report* 15, no. 2 (Spring 1989): pp. 20–23.
82. *Ethics Digest* 6, no. 6 (December 1989).
83. R. Edward Freeman, Darden School video interview, 17 June 2003.
84. *Darden Report* 15, no. 2 (Spring 1989): p. 17.

INTERLEAF: THE CASE METHOD

1. Cruikshank, *A Delicate Experiment*, pp. 74–78.
2. Snavely Committee Report, p. 17.
3. Hammaker, Darden School video interview, 25 June 2000.
4. Abbott, Annual Report, 1955, pp. 4–5.
5. Robert F. Bruner, Darden School video interview, 8 May 2003.
6. Christopher Gale, Darden School video interview, 8 May 2003.
7. Bruner, Darden School video interview, 8 May 2003.
8. John L. Colley, Jr., Darden School video interview, 8 May 2003.
9. Hammaker, Darden School video interview, 25 June 2000.
10. Leslie E. Grayson, Darden School video interview, 25 October 2001.
11. Paul W. Farris, Darden School video interview, 17 September 2003.
12. Edward W. Davis, Darden School video interview, 17 September 2003.

CHAPTER 3: TAKING ROOT, 1973–1994

Dean C. Stewart Sheppard
1. *Charlottesville Daily Progress*, 13 March 2002; C. Ray Smith, Eulogy for C. Stewart Sheppard, 23 March 2002.
2. *Darden Report* 6, no. 2 (Spring–Summer 1980): p. 28.

Honoring Colgate Darden
3. *Darden Report* 1, no. 1 (Fall–Winter 1974): p. 4.

4. *Richmond Times-Dispatch*, 1 June 1974.
5. Darden School Archives; *UVA Alumni News*, July–August 1974, pp. 7–8.

The 20th Anniversary
6. *Darden Report* 2, no. 1 (Fall–Winter 1975): pp. 2–3.
7. *Darden Report* 2, no. 1 (Fall–Winter 1975): pp. 12–23.

The North Grounds Building
8. *Darden Report* 2, no. 1 (Fall–Winter 1975): pp. 9, 12–23.

Expansion of the Student Body
9. *Darden Report* 4, no. 2 (Spring–Summer 1978): p. 4.
10. *Darden Report* 3, no. 1 (Fall–Winter 1976): p. 1.
11. Sheppard, *First Twenty Years*, p. 136.
12. *Darden Report* 2, no. 2 (Spring–Summer 1976): p. 24.
13. *Darden Report* 4, no. 2 (Spring–Summer 1978): pp. 8–9.

The Darden Case: Strategic Self-Examination
14. *Darden Report* 5, no. 1 (Winter 1979): p. 2; Faculty Meeting Minutes, 1 April 1977, pp. 1–2; "The Darden School," case study, 22 March 1977, Darden School Archives.
15. *Darden Report* 5, no. 1 (Winter 1979): p. 2; Faculty Meeting Minutes, 21 September 1977, p. 2.
16. *Darden Report* 6, no. 1 (Winter 1980): p. 1.

Women at Darden
17. *Darden Report* 9, no. 1 (Winter 1983): p. 33; *Darden Report* 10, no. 1 (Winter 1984): p. 56.
18. *Darden Report* 2, no. 1 (Fall–Winter 1975): p. 27.
19. *Darden Report* 4, no. 1 (Fall–Winter 1977): p. 2.
20. Derek A. Newton, *Think Like a Man, Act Like a Lady, Work Like a Dog* (Garden City, NY: Doubleday, 1979); *Darden Report* 5, no. 1 (Winter 1979): pp. 7–12.
21. *Darden Report* 5, no. 1 (Winter 1979): p. 1.

Minority Students
22. William E. Zierden, "Minority Student Enrollment at the Darden School: Review and Recommendations," 21 April 1977, Darden School Archives.
23. *Darden Report* 3, no. 1 (Fall–Winter 1976): p. 24; *Darden Report* 3, no. 2 (Spring–Summer 1977): p. 23; *Darden Report* 4, no. 2 (Spring–Summer 1978): p. 19; *Darden Report* 7, no. 1 (Winter 1981): pp. 2–3.
24. Darden Association of Black Business Students, By-Laws, Darden School Archives.
25. *Darden Report* 6, no. 2 (Spring–Summer 1980): p. 48.
26. *Darden* 23, no. 1 (Winter 1997): pp. 12–13; *Darden* 23, no. 2 (Spring 1997): p. 4.

Globalization
27. Sheppard, *First Twenty Years*, pp. 44–45; *Darden Report* 2, no. 2 (Spring–Summer 1976): p. 9.
28. *Darden Report* 3, no. 1 (Fall–Winter 1976): p. 3.
29. *Darden Report* 5, no. 2 (Spring–Summer 1979): pp. 28–29.
30. *Darden Report* 12, no. 3 (Fall 1986): p. 9; Darden School Archives.
31. Sherwood C. Frey, Jr., Darden School video interview, 25 February 2003.
32. *Darden* 29, no. 2 (Fall 2003): p. 8.
33. *Darden Report* 11, no. 2 (Summer 1985): pp. 24–25; *Darden Report* 12, no. 3 (Fall 1986): p. 33; *Darden Report* 13, no. 2 (Spring 1987): pp. 9–13; *New York Times*, 19 May 1987, quoted in *Darden Report* 13, no. 3 (Summer 1987): p. 48; Leslie E. Grayson, "A Missionary for Globalization at the Darden School, 1971–2004," unpublished manuscript, Darden School Archives.
34. *Darden Report* 17, no. 2 (Spring 1991): pp. 18–25.

35. *Darden* 23, no. 2 (Spring 1997): p. 8.
36. *Darden* 23, no. 4 (Fall 1997): p. 17; *Darden Report* 18, no. 1 (Winter 1992): pp. 18–21.

MBA Tournament, 1979
37. *Darden Report* 5, no. 2 (Spring–Summer 1979): pp. 5–6; *Darden Report* 5, no. 1 (Winter 1979): p. 30.

Student Activities
38. *Darden Report* 6, no. 1 (Winter 1980): p. 31.
39. Frey, Darden School video interview, 25 February 2003.

Sponsors Hall
40. Fair, *Some Memories*, pp. 140–42; *Darden Report* 3, no. 1 (Fall–Winter 1976): p. 17; *Darden Report* 3, no. 2 (Spring–Summer 1977): pp. 4–5; *Darden Report* 6, no. 1 (Winter 1980): pp. 2, 5.

Dean Robert Haigh
41. *Darden Report* 7, no. 1 (Winter 1981): pp. 9–10.
42. *Darden Report* 7, no. 2 (Summer 1981): p. 1.
43. *Darden Report* 7, no. 2 (Summer 1981): pp. 1–3.

Dean John Rosenblum
44. *Darden Report* 9, no. 1 (Winter 1983): p. 2.
45. Jeremy Main, "B-Schools Get a Global Vision," *Fortune*, 17 July 1989, pp. 78–80.
46. Brian O'Reilly, "What's Killing the Business School Deans of America?" *Fortune*, 8 August 1994, pp. 67–68.

The Second Faculty Generation
47. *Darden Report* 2, no. 2 (Spring–Summer 1976): p. i.
48. Charles O. Meiburg, Darden School video interview, 9 February 2001.

The Center for International Banking Studies (CIBS)
49. Henry Mueller, *In a Nutshell: A Memoir* (New York: Vantage Press, 2002), pp. 114–17.

C. Ray Smith
50. *Darden* 29, no. 1 (Spring 2003): pp. 16–20.

INTERLEAF: MBA PROGRAM RIGOR

1. Lemuel E. Lewis, Darden School video interview, 18 October 2002.
2. *Darden Report* 6, no. 2 (Spring–Summer 1980): p. 24.
3. James C. Dunstan, Darden School video interview, 25 July 2001.
4. John D. Forbes, Darden School video interview, 1 June 2002.
5. Hammaker, Darden School video interview, 25 June 2000.
6. *Darden Report* 2, no. 2 (Spring–Summer 1976): p. 8.

CHAPTER 4: FLOWERING, 1995–2004

The Darden School Mission Statement
1. Darden School Archives; Sheppard, *First Twenty Years*, p. 123.
2. *Academic Policies & Procedures Manual* (Charlottesville: Darden School, 1992 and all later eds.); Faculty Meeting Minutes, 13 November 1991.

The William H. Goodwin, Jr., Darden School Grounds
3. Darden School Archives.

Robert A. M. Stern
4. Darden School Archives.

Dean Leo Higdon
5. *New York Times*, 16 July 1993.

6. *Virginian-Pilot and Ledger-Star*, 12 November 1995, pp. D1–D2.
7. Leo Higdon, "Strategic Overview," June 1994, Darden School Archives.
8. *BusinessWeek*, 21 September 1996, pp. 110–22.

Philanthropy
9. *Darden Report* 3, no. 1 (Winter–Fall 1976): p. 2.
10. *Darden Report* 3, no. 1 (Winter–Fall 1976): p. 2.
11. *Darden Report* 6, no. 2 (Spring–Summer 1980): pp. 10–11; *Darden Report* 4, no. 1 (Fall–Winter 1977): p. 80.
12. *Darden Report* 9, no. 1 (Winter 1983): p. 4; *Darden Report* 10, no. 1 (Winter 1984): pp. 30–32.
13. *Darden* 27, no. 2 (Spring 2001): p. 6.
14. "Campaign for Darden Newsletter," October 1999; *Darden* 27, no. 2 (Summer 2001): p. 4; *Darden* 30, no. 1 (Summer 2004): p. 18.

William H. Goodwin, Jr.
15. William H. Goodwin, Jr., transcript of dedication ceremony video interview by Dennis Powers, 1996, p. 5.
16. Goodwin, interview, p. 9.
17. *Darden Report* 20, no. 1 (Winter 1994): p. 25; *Darden Report* 26, no. 1 (special issue, 2000): pp. 14–16.

George David
18. "The Best and Worst Managers of the Year," *BusinessWeek*, 12 January 2004, pp. 55–56.
19. Diane Bradly, "The Unsung Hero," *BusinessWeek*, 25 October 2004, pp. 74–84.
20. *Fortune*, 3 February 1986, quoted in *Darden Report* 12, no. 1 (Winter 1986): p. 29.
21. *BusinessWeek*, 12 January 2004, pp. 55–56.
22. *Darden* 23, no. 4 (Fall 1997): p. 49.
23. George A. L. David, transcript of dedication ceremony video interview by Dennis Powers, 1996, p. 4.

Dean Edward Snyder
24. Steven Ginsberg, "Selecting Business School Deans 101," *Washington Post*, 13 July 1998.
25. *Inside UVA*, 22 October 1999, p. 5.

Scale and Scope: Expansion of the MBA Program
26. Edward A. Snyder, "The Scale and Scope of Management Education Programs at the University of Virginia's Darden School," 1 July 1999, Darden School Archives.
27. Leslie E. Grayson to Darden Faculty, "Re: Scale and Scope," 10 November 1999, Darden School Archives.
28. "Dean Announces Expanded MBA Program," *Cold Call Chronicle*, 8 December 1999, p. 1.

Financial Self-Sufficiency
29. University of Virginia Board of Visitors Agenda Summary, Educational Policy Committee, 10–11 November 1995; Darden School Archives.

Chips and Quips
30. *Cold Call Chronicle*, 25 March 2004, pp. 21–22.
31. *Darden Report* 13, no. 3 (Summer 1987): p. 33.

Batten Institute
32. Darden School Archives, "Strategic Overview," June 1994.
33. "Strategic Overview," June 1994.
34. Frank Batten to Leo I. Higdon, 10 October 1995, Darden School Archives.
35. Darden School Archives.
36. Bruner, Darden School video interview, 8 May 2003.

37. Bruner, Darden School video interview, 8 May 2003.
38. Bruner, Darden School video interview, 8 May 2003.

Frank Batten
39. *Charlottesville Daily Progress*, 11 December 1999, p. 1.
40. *Darden* 26, no. 1 (special issue, 2000): p. 18.
41. *Darden* 26, no. 1 (special issue, 2000): pp. 17–19.
42. *Darden* 26, no. 1 (special issue, 2000): p. 19.
43. Frank Batten, *The Weather Channel* (Boston: Harvard University Press, 2002).
44. Darden School Archives.

Dean Robert Harris
45. University of Virginia, press release, 3 October 2001.
46. Smith, Darden School video interview, 26 September 2002.
47. Darden School Archives; Faculty Meeting Minutes, 13 October 2004.

The Third Faculty Generation
48. Darden School Archives.

Instructional Technology
49. Application for Accreditation to the American Assembly of Collegiate Schools of Business, 1970, Darden School Archives, pp. 217–18.
50. *Darden Report* 8, no. 2 (Summer 1982): pp. 8–9.
51. *Darden Report* 10, no. 2 (Summer 1984): pp. 7–9.
52. *Darden Report* 13, no. 3 (Summer 1987): p. 6.
53. *Darden Report* 15, no. 2 (Spring 1989): pp. 14–18.
54. David, interview, p. 14.

Darden Business Publishing
55. *Darden Report* 13, no. 1 (Winter 1987): pp. 8–11.
56. Darden School Archives.

Business Roundtable Institute for Corporate Ethics
57. *Darden* 30, no. 1 (Spring 2004): pp. 28–31.
58. *Darden Report* 6, no. 2 (Spring–Summer 1980): p. 7.
59. Darden School Archives; *Darden* 30, no. 1 (Spring 2004): pp. 28–31.

Alumni Showcase
60. *Cold Call Chronicle*, 22 April 2004, p. 10.
61. *Darden Report* 15, no. 4 (Fall 1989): p. 22; "Remarks by Thomas A. Saunders III," 12 April 1996, Darden School Archives; *Darden* 22, no. 1 (Winter 1996): p. 23.
62. *Darden Report* 15, no. 3 (Summer 1989): p. 2; *BusinessWeek*, 14 January 2002; *BusinessWeek*, 10 January 2005, pp. 56–57.
63. *Darden* 27, no. 1 (Winter 2001): p. 89; *BusinessWeek*, 27 September 1999.
64. *Darden* 27, no. 2 (Spring 2001): p. 69; *Black MBA Magazine* (Summer 2003).

The Darden Experience
65. Smith, Darden School video interview, 26 September 2002.
66. Davis, Darden School video interview, 17 September 2003.
67. James G. Clawson, Darden School video interview, 24 September 2003.
68. Catherine H. Smiley, Darden School video interview, 14 August 2002.
69. E. Richard Brownlee II, Darden School video interview, 24 September 2003.
70. Jeremy Shinewald, "Address at Final Exercises," 18 May 2003.

EPILOGUE: THE PROMISE OF THE FUTURE

1. Sheppard, *First Twenty Years*, p. 9.
2. Sheppard, *First Twenty Years*, p. 122.

My thanks to the many fine photographers who contributed to this volume by recording Darden's history in images over the past five decades. — M. R.

Cover: Jack Mellott
Endsheet: Jon Golden
ii–iii: Robert Redifera
iv–v: John Consoli
vi–vii: Jon Golden
viii–ix: Jack Mellott
x–xi: Jack Mellott
xii–xiii: Peter Anron, Esto Photographics
xiv–xv: Peter Anron, Esto Photographics
xvi: Jon Golden
xviii: (top) Darden Photography Collection
xviii: (bottom left) Darden Photography Collection
xviii: (bottom right) Jon Golden
1: Prints Collection, Special Collections, University of Virginia Library
2: Prints Collection, Special Collections, University of Virginia Library
3: Prints Collection, Special Collections, University of Virginia Library
5: Prints Collection, Special Collections, University of Virginia Library
6: Jon Golden
7: Prints Collection, Special Collections, University of Virginia Library
8: Prints Collection, Special Collections, University of Virginia Library
11: Jon Golden, photographer; Ned Bittinger, artist
13: Trish Crowe, artist. Reprinted from Darden Report (Fall–Winter 1974)
14: Foster Studio, Richmond, VA
16: Prints Collection, Special Collections, University of Virginia Library
18: Prints Collection, Special Collections, University of Virginia Library
19: Prints Collection, Special Collections, University of Virginia Library
20: (top left) Jon Golden
20: (bottom) John Wade
20: (top right) Stephanie Gross
21: (top) Darden Photography Collection
21: (bottom) John Wade
22: Courtesy McIntire School of Commerce, University of Virginia
22: (insert) Reprinted with permission from the New York Times, 2 December 1954
23: Darden Photography Collection
24: Robert Llewellyn
25: Darden Photography Collection
26: John Wade
27: Prints Collection, Special Collections, University of Virginia Library
28: Robert Llewellyn
29: (top) Prints Collection, Special Collections, University of Virginia Library
29: (bottom left) Robert Llewellyn
29: (bottom right) Robert Llewellyn
30: Robert Llewellyn
31: Triad Photography Group, San Francisco, CA

32: Prints Collection, Special Collections, University of Virginia Library
33: Darden Photography Collection
34: John Wade
36: (top) Jon Golden
36: (bottom) Prints Collection, Special Collections, University of Virginia Library
37: Darden Photography Collection
38: John Wade
39: Gary Alter
40: John Wade
41: Darden Photography Collection
42–43: Darden Photography Collection
43: (bottom) Darden Photography Collection
44: Darden Photography Collection
46: Jon Golden
47: Ralph Thompson. Reprinted from Charlottesville Daily Progress, 24 March 1960
48: Darden Photography Collection
49: Darden Photography Collection
50–51: Jim Gibson
52: Prints Collection, Special Collections, University of Virginia Library
53: (top) John Wade
53: (next to top) John Wade
53: (next to bottom) John Wade
53: (bottom) Elaine Ruggieri
54: (top) Elaine Ruggieri
54: (next to top) Elaine Ruggieri
54: (next to bottom) Darden Photography Collection
54: (bottom) Jon Golden
55: John Wade
56: Elaine Ruggieri
58: Prints Collection, Special Collections, University of Virginia Library
59: John Wade
60: Jon Golden
61: John Wade
62: Gary Alter
63: Gary Alter
65: Darden Photography Collection
67: Elaine Ruggieri
68: John Wade
69: Elaine Ruggieri
70: David Price
71: Jon Golden
73: John Wade
74: Prints Collection, Special Collections, University of Virginia Library
75: Darden Photography Collection
76: Jon Golden
77: Prints Collection, Special Collections, University of Virginia Library
78: Jon Golden
80: Jon Golden
81: Jon Golden
83: Elaine Ruggieri
84: (top) David Price
84: (next to top) David Price
84: (next to bottom) Jack Mellott
84: (bottom) Elaine Ruggieri
85: David Price
86: Jon Golden
87: Jon Golden
88: David Price
88: (insert) John Wade
89: John Wade
90: Prints Collection, Special Collections, University of Virginia Library
91: John Wade
92: John Wade
93: Jon Golden

94: (top) John Wade
94–95: Darden Photography Collection
95: (bottom) John Wade
96: (left) Elaine Ruggieri
96: (right) John Wade
97: Elaine Ruggieri
98–99: Darden Photography Collection
100: Jon Golden
101: Prints Collection, Special Collections, University of Virginia Library
103: (top) Darden Photography Collection
103: (insert) Woodallen Photography, Houston, TX
104: Elaine Ruggieri
105: Elaine Ruggieri
106–7: John Consoli
108: Jon Golden
109: (top) Elaine Ruggieri
109: (bottom) Darden Photography Collection
110: Darden Photography Collection
111: John Consoli
112: David Price
113: Elaine Ruggieri
114: John Wade
115: David Price
116: Jon Golden
117: Stephanie Gross
119: Reprinted from Darden Report (Spring–Summer 1979)
120: (left) Randall Brown (MBA '78)
120: (center) Elaine Ruggieri
120: (right) Elaine Ruggieri
121: (left) Christopher C. Quarles III (MBA '90)
121: (center) Jon Golden
121: (right) Peggy Harrison
122: Peggy Harrison
124–25: Frank Moore Design
126: (top) John Wade
126: (bottom) Erin Garvey
127: Prints Collection, Special Collections, University of Virginia Library
129: Elaine Ruggieri
130: Jon Golden
133: Katherine Lambert. Reprinted from Fortune, 17 July 1989
134: (top) Tom Cogill
134: (center) Reprinted from Darden 10K, 1987
135: Elaine Ruggieri
136: (left) Jon Golden
136: (right) Diane Nelson
137: Prints Collection, Special Collections, University of Virginia Library
137: (right) Prints Collection, Special Collections, University of Virginia Library
138: (left) John Wade
138: (center left) David Price
138: (center right) Jon Golden
138: (right) Jon Golden
139: Stephanie Gross
140: (top) John Consoli
140: (bottom left) Andrew Shurtleff
140: (bottom right) John Consoli
141: (top) Jon Golden
141: (bottom left) Darden Yearbook, 1981
141: (bottom left center) David Price
141: (bottom right center) Gary Alter
141: (bottom right) Jack Mellott
142: Elaine Ruggieri
143: Stephanie Gross
144: Darden Photography Collection
145: Robert Llewellyn
146: Cartoon by S. Huntington Hobbs IV (MBA '79)
147: Jack Mellott

148: Cartoon by S. Huntington Hobbs IV (MBA '79)
149: (top) Darden Photography Collection
149: (bottom) Cartoon by S. Huntington Hobbs IV (MBA '79)
150: John Consoli
151: Stephanie Gross
152: Jon Golden
153: Jon Golden
154: Jack Mellott
155: Jack Mellott
156: John Consoli
157: William Sublette
158–59: John Consoli
160: Jack Mellott
161: Seamane Flanagan
162: Courtesy Robert A. M. Stern Architects
163: Jon Golden
164: Jon Golden
165: (top) Jon Golden
165: (bottom) Rick Miller and Jeff Weigand
166–67: Jon Golden
168: John Consoli
169: Douglas Miller. Reprinted from Albemarle magazine (April–May 1996)
170–71: John Consoli
170: (insert) Jon Golden
172: John Consoli
173: David Price
174: John Consoli
175: Stephanie Gross
176: Jon Golden
177: Jon Golden
178: Stephanie Gross
180: Jack Mellott
182: Photoworks
183: David Price
184: John Consoli
186: John Consoli
187: Courtesy of the Cold Call Chronicle
189: Tom Cogill
190: Tom Cogill
193: Courtesy Landmark Communications
194: Stephanie Gross
196: (left) Tom Cogill
196: (center) John Consoli
196: (right) Seamane Flanagan
197: (left) John Consoli
197: (center) Stephanie Gross
197: (right) John Consoli
198: Elaine Ruggieri
199: Elaine Ruggieri
200: Jon Golden
201: Jon Golden
202: John Consoli
203: Darden Photography Collection
204: Tom Cogill
205: Jon Golden
206: Andrew Shurtleff
207: Jon Golden
208–9: Jon Golden
210: Jon Golden
211: Michael Bailey
212: (left) Jack Mellott
212: (right) Michael Bailey
213: Reprinted from Black MBA (Summer 2003)
214: Stephanie Gross
215: Susan Wormington
216–17: Michael Bailey
218: Stephanie Gross
219: Jon Golden
220: David Price
221: John Consoli

INDEX